Women Writers and Journalists in the Nineteenth-Century South

The first study to focus on white and black women journalists and writers both before and after the Civil War, this book offers fresh insight into southern intellectual life, the fight for women's rights, and gender ideology. Based on new research into southern magazines and newspapers, this book seeks to shift scholarly attention away from novelists and toward the rich and diverse periodical culture of the South between 1820 and 1900. Magazines were of central importance to the literary culture of the South because the region lacked the publishing centers that could produce large numbers of books. Easily portable, newspapers and magazines could be sent through the increasingly sophisticated postal system for relatively low subscription rates. The mix of content, from poetry to short fiction and literary reviews to practical advice and political news, meant that periodicals held broad appeal. As editors, contributors, correspondents, and reporters in the nineteenth century, southern women entered traditionally male bastions when they embarked on careers in journalism. In so doing, they opened the door to calls for greater political and social equality at the turn of the twentieth century.

Jonathan Daniel Wells is associate professor of History at Temple University. He is the author or editor of six books, including *The Origins of the Southern Middle Class: 1820–1861* and *Entering the Fray: Gender, Politics, and Culture in the New South.* He is a co-editor of a forthcoming collection of essays, *The Southern Middle Class in the Nineteenth Century.* He has published several reviews and articles on nineteenth-century America, the Civil War, slavery, gender, politics, class, and intellectual life, in journals such as *The Journal of Southern History*, *American Nineteenth-Century History*, and the *Maryland Historical Magazine.*

CAMBRIDGE STUDIES ON THE AMERICAN SOUTH

Series Editors

Mark M. Smith, *University of South Carolina, Columbia*
David Moltke-Hansen, *Center for the Study of the American South, University of North Carolina at Chapel Hill*

Interdisciplinary in its scope and intent, this series builds on and extends Cambridge University Press's long-standing commitment to studies on the American South. The series not only will offer the best new work on the South's distinctive institutional, social, economic, and cultural history but also will feature works in a national, comparative, and transnational perspective.

Titles in the Series

Robert E. Bonner, *Southern Slaveholders and the Crisis of American Nationhood*
Peter McCandless, *Slavery, Disease, and Suffering in the Southern Lowcountry*

Women Writers and Journalists in the Nineteenth-Century South

JONATHAN DANIEL WELLS
Temple University

CAMBRIDGE
UNIVERSITY PRESS

CAMBRIDGE UNIVERSITY PRESS
Cambridge, New York, Melbourne, Madrid, Cape Town,
Singapore, São Paulo, Delhi, Tokyo, Mexico City

Cambridge University Press
32 Avenue of the Americas, New York, NY 10013-2473, USA

www.cambridge.org
Information on this title: www.cambridge.org/9781107012660

First published 2011

Printed in the United States of America

A catalog record for this publication is available from the British Library.

Library of Congress Cataloging in Publication data
Wells, Jonathan Daniel, 1969–
Women writers and journalists in the nineteenth-century south / Jonathan Daniel Wells.
p. cm. – (Cambridge studies on the American south)
Includes bibliographical references and index.
ISBN 978-1-107-01266-0 (hardback)
1. Women in journalism – Southern States – History – 19th century. 2. Journalism – Southern States – History – 19th century. 3. Periodicals – Publishing – Southern States – History – 19th century. 4. Women's periodicals, American – Southern States – History – 19th century. 5. Literature – Publishing – Southern States – History – 19th century. 6. Women – Press coverage – Southern States – History – 19th century. 7. American literature – Women authors – Southern States – History and criticism. 8. American literature – 19th century – History and criticism. 9. Journalism and literature – United States – History – 19th century. I. Title.
PN4888.W66.W48 2011
810.9'92870975–dc22 2011010350

ISBN 978-1-107-01266-0 Hardback

This book is dedicated to Frank Thompson, Ann Curry Thompson, Saskia Thompson, and Isabel Thompson

Contents

Acknowledgments

Generous funding underwrote the research for this book, including a Franklin Research Grant from the American Philosophical Society and a fellowship from the Virginia Historical Society; visiting scholar status at the American Antiquarian Society allowed me to tie up many loose ends. My sincere thanks to these institutions for helping defray the costs of research and travel. Library staffs across the country, especially at the University of North Carolina, Duke University, the University of South Carolina, the Virginia Historical Society, the University of Michigan, the New York Historical Society, and the South Caroliniana Library, graciously offered invaluable help in tracking down obscure periodicals, writers, and editors.

Over the years, some of the material in this book has been presented at various conferences, and many friends have read and commented on the manuscript in one form or another. I especially want to thank for their encouragement and support Mills Thornton, David Colburn, Bertram Wyatt-Brown, Mark M. Smith, Daniel Dupre, Karen Cox, Michael O'Brien, Cynthia Kierner, Nancy Hewitt, Deborah Gray White, Patricia Schecter, Steve Lawson, Drew Isenberg, Liz Varon, Beth Bailey, David Watt, and the anonymous readers for Cambridge University Press for their thoughtful suggestions on improving the manuscript. Bruce E. Baker and Routledge generously allowed me to republish material in Chapter 5 that was first published in *American Nineteenth-Century History*. I was fortunate enough to deliver the keynote lecture for the 2008 Symposium of the 19th-century Press, the Civil War, and Free Expression at University of Tennessee Chattanooga, and I thank David B. Sachsman and the organization for the chance to present some of my research on southern women editors.

The editors and staff at Cambridge have been professional and diligent in every way. I thank Lew Bateman, Anne Lovering Rounds, Jayashree Prabhu, and the skilled editors of the press.

Personally, I am incredibly fortunate to have the love and support of many friends and family members. Thanks as always to Daniel Wells, Elizabeth Wells, Caroline Wells, and Brynne for their unfaltering encouragement. They taught me early on that scholarship does not have to be a lonely pursuit and the importance of being supportive and loving parents. This book is dedicated to my father-in-law and mother-in-law, Frank Thompson and Ann Thompson, and to my sister-in-law, Saskia Thompson, and to my niece, Isabel. All of them know the importance of family and from all of them I have learned more than I could ever fully repay. Their commitment to social justice, their powerful dedication to the welfare of others, and their graciousness are qualities we should all emulate.

Finally, without the love of my wife, Heather Thompson, life in all its craziness would be hard to manage. Somehow she is both passionate and levelheaded, dedicated but fun, smart and beautiful yet unpretentious. She is my best friend, best editor, and so much more. Our children, Dillon, Wilder, and Ava, never cease to amuse, inspire, and exhaust us. We could not imagine life without them and all the joys they bring to their parents.

Introduction

In the beginning of William Faulkner's *Absalom, Absalom!*, twenty-year-old Quentin Compson wonders why the elderly Rosa Coldfield selected him as her partner in the excavation of the Sutpen and Coldfield family histories. There were other family members whom she could have chosen as her confidant and others for whom the names Thomas Sutpen and Ellen Coldfield would have had immediate resonance. "Why tell me about it?" the puzzled Quentin asks his father. "Ah," Mr. Compson replies, "Years ago we in the South made our women into ladies. Then the war came and made the ladies into ghosts. So what else can we do, being gentlemen, but listen to them being ghosts?"[1]

Since the 1980s, an explosion of interest in southern women's history has helped to turn Mr. Compson's "ghosts" into real, flesh-and-blood historical actors. Scores of biographies and monographs as well as edited volumes of women's writings have shed considerable light on the intellectual lives of women, particularly the wealthy mistresses of the plantation.[2] Through such

[1] William Faulkner, *Absalom, Absalom!* (Vintage International ed., New York, 1990), 7–8.

[2] Building on earlier works such as Julia Cherry Spruill's *Women's Life and Work in the Southern Colonies* (Chapel Hill, 1938) and Anne Firor Scott's *The Southern Lady: From Pedestal to Politics* (Chicago, 1970), historians in the last two decades, and especially within the last few years, have produced numerous valuable studies of southern women. See Catherine Clinton, *The Plantation Mistress: Woman's World in the Old South* (New York, 1982); Suzanne Lebsock, *Free Women of Petersburg: Status and Culture in a Southern Town, 1784–1860* (New York, 1984); Elizabeth Fox-Genovese, *Within the Plantation Household: Black and White Women of the Old South* (Chapel Hill, 1988); Christie Anne Farnham, *The Education of the Southern Belle* (New York, 1994); Laura F. Edwards, *Gendered Strife and Confusion: The Political Culture of Reconstruction* (Urbana, 1997); Elizabeth R. Varon, *We Mean to be Counted: White Women and Politics in Antebellum Virginia* (Chapel Hill, 1998); Susanna Delfino and Michele Gillespie, eds., *Neither Lady nor Slave: Working Women in the Old South* (Chapel Hill, 2002); Giselle Roberts, *The Confederate Belle* (Columbia, 2003); Christine Jacobson Carter, *Southern Single Blessedness: Unmarried Women in the Urban South, 1800–1865* (Urbana, 2006); Anya Jabour, *Scarlet's Sisters: Young Women in the Old South* (Chapel Hill, 2007); Rosemarie Zagarri, *Revolutionary Backlash: Women and Politics in the Early American Republic* (Philadelphia, 2007); and Victoria E. Ott, *Confederate Daughters: Coming of Age During the Civil War* (Carbondale, 2008). Recent collected letters

analyses, historians have found a lively literary culture in the region, a culture to which women contributed significantly.

The full story of women and the mind of the South, however, has yet to be told, for much of the work on southern women and literature has focused on novel writing and novel reading. Understandably, scholars have turned to novels as the key to understanding women's intellectual life; after all, southerners constantly debated the merits of and problems with reading book-length fiction. Many southern men and women appreciated novel reading as an innocuous pursuit of pleasure and relaxation; others treated the fantasy world of fiction as a dangerous diversion from the sobriety of real life and accused novelists of corrupting young (particularly female) minds. Recent work on southern intellectual history more broadly has reinforced the focus on the roles that novels played in the life of the mind for women. Beginning with Nina Baym's landmark study *Woman's Fiction* (1978), scholars have turned to novels to gain insight into contemporary thinking about gender roles.[3] More recently, scholars such as Drew Faust and Elizabeth Moss have illuminated the careers of important female southern novelists such as Caroline Lee Hentz and Augusta Jane Evans.[4]

This book seeks to shift the scholarly focus away from novels and novelists and toward the incredibly rich, diverse, and fascinating world of white and black women's work in journalism. Historian Catherine Kerrison has recently called for an intellectual history of southern women that is broad enough to encompass the diversity of women's reading and interests.[5] A relatively unexplored source of information on southern culture, magazines and newspapers published in the southern states provide a fuller, more comprehensive perspective on women and southern literary culture. Because novels were often

and reprinted works by southern women include Giselle Roberts, ed., *The Correspondence of Sarah Morgan and Francis Warrington Dawson* (Athens, 2004); Terrell Armistead Crow and Mary Moulton Barden, eds., *Live Your Own Life: The Family Papers of Mary Bayard Clarke, 1854–1886* (Columbia, 2003); Augusta Jane Evans, *Beulah*, edited by Elizabeth Fox-Genovese (Baton Rouge, 1992) and *Macaria, or, Altars of Sacrifice*, edited by Drew Gilpin Faust (Baton Rouge, 1992); Joan E. Cashion, ed., *Our Common Affairs: Texts from Women in the Old South* (Baltimore, 1996); Richard Lounsbury, ed., *Louisa S. McCord: Poems, Drama, Biography, Letters* (Charlottesville, 1996) and *Louisa S. McCord: Political and Social Essays* (Charlottesville, 1995).

3 Nina Baym, *Woman's Fiction: Popular Novels by and about Women, 1820–1870* (Ithaca, 1978). Michael O'Brien's *Conjectures of Order* (Chapel Hill, 2004), the most important work on the mind of the South written in more than half a century, is a remarkably wide-ranging work that addresses important southern female thinkers such as Louisa McCord, the arch defender of the South and slavery whose essays appeared in regional magazines, and Mary Boykin Chesnut, the insightful observer of southern society. On McCord, see especially pp. 274–84 and 714–18; on O'Brien's superb analysis of Chesnut's importance to understanding southern intellectual culture, see pp. 1185–98.

4 Elizabeth Moss, *Domestic Novelists in the Old South: Defenders of Southern Culture* (Baton Rouge, 1992).

5 Catherine Kerrison, *Claiming the Pen: Women and Intellectual Life in the Early American South* (Ithaca, 2006), 1–33.

serialized in periodicals first, longer works of fiction are encompassed in the pages of periodicals. An examination of magazines provides a more complete picture of southern intellectual life because journals also included short stories, translations, poems, essays, editorials, advice, and critical reviews. As Mildred Lewis Rutherford, a Georgia native, wrote around the turn of the twentieth century, "When we realize that the press of the day sets the standard for literature more than books, and that we are influenced more by its opinion than by any one power, it behooves us to inquire into the character of the papers and magazines we read and have in our homes."[6] As Rutherford knew well, the numbers of magazines specifically designed for women increased dramatically after 1820 and expanded throughout the rest of the nineteenth century. Despite contemporaries' recognition of their importance, remarkably most of the hundreds of magazines published in the nineteenth-century South remain largely unexamined by modern historians and literary scholars.

That such neglect should be the rule is surprising given the richness of the content of southern literary periodicals. Compared to novels, the content that made up most of the pages of southern literary magazines was on the whole more freewheeling, more open to questioning received traditions, and broader in the range of topics discussed. This is not to say that southern periodicals were bastions of radicalism. On the contrary, periodical contents – especially those magazines aimed at white readers – reflected the values and customs of the southern society in which they were published. However, more commonly than in longer works of fiction, women felt at liberty in magazines to espouse their thoughts on a wide variety of issues. Such periodicals were by their nature more democratic than novels. Rather than the work of one author, magazines were usually a compilation of many different authors, some famous and others obscure. Southern magazines show just how widespread periodical writing and reading was in the nineteenth century; literally thousands of names of subscribers and contributors, some of them appearing just once, are recorded in print, testimony to a rich and diverse literary culture.

Magazines were of central importance to the literary culture of the South because the region lacked the publishing centers that could produce large numbers of books.[7] Published weekly, monthly, or quarterly, periodicals gained popularity in the opening decades of the nineteenth century because of their accessibility. Easily portable, newspapers and magazines could be sent through the increasingly sophisticated postal system for relatively low subscription rates. Modeled after prominent northern and European journals like *Graham's Magazine* and the *Edinburgh Review*, southern periodicals

[6] Mildred Lewis Rutherford, *The South in History and Literature* (Athens, 1906), 817.

[7] For an overview of the history of periodicals in the South to 1935, see Jay B. Hubbell's "Southern Magazines" in *Culture in the South* (Chapel Hill, 1935) edited by William T. Couch. See also Frank Luther Mott's seminal multi-volume work, *A History of American Magazines, 1741–1850*, especially volume 2 (Cambridge, 1966). See also Michael Winship, *American Literary Publishing in the Mid-Nineteenth Century: The Business of Ticknor and Fields* (Cambridge, UK, 1995).

combined poetry, short stories, and book reviews with essays on various topics. In addition, many southern periodicals provided religious news and were often affiliated with a particular faith. As Amy Beth Aronson has argued, by the antebellum period many magazines for women "had achieved the first form of best-seller status, reaching audiences across state lines, reaping consistent profits for their owners, making names for their writers and editors, and gaining substantial notice from the press and the general public."[8] Relatively affordable, with subscription rates ranging from one dollar to five dollars per year, periodicals were within the reach of the emerging middle class in both the North and South and thus spread quickly throughout the young nation. In addition, the compact size, which varied between a few pages and one hundred pages or more, rendered journals easily sent to large towns and rural areas alike. Indeed, as the postal records left behind indicate, magazines published in New York found their way into the smallest southern and western towns, and editors and authors could obtain national reputations shaped almost exclusively by their contributions to the popular and widely read magazines of the day.[9] Although it is true that some women shunned celebrity and used pen names to hide their identity, it is often mistakenly assumed that southern female authors universally veered from the public eye or wrote primarily for private consumption. As Mary Kelley argues in *Learning to Stand and Speak*, young white women had ample opportunity to demonstrate intellectual vigor in the public eye.[10] Research on women journalists bolsters this claim, proving that female authors harbored ambitions that drove them to seek lasting careers and even fame. They understood clearly that the short fiction and novels they penned, and the periodicals they edited, would endure far beyond their own lifetimes.[11]

One should not exaggerate the openness of southern literary culture; magazines and newspapers were limited to those who were educated, literate, and to those who had the disposable income to devote to subscriptions. Women from African American or laboring white families were less likely to obtain an education, less likely to be literate, and so less likely to become literary consumers. However, a broadening of southern literary culture can be attributed

[8] Amy Beth Aronson, *Taking Liberties: Early American Women's Magazines and their Readers* (Westport, 2002), 2. See also Jan Whitt, *Women in American Journalism: A New History* (Urbana, 2008) and Kathryn Shevelow, *Women and Print Culture: The Construction of Femininity in the Early Periodical* (London, 1989).

[9] Richard R. John, *Spreading the News: The American Postal System from Franklin to Morse* (Cambridge, MA, 1995). Numerous studies have underscored the great extent to which periodicals were sent to subscribers through the postal system, particularly after 1820. See Jonathan Daniel Wells, *The Origins of the Southern Middle Class, 1800–1861* (Chapel Hill, 2004), 42–57, and Amy M. Thomas, "Who Makes the Text? The Production and Use of Literature in Antebellum America," (Ph.D. diss., Duke University, 1992).

[10] Mary Kelley, *Learning to Stand and Speak: Women, Education, and Public Life in America's Republic* (Chapel Hill, 2006).

[11] Anne E. Boyd, *Writing for Immortality: Women and the Emergence of High Literary Culture in America* (Baltimore, 2004).

to the emergence of a middle class in the early nineteenth-century South. Recently scholars have come to appreciate the importance of the professional and commercial middle class in the region. Considerable scholarly attention has been and continues to be directed at the planter class, but researchers are also beginning to examine the culture of middle-class doctors, merchants, teachers, lawyers, and editors. The emerging middle class in the nineteenth century provided a new and important readership for magazines, and the increase in the number of publications after 1820 coincides with the similarly rapid expansion of this new literate and enterprising southern middle class.[12] Middle-class women were central to the expansion of southern intellectual and literary culture as editors, contributors, and subscribers.

Whereas readership was largely limited to the upper and middle classes, whiteness also circumscribed southern periodical culture, at least in the antebellum era. Early nineteenth-century southern periodicals were almost exclusively limited to a white readership; and throughout the pre-Civil War South and in the immediate postbellum era, white women were in a much better position to make literary contributions as writers and editors. If, as Faulkner suggests, white women remain mere apparitions, then black women writers in the late nineteenth-century and early twentieth-century South are even more phantom-like. We have learned a great deal from important studies by scholars such as Valerie Smith, Frances Smith Foster, Henry Louis Gates, Jr., Dickson Bruce, and others; and Oxford University Press' series reprinting many key works by African American women authors of the late 1800s and early 1900s represents a seminal contribution to our understanding of southern writers of color.[13] Aside from the important work of Ida B. Wells, however, we still know little about the contributions of black women editors and journalists in the late nineteenth-century South. The antebellum period was much more open to the participation of white rather than black women in the literary and intellectual culture of the region, and thus these women dominate the first part of the book. But even in the pre-Civil War years, one can point to important contributions made by African American women such as Hannah Crafts (which may have been a pen name for Jane Johnson) and Harriet Jacobs.

There were a few African American journals published in the antebellum North but none that we know of in the South until the Civil War. In the Old South, African Americans usually appeared in the pages of magazines only as the subjects of political discussions over slavery. There are rare exceptions to this rule, such as the publication of two poems by the North Carolina slave

[12] On the southern middle class, see Wells, *The Origins of the Southern Middle Class*, Jennifer R. Green, *Military Education and the Emerging Middle Class in the Old South* (Cambridge, 2008), and Frank J. Byrne, *Becoming Bourgeois: Merchant Culture in the South, 1820–1865* (Lexington, KY, 2006).

[13] See, for example, Valerie Smith, *Self-Discovery and Authority in Afro-American Narrative* (Cambridge, 1987); Dickson D. Bruce Jr., *The Origins of African American Literature, 1680–1865* (Charlottesville, 2001); Frances Smith Foster, *Written by Herself: Literary Production by African American Women, 1746–1892* (Bloomington, 1993).

George Moses Horton in the pages of Richmond's *Southern Literary Messenger* in 1841. As literary subjects, slave women are almost totally absent in such journals. Emancipation, however, gradually opened an entirely new world of journalism to former slaves. In the latter half of the nineteenth century, journalism became for black women a path to self-expression, expanded rights, and public prominence, just as it had for white southern women. Aided by a new phalanx of black women editors and writers, a wide range of periodicals for African American readers persisted in the late nineteenth-century South. Penelope Bullock found that nearly a hundred African American journals were launched between 1838 and 1909, many of which originated in the South.[14] Magazines and newspapers associated with religious denominations, literary clubs, temperance reform, and other groups were vital forums for the black community. As Evelyn Brooks Higginbotham has argued, for women periodicals "affirmed their bond with one another, informed readers of their goals and periodic meetings, and featured news of general interest to their sex."[15]

Historians have enhanced our understanding of emancipation by analyzing the South's transition to free labor after the war. According to Tera Hunter, African American women in the decades after slavery's end moved to cities like Atlanta in pursuit of work that allowed them to enjoy freedom. Unfortunately, racism funneled these women into domestic service. Despite limited occupational opportunities, and the continued subjugation of rural blacks in the form of sharecropping and tenant farming, there were also victories as Hunter highlights women's quest for independence.[16] Such quests were to pay dividends. In the late 1800s, black readers, writers, and editors began to create a flourishing periodical culture that grew in size and importance by the turn of the twentieth century. After the first periodicals aimed at a black readership were published sporadically in the 1860s, magazines and newspapers became a vital part of African American life in the 1870s and 1880s. In fact, the growth of the black periodical press in the late 1800s and early 1900s should be seen as part of an emerging black middle-class culture, just as periodicals were vital to the rise of the white southern middle class in the early period. African American teachers, clergy, businessmen, and professionals subscribed to the new magazines, and black women pioneers helped to shape this black middle class as editors and writers. Thus, the expansion of the region's literary culture was a gradual process, beginning first with the journalistic efforts of white women in the antebellum years and culminating in the early twentieth century with the vigorous work of southern black women.

Early white feminists failed to see the crucial importance of joining their African American sisters in the fight for gender equality. Because of rigid

[14] Penelope L. Bullock, *The Afro-American Periodical Press, 1838–1909* (Baton Rouge, 1981), 2.

[15] Evelyn Brooks Higginbotham, *Righteous Discontent: The Women's Movement in the Black Baptist Church, 1880–1920* (Cambridge, 1993), 76.

[16] Tera W. Hunter, *To 'Joy My Freedom: Southern Black Women's Lives and Labors after the Civil War* (Cambridge, 1997).

segregation, white and black women journalists and writers seemingly inhabited two separate worlds, rarely communicating or even acknowledging one another. The historian of southern journalism searches largely in vain for evidence of cross-racial collaboration or even cross-racial dialogue. As historians of the southern women's movement have shown, segregation posed substantial barriers to racial and gender justice. Black women writers and editors contributed much that was powerful, heartfelt, and potentially quite useful in the push for gender equality. White women generally refused to acknowledge these contributions. Using the hindsight of the historian, however, the writings of black and white women reveal a common purpose: to prove, through literary endeavors, that women could compete intellectually with men. It was this goal, this effort to convince readers of their talents, that drove women authors, journalists, and editors to make the case for the intellectual equality that would become the basis for calls for greater political equality.

Even in the colonial period, a few women could be found serving as newspaper or magazine editors. Perhaps the first southern woman to head a newspaper was Charleston's Elizabeth Timothy. Born in Holland, Timothy moved to Philadelphia in 1731 and then to Charleston in 1734 where Elizabeth and her newspaperman husband, Louis, founded the *South Carolina Gazette*. Louis was killed tragically at the end of 1738, and Elizabeth elected to continue the biweekly paper until 1746. Soon after she took control of the paper, Timothy stated that she "hoped to make the paper as entertaining and correct as may be reasonably expected.... I flatter myself that persons who assisted my Husband will be kindly pleased to continue their favours to his poor afflicted widow and six small children."[17] In 1746, she passed on the editorial duties to her son Peter, and later her daughter-in-law edited the paper as well.[18] Timothy was not alone; other colonial women in the South edited papers as well, though their numbers never grew beyond a handful.[19]

Although women editors existed before 1800, the antebellum era witnessed unprecedented numbers of white women who actively participated in the

[17] Timothy quoted in Marjorie Barlow, ed., *Notes on Woman Printers in Colonial American and the United States, 1639–1975* (Charlottesville, 1976), 66.

[18] Barlow, *Notes on Woman Printers*, 66–7; John Clyde Oswald, *Printing in the Americas* (New York, 1937), 182–3; Elizabeth Williams Anthony Dexter, *Career Women of America, 1776–1840* (Francetown, NH, 1950), 102; Edward T. James, *Notable American Women, 1607–1950* (Cambridge, 1971), 465–6; Leona M. Hudak, *Early American Women Printers and Publishers, 1639–1820* (Metuchen, NJ, 1978), 131–63. Elizabeth Timothy also ran a store in Charleston that sold books and stationery.

[19] Mary Wilkenson Crouch edited the *Charleston Gazette* between 1778 and 1780. Barlow, *Notes on Woman Printers*, 65–6. Anne Catherine Green edited the *Maryland Gazette* from 1767 to 1772, Mary Katherine Goddard of Maryland edited the *Maryland Journal & Baltimore Advertiser* during the Revolution, and Phoebe Herbert ran the *Washington Spy* from 1795 to 1797. Barlow, *Notes on Woman Printers*, 30–2; Oswald, *Printing in the Americas*, 184–5; Dexter, *Career Women of America*, 102–4; Hudak, *Early American Women Printers and Publishers*, 602–8.

South's literary culture as writers and readers. The importance of women as a market of literary consumers rose with the proliferation of female educational institutions. As the antebellum cause of female education became the battle cry of the southern orator and author alike, and southerners backed up the rhetoric with greater numbers of women's schools, the market for women's periodicals grew in proportion. The development of educational opportunities for women before the Civil War, motivated initially by conservative attachments to women's domestic duties, opened up the literary culture of the Old South to which women contributed significantly as students, authors, and editors.[20]

Southerners established literary magazines for women for many different reasons. Some began in conjunction with a female college or to spread the word of a particular religion. Others were inaugurated to promote the cause of an independent southern literature, while still others became a forum for women's creative talents. In addition to the open nature of periodicals that encouraged women contributors, women also filled roles as editors. About a dozen southern women edited their own periodicals before the Civil War, and many more did so in the late nineteenth century. Although few women would have called themselves "journalists" before the war, the late nineteenth century witnessed the evolution of the title until by the 1870s and 1880s women not only referred to themselves with the professional appellation of "journalist," but they also formed professional press associations. Thus, by examining female writers and editors over the course of the 1800s, we see the growing acceptance of women first as literary consumers, then as contributors, followed by roles as associate or assistant editors to male publishers, then as chief editors of newspapers and magazines themselves. Of course, this evolution was hardly a linear one; in some ways white women editors like Mary Chase Barney, Anne Newport Royall, and Rebecca Hicks, all of whom edited magazines in the early nineteenth-century South, were the boldest editors of the entire century. Slavery and racism prevented black women from becoming journalists and editors in the South until after the war, but they quickly became active in writing for and editing periodicals beginning in the 1870s. So despite the different paths black and white women took to journalism over the course of the nineteenth century, and despite the uneven and nonlinear progression of white women in becoming members of the press, the broader advance of women from literary consumers to literary producers is clear.

In embarking on careers in journalism, southern women were pushing against traditional boundaries. Whatever the impetus, these periodicals became important avenues for female self-expression. As Amy Beth Aronson points out, "The early women's magazines made available to all women theoretically – but to some influential women realistically – the opportunity to break through a gender-imposed silence in the public sphere."[21] As

[20] Mary Kelley, "Reading Women/Women Reading: The Making of Learned Women in Antebellum America," *Journal of American History* 83 (September 1996), 401–24.

[21] Aronson, *Taking Liberties*, 12.

editors, contributors, correspondents, and reporters in the nineteenth century, women were entering traditionally male bastions. Particularly in the late 1700s and early 1800s, the periodical business was characterized often by rough political maneuvering, with newspapers and magazines publishing wildly partisan accusations against political opponents even as they also offered readers news, poems, and short stories. Joseph Dennie's *Portfolio*, for example, leveled a constant barrage of attacks against Republicans in support of the Federalist cause in the early 1800s.[22] Thus, when women engaged in the world of periodical publishing, they were stepping into an arena that had been almost the exclusive province of men since the first magazines and newspapers were printed.

At the same time, however, journalism for women was often an outgrowth of their careers as authors, and here women were apt to encounter less resistance. From the earliest days of the colonial period, but especially in the early republic, women were recognized for their talents in poetry and prose. Women writers were widely accepted, praised, and promoted in the early nineteenth century, and writers such as Connecticut's Lydia Huntley Sigourney were universally welcomed in the pages of both northern and southern magazines. Women, in fact, were believed to be well-suited to careers as authors because they were thought to be more attuned to their emotions, and the ability to convey feelings through literature was an asset in the Romantic Age. As historian Joan E. Cashin has argued, white women's "culture fostered high expectations about expressing feelings in private relationships."[23] According to prevailing gender ideology, emotional effusiveness facilitated the writing of poetry. Many of the late nineteenth-century black and white women journalists began their careers earlier in the century as poets and authors of short fiction. The acceptance of women writers in the Old South was an important foundation for their later acceptance as members of the press.

Still, the process was a gradual one. Not until the late nineteenth century did women begin to form press associations and to think of themselves as professional journalists.[24] What may be most surprising to the modern observer is the significant level of acceptance, encouragement, and even admiration that southern women journalists experienced. Although the odd curmudgeon opposed to career women could be found in both the North and South, there were remarkably few complaints against women contributors or editors before or after the Civil War in the South. "There should not be any essential functional disparity between the journalist male and the journalist female," maintained

[22] William C. Dowling, *Literary Federalism in the Age of Jefferson: Joseph Dennie and The Portfolio, 1801–1812* (Columbia, 1999).

[23] Joan E. Cashin, ed., *Our Common Affairs: Texts from Women in the Old South* (Baltimore, 1996), 18.

[24] For a useful discussion of journalism and women in the British context, see Hilary Fraser, Stephanie Green, and Judith Johnston, *Gender and the Victorian Periodical* (Cambridge, 2003), ch. 3.

E. A. Bennett at the end of the 1800s.[25] Bennett added that "women journalists as a body have faults.... But I deny that these faults are natural.... They are due not to sex, but to the subtle, far-reaching effects of early training."[26] One should not proclaim that the nineteenth-century South was more open to transcending traditional boundaries than it in fact was. But neither should its differences with the North in the same time period be exaggerated. Southern women, like their northern counterparts, expressed in public and private their desires to venture beyond traditional roles in every decade from the 1820s through the 1890s. Particularly after the women's exposition at the World's Fair in Chicago in 1893, southern women considered themselves as members of the press on a par with men.

Women became journalists, editors, and authors through careful planning or by happenstance, and the wide-ranging characteristics of female members of the press is one of the findings of this study. As we shall see, many southern women, particularly in the antebellum era, found themselves heading up a newspaper or magazine after the death of their journalist husbands. Widows had children to support and felt pressed, often against their own judgment and despite significant feelings of inadequacy, to take over for their husbands. For other women editors and journalists, careers were the result of careful planning and working their way up from contributors to periodicals to perhaps heading up a literary department to the uppermost step of taking on a role as editor. This latter path was more common in the later nineteenth century, for by the 1880s educated women were beginning to see journalism as a respected professional pursuit in which learning, reading, and literary talents could combine to make a woman suited to a career.

"Editorship as a Profession for Women," a late nineteenth-century essay by Margaret Sangster, a newspaper journalist known on both sides of the Atlantic, provides some insight into how women prepared themselves for careers in journalism. In encouraging young women to consider journalism as a profession, Sangster grouped journalism together with other middle-class pursuits open to "the woman of good family and liberal education."[27] "A wife," Sangster noted, "often supplements the family purse by her own exertions, and is honored in doing so. Women are doctors, ministers, lawyers, college presidents, and journalists." In addition to female members of the press who served as reporters, literary contributors, and correspondents, women editors were growing in number and prominence in the late 1800s, and Sangster focused on encouraging more young women to enter the field. She was careful to warn her readers that a career in editing was not to be taken lightly but instead entailed numerous hardships: "Editorship presents a most inviting opportunity to the woman who dares to undertake its duties and fulfill its arduous

[25] E. A. Bennett, *Journalism for Women: A Practical Guide* (London, 1898), 9.

[26] *Ibid.*, 11.

[27] Margaret Elizabeth Sangster, "Editorship as a Profession for Women," *Forum* (December 1895), 446.

exactions. Strenuous in obligation, unremitting in requirement, peremptory in the task-master-taking of tolls from body and mind, bristling with difficulties, and beset with drudgeries, it nevertheless repays the worker in multiplied measure."[28] Sangster argued that only particular personality characteristics were suited to careers in journalism, and successful women editors possessed a unique blend of qualities and skills of which only a few could boast. "The personality of the woman seeking editorship," she claimed, "if not winning, should at least be impressive. She needs to be intellectual, receptive, alert, sympathetic; in touch with issues of current thought and action, and with the drifts of current enterprise and discovery. As for her body, it must fitly sheathe so vital and so dominant a soul. Steel and India-rubber are not too strong or too flexible for the physical make-up of the woman in this case.... An editor is, in one bundle, doctor, mother, friend, counselor, physician, comrade, companion, and consoler."[29] As she makes clear, women in the nineteenth-century South, like their northern counterparts, were expected to be "Renaissance women," able to converse intelligently on an expansive range of subjects while at the same time fulfilling all of their duties as wives and mothers. Young women's education, even in the early decades of the nineteenth century, was designed to prepare southern girls for genteel society but to train them as well for their roles as teachers to their children.

There were, however, limits to what was expected or even desired in southern women authors and journalists, and Sangster openly acknowledged these limitations on women as proper and wise. She chastised those female editors who proclaimed that "'I will do my work like a man.'" Sangster was careful to explain that women and men were physically different, requiring different approaches to work in an office. "Few women," she claimed, "can work as relentlessly and with as sternly rigid endeavor as most men may safely do.... She cannot do it in precisely the same way, nor should she do violence to her sex by the attempt.... No woman can with safety work all day long in an office."[30] Thus, as late as 1895, even with women editors commonly found throughout the North and South, and with women's press associations already operating as professional organizations, Sangster felt compelled to counsel women to avoid the strains of overworking in an office environment. In fact, she argued that the bodies of female editors required proper eating, considerable exercise, and constant monitoring to ensure they were not jeopardizing their health. Thus, even the most vigorous supporters of female journalists presented caveats to ensure that men and women were not viewed in precisely the same way.

On the other hand, many female editors and journalists in the nineteenth-century South, especially by the 1880s and 1890s, were bold and persistent advocates of the suffrage movement and for gender equality more broadly. Corinne Stocker, for example, was born in Orangeburg, South Carolina, but

[28] *Ibid.*, 447.
[29] *Ibid.*, 448–9.
[30] *Ibid.*, 453.

earned fame throughout the South as an editor for the *Atlanta Journal*. Like other southern female members of the press, she helped organize women and served as a delegate to the National American Woman's Suffrage Association in Washington in 1896.[31] Importantly, many of these women used their education and literary talents to venture beyond traditional limitations just as they did in the North. Particularly in public roles as editors of literary magazines and newspapers, antebellum women helped to lay the foundations for later nineteenth-century crusades for equality. In fact, as Marjorie Spruill points out, many advocates of female suffrage in the 1890s, including Sue Shelton White, Rebecca Latimer Felton, and Mary Johnston, had backgrounds in journalism or literature.[32] Long before calls for women's political equality emerged in the early twentieth century, and even well before late nineteenth-century women's involvement in clubs and associations, southern women asserted the intellectual equality of the sexes.

This is the first study to examine collectively women journalists and writers in the nineteenth-century South. It offers new perspectives on women and intellectual life in the region, the roots of the southern movement for women's rights, and sectional distinctiveness.

The study advances several key arguments. First, female journalists and periodical culture were fundamentally important to the southern movement for women's rights. Whereas scholars have illuminated the role of the club movement and other factors in facilitating the development of a cohort of pro-suffrage activists, the crucial roles played by women's magazines, journalists, editors, and contributors have not been appreciated. In fact, even given the importance of the club movement in the late nineteenth century, understanding the part played by female journalists and authors in promoting gender equality contributes to the broader sense of how such a movement emerged in the South. Whereas scholars have long mined the archives of a few southern periodicals, most notably *The Southern Literary Messenger*, *The Southern Quarterly Review*, and *De Bow's Review*, in important ways the richness of periodical culture is to be found in more obscure magazines. When one examines the diverse contents of women's magazines, it quickly becomes clear that women were willing to express sentiments in periodicals that they rarely offered elsewhere. Some female editors, such as the Old South's Mary Chase Barney or the New South's Ida B. Wells, were outspoken on politics, gender inequality, or racial injustice.

In addition to their contribution to the cause of expanding women's rights, journalism and periodicals were important vehicles for black and white women's self-expression, helping to enrich and enliven the region's literary

[31] Margherita Arlina Hamm, "Woman's Broader Life," *Arthur's Home Magazine* 46 (January 1896), 24.

[32] Marjorie Spruill Wheeler, *New Women of the New South: The Leaders of the Woman Suffrage Movement in the Southern States* (New York, 1993), 40–1.

and intellectual culture. The magazines and newspapers of the nineteenth-century South are testimony, not only to the existence of women journalists and authors, but also to their productive and creative abilities. Although scholars have studied female novelists such as Mary Virginia Terhune and Augusta Jane Evans, little is known about the female editors and journalists of the late nineteenth century, and even less is known about the several southern women who edited their own periodicals before the Civil War. The literary and intellectual achievements of women journalists emanated from the movement for female education beginning in the early 1800s and the concomitant debate over to what extent men and women were intellectually equal. A newly educated generation of women in the first decades of the nineteenth century became writers who contributed to magazines and literary newspapers, which in turn provided a path to careers as editors and associate editors and, by the late 1800s, became the basis for professional black and white women journalists who headed nationally known periodicals and formed their own press associations. These important aspects of the nineteenth-century southern culture are almost completely forgotten. This volume will hopefully add to our understanding of and appreciation for the literary life of the nineteenth-century South.

A related point is that women engaged in many literary and intellectual activities at once. While writing for or editing periodicals, women were also often teachers, lecturers, or engaged in other professional pursuits, in addition to their domestic duties. African American women writers and journalists, including Anna Julia Cooper, Mary Church Terrell, Mary Virginia Cook, and Frances Harper, won acclaim for their oratorical skills as well as their literary work. A chief aim of this book is to convey to the reader the importance of examining the full range of southern magazines.

Finally, the chapters that follow argue that the difference between the North and South on matters of gender has been exaggerated, in both the antebellum and postbellum eras. To be sure, vast differences over slavery and economic development divided the sections, but northerners and southerners largely shared a common gender ideology. Scholars have recently come to question the value of thinking about nineteenth-century notions of gender in terms of separate spheres for men and women, and have criticized Jürgen Habermas for largely leaving women out of his understanding of these spheres. However, the notion of separate spheres for men and women does reflect to some degree how nineteenth-century Americans themselves understood their world.

Scholars have viewed the creation of separate spheres for men and women as a product of the early nineteenth-century urbanization and industrialization, changes that carried the husband and father outside the home to find work and left the domestic sphere to women.[33] Nineteenth-century southerners, however, with a far less industrialized and urbanized society than existed

[33] Linda Kerber, "Separate Spheres, Female Worlds, Woman's Place: The Rhetoric of Women's History," *Journal of American History* 65 (June 1988), 9–39.

in the North, believed strongly in the notion of separate public and private spheres for men and women and promulgated the same ideas in newspapers and magazines. Thus, the notion of separate spheres, a powerful and pervasive component of southern thinking, should not be attributed to economic trends but instead to long-held ideas regarding the biological nature of the sexes. In short, the innate characteristics of men, including aggressiveness, ambition, boldness, and physical vigor allegedly rendered them better suited to the public world of politics and work. The natural tendencies of women, so the thinking went, veered toward shyness, emotion, and physical and mental delicacy, making them more adapted to the domestic arena. These widely cherished ideas regarding gender difference were the origins of separate sphere ideology and thus could be shared by the largely agricultural nineteenth-century South with a vigor and tenacity equal to northerners.[34] As the present work demonstrates, however, the ideology of separate spheres harbored the seeds of its own demise. The notion of a separate domain for women provided an alternate road to female activism that helped to spur greater calls for gender equality in the post-Civil War era.

The book is divided into three sections, the first of which provides historical context for the emergence of women journalists and editors in the nineteenth-century South. Part I is more thematic than chronological. Chapters 1 and 2 address the push for female education and the effect of such efforts on southern girls and young women. Interestingly, the movement for greater educational opportunities for southern women arose from the widespread recognition that mothers needed to be learned in a wide range of disciplines in order to be properly suited to teach their children, who, after all, were the future citizens and statesmen of the Republic. The emphasis on educating white women was so powerful that the theme is ubiquitous in southern periodicals, speeches, and pamphlets. Though perhaps somewhat cursory due to the emphasis on breadth rather than depth, the schooling southern girls received left them at least partially educated but with precious few outlets for that knowledge outside of motherhood. Through reading and by stressing that men and women were intellectually equal, literary culture was the one arena in which women could find individual achievement, professional rewards, and public acknowledgment.

Parts II and III then offer chronological as well as thematic approaches to understanding women authors, literary periodicals, and editors. Part II focuses on women writers, journalists, editors, and periodicals in the South between roughly 1820 and 1860. Although there were a few notable women printers and editors in the southern states before 1820, during the antebellum period white women began to create a professional niche in the world of magazines

[34] Examples will follow in later chapters, but a good starting point for exploring separate sphere ideology in the South can be seen in "Woman – Her Sphere," Charleston *Southern Patriot* 39 (March 30, 1838), 2.

and newspapers. Key to the importance of the 1820s and 1830s for this growth of women journalists was the improved postal system, which was aided significantly by advances in transportation. Such progress rendered periodicals easily transportable, relatively inexpensive, and well-suited to the developing literary culture of the Old South. The 1830s witnessed the emergence of pioneer white female editors like Mary Barney, Anne Royall, Frances Bumpass, Caroline Gilman, Virginia Smith French, and Rachel Jones Holton.

The final chapters offer insight into postwar women editors and journalists as well as the formation of press associations for women. Part III addresses the increasing professionalization of the field, indicated not just by the greater numbers of female members of the press after 1865 but also by the establishment of specialized groups and organizations. In addition, as many of these women were also advocates for female suffrage and equality, journalists played an underappreciated role in the southern movement for women's rights. Mary E. Bryan, Ellen Dortch, Elia Goode Byington, Eliza Nicholson, and Martha R. Field were all leading journalists who provided important models for the hundreds of other female journalists in the New South to follow. Perhaps more importantly, the postwar South also harbored the first southern black women journalists, the most significant of whom, Ida B. Wells-Barnett, wrote about racial as well as gender injustice. The stories of these white and black female journalists, too long untold, add richly to our understanding of gender roles, the evolution of the southern movement for women's rights, and the literary culture of the nineteenth-century South.

PART ONE

FOUNDATIONS

Sarah Cooper, a young white woman living in Virginia in the early 1820s, dreamed of a life beyond the confines of her family's farm. Cooper fashioned herself a future journalist, the editor of some important big-city daily. Too young perhaps to realize fully the limits placed on her gender by society, Cooper – probably inspired by the many newspapers and magazines read by her parents and neighbors in Fairfax County – went beyond simply daydreaming of a future career as an editor. With painstaking effort, she handwrote her own edition of a literary magazine. The first of her attempts that survive, an unnamed four-page journal, consisted of a mix of poetry, stories, and short selections, all meticulously written in columns just as they might appear if published. Her opinions and personality show through; one selection referred to men as "the vain things." Two years later, still fashioning herself an editor, she composed by hand another homemade magazine entitled "The Fulminator." In addition to composing poems and short stories, Cooper carefully illustrated a masthead, complete with the title, subscription terms, and volume number, and even took the trouble to draw ersatz advertisements.[1]

Cooper's considerable efforts are both saddening and telling. Saddening, because despite grand designs and obvious talent, girls and young women like Cooper were unlikely to become journalists, at least before the Civil War. Yet, Cooper's ambitions are also telling, for women yearned for careers outside the home, for outlets for creative expression and opportunities to earn fame. A few would even beat the odds and realize their dreams. Although there is no evidence that Sarah Cooper ever became a journalist, other nineteenth-century southern women, both black and white, did fulfill such dreams, against considerable odds and overcoming significant barriers.

Because so little has been written about them, however, the emergence of female journalists in the nineteenth-century South warrants considerable

[1] Homemade magazines deposited in the Cooper Family Papers, Virginia Historical Society. Many thanks to Lee Shepard of the society for bringing the handcrafted periodicals to my attention.

explanation. How did a society with conservative views on gender, a society that placed the belle on a pedestal, come to harbor women journalists? How did white women embark on such careers and yet remain largely excluded from other professional pursuits? How did many southerners come to see men and women as intellectual equals? To answer such questions, and to understand the context for the appearance of southern women writers and journalists in the 1800s, we must appreciate and come to grips with the debates over female education, reading, and the intellectual equality of the sexes that pervaded antebellum southern culture.

1

Reading, Literary Magazines, and the Debate over Gender Equality

In an 1855 editorial in her magazine *The Kaleidoscope*, Virginia's Rebecca Hicks asked her readers to question the validity of traditional perceptions of gender, especially in regard to intellectual ability: "Why all this ado about the natural superiority of men's minds? They are *sometimes* superior, I grant, but that they are often hopelessly inferior, nobody with a pair of eyes in his head, can ever pretend to deny. Men are sometimes stupid, and women are sometimes wonderfully gifted, and there's no use in denying it, and all we ask of the men is to stand back and give us fair play."[1] Hicks denied that significant, inherent intellectual differences existed between men and women and instead attributed disparities in accomplishments to discrimination and cultural biases. "The man who would deny to women," Hicks asked in another editorial, "the cultivation of her intellect ought, for consistency, to shut her up in a harem." Her frustrations with gender inequality came through the pages of her magazine clearly. "In *what*, besides physical strength, are we inferior to man? Can any one tell us where *his* domain ends, and ours begins? What has he done, with all his advantages, that we have not done with all our disadvantages?"[2]

Hicks argued that women deserved a thorough education on a par with men, and many southerners agreed.[3] Yet nineteenth-century southerners were also deeply conflicted about the meaning and nature of gender. How well were women mentally prepared for such a broad, liberal education? Were women intellectually capable of understanding philosophy, science, and mathematics? Nineteenth-century southerners devoted a great deal of time and energy to exploring the limitations and possibilities of the female mind, and women writers contributed significantly to these debates. In doing so, women authors subtly argued that intellectual equality was a precursor to political equality.

[1] Rebecca Hicks, "Woman's Rights," *The Kaleidoscope* 1 (February 7, 1855), 29.

[2] Hicks, "Literary Women," *The Kaleidoscope* 1 (March 14, 1855), 68.

[3] Christine Jacobson Carter, *Southern Single Blessedness: Unmarried Women in the Urban South, 1800–1865* (Urbana, 2006), 41–64.

Importantly, magazines were the primary vehicles through which these issues and questions on the meaning of gender difference were debated.

Southern intellectuals explored the similarities and differences between men and women and were often uncertain in their conclusions. On the one hand, women were often depicted in southern novels, poems, and essays as possessing stronger emotions than men. It was widely assumed, not just in the South but also in the broader Western world, that women were more maudlin, more often given to weeping and melancholy, and more easily swayed by appeals to the heart. As historian Kirsten Fischer has shown, the belief that men and women were two fundamentally different beings was rooted in eighteenth-century European Enlightenment thought.[4] Yet if women were closer to their feelings, and could draw on a wealth of emotional power to enrich their fiction, then perhaps they were even more temperamentally well-matched to the act of writing than men. Although their physical makeup was different, this did not necessarily translate in the minds of some southerners into mental inferiority. As one Florida man wrote to his granddaughter, "Generally speaking, the women have not been treated with justice by the male sex.... But if the woman be inferior to the man in bodily strength, her mind is equally vigorous as his.... The fact appears to be this, the men have entered into a kind of conspiracy to keep the women in the background."[5] To what extent were the differences in accomplishments between men and women a result of gaps in educational opportunities? Were there substantive distinctions between the mental abilities of men and women or merely differences based on cultural experience and upbringing? Southerners debated such questions with dynamism and often keen insight in the mid-nineteenth century.

Whereas many southerners continued to assert that there were differences in the mental aptitudes of the sexes rooted in biology, others recognized that custom and culture, not innate differences, were responsible for creating disparate levels of intellectual achievements for men and women. As a commentator noted in an 1834 edition of the *Nashville Banner and Nashville Whig*, "Much is said about the inherently distinctive differences existing between men and women. I believe them to be few; and that they are neither mental nor moral ones. Till the respective discipline under which male and female children are trained begins to operate, no dissimilarity is discernable."[6] The issue of whether or to what extent gender was a factor in mental acuity is one that historians have largely neglected but one that contemporary southerners believed was central to establishing the proper roles for men and women.

Understanding the debate over the intellectual equality of men and women has a number of important implications for our broader understanding of the

[4] Kirsten Fischer, *Suspect Relations: Sex, Race, and Resistance in Colonial North Carolina* (Ithaca, 2002), 10–13.

[5] Marcus Cicero Stephens to Mary Ann Primrose, Marcus Cicero Stephens Letters, Southern Historical Collection, University of North Carolina, Chapel Hill.

[6] "Men and Women," *Nashville Banner and Nashville Whig* 22 (November 5, 1834), 3.

South and its female writers and journalists. First, acknowledging the extent to which southerners were willing to debate publicly the notion of gender equality complicates our picture of dissent in the region. In fact, numerous recent books indicate that a more vibrant culture of dissent existed in the South than was believed previously. William Freehling, Margaret Storey, James Alex Baggett, and other scholars have identified a vocal and influential minority of southerners in the mid-nineteenth century who questioned the fundamental tenets of southern society.[7] Similarly, the heretofore unexplored discussions of comparative intellectual ability complicates the popular image of a region closed to ideas that ran counter to tradition and helps to bolster the conclusions of recent scholarship that dissent existed in the region before, during, and after the Civil War.

Race complicated the issue of gender difference even further. At the same time that southerners debated the meaning of gender, southerners engaged in a parallel discussion over race. White southerners argued that slaves and free blacks were inherently intellectually inferior, a point that even lukewarm supporters of slavery failed to question. In fact, much of the deliberations on race merely assumed white racial superiority and sought instead to understand the origins of the assumed differences in the intellectual capacity of the races. White southerners proved much more willing to believe that any differences in the accomplishments of white men and women were the product of culture, upbringing, and education. They did not apply the same rationale to perceived distinctions between the achievements of blacks and whites.

If in fact many southerners openly accepted or at least were willing to entertain the notion that women were the intellectual equals of men, then our view of the antebellum South as the uniquely staunch defender of traditional roles must be reexamined. In fact, the close ties between the North and South, particularly the cultural links forged between readers of periodical literature, suggest that sectional distinctions on matters of gender may be overstated. The ties between the sections provided the foundation for a shared intellectual culture that blurred sectional boundaries.

The debate over gender and intellectual ability included some of the region's leading thinkers. Thomas R. Dew, the Virginia professor of history who became president of William and Mary College, published a lengthy treatise on the intellectual equality of the sexes in the region's leading monthly magazine, the *Southern Literary Messenger*, in 1835. Dew clearly discerned differences, he believed, in the intellectual abilities of men and women. He argued that

[7] See, for example, Margaret M. Storey, *Loyalty and Loss: Alabama's Unionists in the Civil War and Reconstruction* (Baton Rouge, 2004); John C. Inscoe and Robert C. Kenzer, eds., *Enemies of the Country: New Perspectives on Unionists in the Civil War South* (Athens, 2004); James Alex Baggett, *The Scalawags: Southern Dissenters in the Civil War and Reconstruction* (Baton Rouge, 2002); William Freehling, *The South vs. the South: How Anti-Confederate Southerners Shaped the Course of the Civil War* (New York, 2002).

men were more properly suited to politics and statesmanship, whereas women possessed "humane feelings" and "kindly sympathies."[8] Like other commentators, Dew viewed woman as man's companion and helpmate.[9] However, Dew found the question of the intellectual differences between the sexes a particularly perplexing one; few questions had so consumed philosophers and thinkers of every age. The debate over men and women's mental capabilities, he argued, had "given rise to more speculation, sophism, and false reasoning, than any others observable between the sexes."[10] Dew maintained that in virtually every past civilization, men were the leaders in both the political and intellectual arenas. Throughout history, "all the great, and learned, and lucrative occupations of life are filled by him."[11] But, Dew asked, "Whence arises this actual superiority? Is it the result of nature? Or is it the result of education ...? Is the capacity of man naturally greater than that of woman? Or are they born with equal natural endowments in this respect?"[12]

Surprisingly, Dew attributed women's seeming inferiority to mere inadequacy of education. "I am inclined to belief, that there is *no natural* difference between the intellectual powers of man and woman, and that the differences observable between them in this respect at mature age, are wholly the result of education physical and moral." "We find," Dew argued, "that the education which boys receive from teachers, is much more scientific and complete than that of the girls."[13] Dew's chief complaint was that girls received only a superficial education in a few ornamental subjects. At too young an age, a girl left school, entering "into all the scenes of gaiety and fashion, and is frequently married before that age at which the boy is sent to college."[14] He maintained that the disciplines requiring a higher level of reasoning, like the sciences, philosophy, and mathematics, were only valuable to students of a certain age (Dew thought that students could only grasp these subjects at about the age of seventeen). It was no wonder, he declared, that relatively few women throughout history could be found as significant contributors to philosophy, physics, or the law. They were not permitted to remain in school long enough to be usefully instructed. Furthermore, Dew pointed out, society more broadly was much more encouraging of boys than girls. "They [boys] are much more stimulated and encouraged by parents, guardians, and friends, to persevere in the arduous, and at first excessively disagreeable career of study and literary labor."[15] Dew fell back on the notion that women were in fact "domestic" in habits, fitted for the social circle, and better able to grasp the importance

[8] Dew, "Dissertation on the Characteristic Differences between the Sexes, and on the Position and Influence of Woman in Society," *Southern Literary Messenger* 1 (August 1835), 672.

[9] *Ibid.*, 673.

[10] *Ibid.*, 675.

[11] *Ibid.*, 676.

[12] *Ibid.*

[13] *Ibid.*

[14] *Ibid.*, 677.

[15] *Ibid.*

of their own family as opposed to the needs of an entire nation, which men, because of their superior ability to form abstract ideas, could consider. Still, even this inability to form abstract arguments he ascribed to the training and experience to which women were subjected at a young age, and less so to any innate differences between the sexes. Overall, Dew's essay exhibited a relatively insightful and sophisticated understanding of the causes of perceived distinctions between men and women.

While Dew offered his opinions in a series of published magazine essays, another careful writer on the subject expressed strong opinions in the same widely read pages of the *Southern Literary Messenger.* Identified only as "N. Carolina," this writer forthrightly stated the case for the intellectual equality of women with unusual boldness. "We cannot see," the author maintained, "why the same means used in the education of girls as in that of boys, should not be productive of the same results."[16] Moving on to satirize the views of those who did not believe women were capable of intellectual pursuits, the author mocked "Oh! No, woman is a poor, frail, *light*-headed creature, and because she has no disposition to take ... she cannot forsooth remain steady under intellectual draughts, that would not be more than a mite's meal to *him* of the more capacious skull!" "N. Carolina" even harshly criticized those men who would refuse women the right to compete intellectually: "These gallants have a shivering horror of a learned female, a blue, a feminine bore. Oh! It perverts lovely, angel woman from her sphere, which is to revolve as an ornamental satellite about their Lord Jupiter.... Such an opinion always indicates envy and jealousy in its possessor of the learned female who incurs his censure. And such a man has reason to fear women of liberal endowments, which, added to their natural quickness and keenness of repartee, makes them dangerous antagonists."[17]

Perhaps most intriguing, not only did these sentiments appear in the region's leading periodical, but also they affixed clear blame for the lower status of women. The authors point to men and their refusal to see women as equals as the main impediments to greater intellectual advancement. In caustic and mocking tones, the promoters of women's intellectual abilities repeatedly cast men as barriers to a woman's right to develop her mind and her abilities.

Other periodicals proved fertile ground for discussions of the intellectual equality of the sexes. Magazines like Georgia's monthly *Orion* shunned discussions of slavery, but they were willing to debate other controversial subjects, including equality between men and women. Similarly, in the *Southern Lady's Companion*, a monthly published in Nashville, a number of essays appeared in the 1840s and 1850s that specifically addressed the sameness in the mental faculties of the sexes. In an article titled "The Claims of Women," an author identified as "W.B.S." denounced those who argued that "by the fundamental law of her intellectual nature, [woman] is

[16] N. Carolina [pseud.], "Female Education," *Southern Literary Messenger* (June 1840), 453.
[17] *Ibid.*, 454.

pronounced to be below the average standard of the masculine intellect; and yet in character and conduct she is held to even a higher law of responsibility than man." This contributor identified a fundamental contradiction in the gender ideology of antebellum America. "A purer and higher life is expected of a sex which at the same time are considered to occupy a lower position in the scale of mental abilities." Improved educational opportunities might be part of the answer, but university education had "to a large extent been denied her." "In addition to her supposed inferiority, she is, to a surprising and ruinous extent, denied the proper means and educational advantages by which she might perchance reach the measure of what society demands at her hands."[18] Not content to let this flawed incongruity go unchallenged, the writer argued forcefully that women must be educated to meet the requirements that society demanded of them. Because woman was "expected to be a living encyclopedia of human endowments and perfections," how could society simultaneously deny her intellectual capabilities? "The fault," W. B. S. pointed out, "lies primarily at the door of the guardians of the public welfare.... Let them, upon the same principles, and with the same earnestness, labor for the improvement and happiness of the one sex, as for that of the other."[19] Thus, southern commentators realized that it was not mental inferiority that held women back from positions of prominence as governmental leaders, scientists, or philosophers.

The readers and authors of the *Southern Lady's Companion* seem to have been particularly attuned to the contradictory nature of southern society's expectations of its wives and mothers. In "Woman's Rights," an essay by Mary J. Coppedge, the inconsistency was laid bare again. Coppedge was especially interested in the conflict that such expectations could cause within the family. For example, tension between brothers and sisters, who were likely to receive different levels of education, must have been acute. "There seems to be no surer method of producing discord in the human family," Coppedge wrote, "than by parents bestowing upon their sons more education than upon their daughters."[20] Hard feelings between husband and wife might also arise if one accepted the notion that women were mentally inferior, particularly if such disparities were aired in public. "Nothing causes deeper pain on the part of the wife, than when her husband is cruel enough to make light of her weakness in company."[21] Coppedge identified some of the familial consequences of unequal education for the sexes. She not only recognized the tensions between men and women that might arise because of traditional gender ideology, but she also put the blame squarely on the contradictions inherent in that ideology. This point is crucial, for such critiques of women's upbringing were not

[18] W. B. S. [pseud.], "The Claims of Woman," *Southern Lady's Companion* 3 (November 1849), 169.

[19] *Ibid.*, 170.

[20] Mary J. Coppedge, "Woman's Rights," *Southern Lady's Companion* 7 (June 1853), 89.

[21] *Ibid.*, 90.

arcane debates or mere philosophical quandaries to ponder; rather they were fundamental attacks on tradition in southern society and as such warrant inclusion in the growing body of works on southern dissent.

Like *The Southern Lady's Companion*, *The Ladies' Pearl* was also a Nashville monthly that weighed in frequently on the topic of the mental aptitude of the sexes. In one essay, Joseph L. Weir, a teacher from White's Creek, Tennessee, denounced men who saw themselves as intellectually superior to women. "The dignified gentleman," Weir declared, "it is true, bows with great apparent respect to the ladies; but at the same time it is obvious that he regards himself as being, intellectually, their superior."[22] He accused contemporary writers, especially men, of "exerting themselves to establish and maintain the false and injurious notion of woman's mental inferiority." Weir questioned these writers' motives, who were "either jealous of female competition in literary pursuits, or else they have ... imbibed a prejudice against the whole sex."[23] As a teacher, Weir attested that he had been "a closer observer of the mental capacity of both sexes" and in so doing concluded "that young ladies progress as fast, in the various branches of science as young gentlemen do." Weir realized that gender differences in intellectual attainments stemmed from the customs and prejudices of society rather than mental ability. "Who, but a wicked ignoramus will dare to impeach woman of weakness and want of intellect, without even giving her a chance to clear herself of the unjust and foul imputation?"[24] Weir thought that because young girls and women had never received an education equal to men, the assertion that they were intellectually inferior "has never been proven." The blame remained with men. The relative paucity of female intellectual achievements, he argued, was not "at all to be attributed to their want of native intellect, but must be imputed to the tyranny which has been exercised over them by the 'lords of creation.'"[25] Weir concluded his essay with a powerful vision of southern women and their future: "They cannot much longer be made to believe that the end for which they were created, is to make an external show, and obtain husbands; but having nobler ends in view, they will shine as brilliant stars, both in the intellectual world and in the domestic circle."[26]

Occasionally, southern publications would present a debate on intellectual equality that spanned a number of issues. The *Southron*, a literary magazine published in 1841 in Gallatin, Tennessee, printed a running discussion of female intellectual equality and gender roles over a number of issues. The discussion began in the March number with an essay by "Urbanus," a resident of Gallatin, titled "The Female Intellectual Faculties Equal to the Male." Admitting that "a very essential difference in the spheres, in which they are

[22] Joseph L. Weir, "Female Education," *Ladies' Pearl* 2 (August 1854), 297.

[23] *Ibid.*

[24] *Ibid.*

[25] *Ibid.*, 298.

[26] *Ibid.*

called to act" governed men and women, "Urbanus" suggested that the differences were in large part generated by custom and not by nature: "This, [intellectual] inequality, however, is evidently referable, to the mode of female education and not to a natural deficiency ... [W]e are told, genius will make its own opportunities. Yes, it will, when it is assisted to a certain extent, and all restraints are thrown off. But woman has never been thus aided. She is universally trained from the start as a female.... The very first bent of the mind is to the female circle and then through life necessity compels her, at least, to share the larger portion of her time this way.... Thus education, domestic duties and the forbidding mandates of man, have ever been combined against her."[27] A *Southron* reader, spurred by the comments of "Urbanus," offered comments on gender equality in the next issue. The author agreed with "Urbanus" that "No man can expect a plentiful harvest who neglects the cultivation of the soil." If women did not receive the same education as men, how could they be expected to be as active intellectually? But the respondent also disagreed that examples of successful women were few by pointing out the names of famous women like Caroline Herschel in astronomy, Mrs. Sommerville in science, and Mrs. Wakefield in botany. "In every instance," the author reiterated, "where she has established her claims to worth or fame, she has done it without these advantages, often struggling against a torrent of prejudice. Until the mind of woman is admitted to equal culture with man, none should suppose it inferior."[28]

The *Southron* continued the debate with an essay by "M.T.," a woman from Gallatin, who assumed the traditional stance that real differences between the sexes were rooted in biology and nature as God intended. "M.T." tied the differences in physical constitution to mental ability: "Experience has taught us that their mental constitution partake respectively of the nature of the physical."[29] M. T. was blunt in her assertions of intellectual difference: "And in the history of the human mind we have never seen females stepping forward to the task of great mental exertion."[30] This letter in turn sparked a retort in defense of women's intellectual abilities from a Gallatin citizen identified only as "R." This writer flatly rejected the linking of the physical and mental: "On the contrary, neither philosophy nor the common belief of mankind, makes the existence or activity of mind dependent upon the 'formation' or 'texture' of the body, however delicate or robust it may be. Neither is muscular volume or vigor, in any case the measure of mind.... To say that the female mind is incapable of equal attainments under equal culture, is to assert that there is between the minds of the sexes, a generic distinction which cannot be demonstrated." "If there is not," the author forcefully stated in opposition to

[27] Urbanus [pseud.], "The Female Intellectual Faculties Equal to the Male," *Southron* 1 (March 1841), 104–5.

[28] See "Editor's Table," *Southron* 1 (April 1841), 142.

[29] M. T. [pseud.], "Consideration of the Comparative Intellectual Powers of the Sexes," *Southron* 1 (May 1841), 162.

[30] *Ibid.*, 163.

the arguments of "M.T.," "a distinct essence forming the matter of minds in males and females – if the essence of their minds is one and the same substance in nature, capable, in both, of vast improvement and polish according to how it is cultivated or neglected ... it is surely not, philosophically, correct to say that the 'economy of nature' has provided weaker minds for weaker bodies."

Agreeing with "Urbanus'" comments on the societal roots of gender distinction, "R." argued, "In the 'economy of nature' the control of politics has been given to man; to woman has been assigned the lesser affairs of society. The custom of all ages and countries has preserved, with rigorous precision, the masculine ascendancy. Hence each has directed their attention to the appropriate pursuits."[31] The *Southron* went on to publish other articles on female education and intellect, including an essay comparing male and female education by Hannah Moore, the British author and thinker.[32]

Such discussions in southern periodicals indicate that despite the ideological hegemony on the issue of slavery, vigorous dissenting voices were raised in the region. In attacking traditional gender ideology, these writers engaged in a broader attack on southern society and its denial of greater education opportunities for women. Southern educators like James M. Garnett of Richmond, a prominent teacher and proponent of women's schools, frequently spoke on the topic of women's role in society. Apparently southern parents found much of value in his collected *Lectures on Female Education* because the volume went through a number of editions in the mid- to late 1820s. In his published lectures, Garnett was highly critical of the cultural limitations placed on women that he felt circumscribed their education. "You may rest well assured," Garnett explained to young women, "... that there is no imaginable reason for thinking any of those mental qualifications which are most praiseworthy in *our* sex, either censurable or unattainable in yours."[33] Indicating that perhaps eating disorders among young women were a problem in the Old South, Garnett warned girls about letting the physical expectations of society influence their eating habits. Some believe, Garnett argued, "that it is altogether incompatible with female delicacy to live upon any thing much grosser than ether itself. Such ladies, in order to acquire what the oracular and silly books which they chiefly consult, call '*a Sylph-Like Form*;' will starve themselves nearly to death; will deluge and corrode their stomachs with acids; and will discipline and excruciate their bodies with corsets, until good health, good spirits, and good principles all sink together ... and [she] dies a martyr to the vain effort of making herself something which nature never intended."[34]

Garnett even questioned the value of marriage for women and criticized harshly those who would prefer that women sacrifice themselves or their

[31] R. [pseud.], "The Female Intellect," *Southron* 1 (July 1841), 235.

[32] Hannah Moore, "Comparison of the Mode of Female Education in the Last Age with the Present," *Southron* 1 (September 1841), 289–93.

[33] James M. Garnett, *Seven Lectures on Female Education* (Richmond, 1824), 39.

[34] *Ibid.*, 68.

individuality for marriage. Young women, Garnett warned, should "turn a deaf ear to any man who would try to persuade you that such frail bipeds as yourselves are really angels and goddesses. Should it ever by your misfortune to be obliged to listen to such language, you will never err in considering it, either the senseless rant of some demented boy who does not know you, or the disgusting folly of some dotard, who had better be thinking of his grave, or the contemptuous ridicule of one who means to laugh at you, as so many silly dolls, destitute of understanding."[35]

Garnett's criticism of marriage was bold and unyielding. Garnett did not oppose marriage in principle, only the notion that women should be married off at the first opportunity. One of the chief reasons for the lack of education of young women was the societal pressure to avoid being single for too long. Indeed, southern society ridiculed the unmarried spinster who with no husband or children of her own was the epitome of loneliness. Still, Garnett believed that social pressures to marry early did a great disservice to young women. "There is another which may dispute the superior power of doing mischief," Garnett wrote in his lectures, "with any that has been named. It is the notion so often calculated ... that the chief earthly purpose for which women 'live, and move, and have their being,' is – *to marry* ... Grammatically speaking, these very provident matrimonisers, will not even allow *woman* to be a *noun-substantive*, but only a miserable conjunction, '*having no signification of herself*,' unless coupled in wedlock to *man*." Marriage, in other words, was not the idyllic domestic life often depicted in novels. On the contrary, marriage was difficult and sometimes disastrous. "How far preferable would it be," Garnett reasoned, "to teach them from the moment they are susceptible of moral instruction, that although more happiness *may be* enjoyed in married, than in single life; yet that more wretchedness *may be*, and often *is*, endured in the first than in the last."[36]

Such strong comments should not necessarily be seen as support for women's political rights. Advocating intellectual equality did not mean to most southern writers and thinkers advocating political equality. Indeed, even those who argued vigorously that women were mentally equally to men often tempered their claims by making sure the reader did not mistake them for champions of women politicians. A writer in the *Southern Quarterly Review* in 1842, for example, was willing to entertain the notion that the intellectual differences between women and men had been grossly exaggerated. However, the same reviewer also argued, "away with the absurd folly of women-governors, women-legislators, women-judges, women-lawyers, women-generals, women-police, &c. All these are crudities of some female closet-speculating fanatic."[37]

[35] *Ibid.*, 109–10.

[36] Garnett, *Lectures on Female Education* (Richmond, 1825), 39.

[37] "Article I," *Southern Quarterly Review* 2 (October 1842), 299.

One of the most prominent advocates of the view that women were not suited for political equality was South Carolina's Louisa S. McCord. In two essays published in 1852, McCord unleashed biting attacks on women's rights, even as she promoted the idea that women could compete with men intellectually.[38] In her essay "The Enfranchisement of Woman," McCord adhered to the notion that women had a distinct place in God's society. "Woman's duty, woman's nature," she maintained, "is to love, to sway by love; to govern by love, to teach by love, to civilize by love!" Women who tried to persuade by employing political tactics, she believed, or who "unsexed" themselves by joining associations and attending conventions whose design was to organize and press for change, acted as men and thus could not elevate women's position in society.[39]

As a conservative writer and thinker, McCord rejected all notions that might raise women to political equality. She denounced those who would apply some "socialistic, communistic, feministic, Mormonistic, or any other such application of chloroform to the suffering patient."[40] She abhorred the "reforming ladies" who falsely claimed that woman was "either the slave or the toy of man." In fact, McCord charges the advocates of political rights for women with "fame-grasping" to promote themselves rather than a worthy cause. "Woman," McCord stated, "was made for *duty*, not for *fame*."[41] With scorn, McCord depicted the household of women politicians: "Duty has gone to the dogs; the husband may go to the devil; and should there be any unlucky brats of things called children, which the feminine individual's spontaneity leaneth not kindly towards, let them also betake themselves to Old Nick, or wherever luck may send them, while the lady spontaneously turns herself to the constructing of some woman's rights constitution in readiness for 'the good time coming.'"[42]

Despite McCord's rejection of women's involvement in movements to promote equality, she engaged in political acts with her writing. Although she may not have realized it, simply by inserting herself into the political debates of the period, McCord asserted that women belonged in the public realm, if not as activists then certainly as intellectuals with worthy contributions to political discourse. Though her views cast her with southern conservatives, McCord's willingness to step into the realm of political opinion served as a bold example for women who wished to express their opinions.

[38] McCord, one of the region's most interesting women, finally has a biographer. See Leigh Fought, *Southern Womanhood and Slavery: A Biography of Louisa S. McCord, 1810–1879* (Columbia, Mo., 2003).

[39] Louisa S. McCord, "Enfranchisement of Woman," *Southern Quarterly Review* 5 (April 1852), 322–41, reprinted in Lounsbury, ed., *Louisa S. McCord*, 109, 110.

[40] McCord, "Woman and Her Needs," *De Bow's Review* (September 1852), 267–92, reprinted in Lounsbury, ed., *Louisa S. McCord*, 126.

[41] *Ibid.*, 128, 131.

[42] *Ibid.*, 139.

For those like McCord who maintained the significance of gender differences in mental ability, the existence of highly intelligent and mentally rigorous women posed an interesting challenge. What to make of such women? Were they simply anomalies, or did they provide evidence that all women were capable of high achievement and only lacked the proper education and guidance? Despite her abolitionism, Margaret Fuller was highly regarded in the South. Southern reviewers, editors, and literary critics grew accustomed in the late antebellum period to northern authors who opposed slavery, and some southerners did not hold such opinions against the authors and were able to assess literary quality based on the merits. Such is the manner in which southern writers dealt with Fuller. In a review of her book *At Home and Abroad*, a commentator in *Russell's Magazine*, a Charleston periodical, noted that Fuller's "allusions to slavery are in the usual style of denunciation and insult." Still, the reviewer gave her credit for her passionate views and managed to "acquit her of hypocrisy."[43] Fuller was no less than a genius, a literary talent whose untimely death was a significant loss to American literature. Yet, her "*massiveness* of mind and character, united to true feminine sensibility, and the warmest poetic instincts, her position, both as woman and author, is one eminently unique."[44] In the eyes of this reviewer, Fuller's genius and gender were a unique combination.

Whereas the antebellum era witnessed open discussion of women's intellectual capabilities, during the Civil War, women continued to make the case for gender equality by lending their literary talents to the Confederacy. Whether they supported secession or not during the tense period between November 1860 and April 1861, the vast majority of southerners joined the cause once their state's decision was made. Numerous examples, from Louisiana diarist Sarah Morgan to North Carolina's Mary Bayard Clarke, demonstrate that even those who stood for the Union in 1860 and early 1861 supported the Confederate war effort once their states seceded. As women wrote essays, poems, and even short stories that bolstered the southern war effort, they made a powerful case that as individuals they were intellectually equal to men.

The significance of women engaged in the political act of advancing the Confederacy through propagandistic writing was not lost on observers during the war. Southerners believed that the crisis provided an opportunity to educate more widely both men and women. As an author in the *Southern Literary Messenger* proclaimed in 1862, "We are now in the midst of a mighty revolution ... let us educate the masses ... [with] a true, solid, education that will enlarge the intellect, elevate the heart, and fit us, as intelligent men and women, to perform our part in the great drama of life."[45] For older women who

[43] "Margaret Fuller Ossoli," *Russell's Magazine* 1 (June 1857), 231.

[44] *Ibid.*, 229.

[45] M. Brooks, "The Intellectual Future of the South," *Southern Literary Messenger* 34 (May 1862), 313–4.

were past school age, however, the lack of a thorough education such as the previous essayist suggested was humiliating and debilitating. Sarah Morgan, who left behind a vivid, detailed diary of her years in Civil War Louisiana, hailed from a wealthy New Orleans and Baton Rouge family, but even she felt inadequately prepared for the new roles women enjoyed as writers during the war. Morgan's diary shows that she had a keen mind, was a thoughtful, questioning individual, and was willing to confront her own strengths and weaknesses. Even though she knew her intellectual abilities were sharp, she felt the sting of an inferior education in a painful incident that she recorded in October 1862. The spark for this critical episode as an intellectual was a conversation she had with Colonel Gustave A. Breaux, commander of the 30th Louisiana and a New Orleans lawyer. As the after-supper talk ranged from topics such as phrenology to health, Morgan began to feel most acutely her own lack of education. "You see," she set down in her diary, "every moment the painful conviction of my ignorance grew more painful still, until it was most humiliating."[46]

Breaux patronized Morgan, asserting that if she wanted to cultivate her mind and equal her male counterparts she would have to devote greater attention to physical activity. Making the dubious claim that a robust frame would aid in building a robust mind, Breaux told Morgan that she needed to spend more time outside with horseback rides and walks in the fresh air. Morgan felt Breaux's condescension keenly and later that evening expressed in her diary her regret at not possessing an education that matched her abilities: "When I lay down, and looked in my own heart and saw my shocking ignorance and pitiful inferiority so painfully evident even to my own eyes, I actually cried. Why was I denied the education that would enable me to be the equal of such a man as Colonel Breaux and the others? He says the woman's mind is the same as the man's, originally, it is only education that makes the difference. Why was I denied that education? Who is to blame?"[47] Morgan was willing to accept part of the blame for not working "to improve the few opportunities thrown in my path," but she also faulted her family for not keeping her in school longer than ten months.[48] It is worth noting that both Breaux and Morgan believed that it was the cultural artifact of gender discrimination in education, not any innate intellectual inferiority on the part of women, that rendered Morgan relatively ill-prepared to hold her own in the conversation with the colonel.

One did not have to deny gender difference to argue that women could be intellectually equal to men. Indeed, throughout the immediate postwar era, many advocates of gender equality continued to base their arguments on the belief that men and women possessed different innate qualities.[49]

[46] October 2, 1862, *Civil War Dairy of Sarah Morgan*, 289.

[47] *Ibid.*, 290.

[48] *Ibid.*

[49] "Boys," *De Bow's Review* n.s. 1 (April 1866), 370.

Acceptance of the intellectual ability of women did not necessarily mean the denial of sexual distinctiveness. Women could articulate ideas on a wide range of subjects, including politics, and yet still remain different from men. But even the acceptance of the power of women's mental aptitudes was an important advance even if based on notions of gender distinctiveness. This advance was recognized at the time, for many southerners in the middle of the 1800s believed that they lived in an enlightened era that acknowledged and appreciated the intellectual abilities of women.[50]

Repeatedly contrasting the position of women in nineteenth-century America with the "unchristian" and "uncivilized" status to which women had been condemned in earlier periods and other nations, southerners boasted proudly that they, unlike other peoples, acknowledged the vital tasks performed by women as teachers, mothers, and wives. "Relic of the dark ages!" is the way one woman described the denial of female intellectual improvement.[51] As Nashville's Anna Willa wrote: "Since the invention of printing and the consequent diffusion of learning, the condition of woman has gradually improved, until it is generally acknowledged, that she requires the same in kind, though hardly in degree, as her brothers."[52] In contrast, past societies and "less-civilized" modern ones were guilty of reducing women to inferior positions. Foreign countries were often juxtaposed unflatteringly with the elevated women of America. Even societies that antebellum Americans revered, such as the Ancient Greeks, earned the scorn of southern writers for their treatment of women. "In married life," a contributor to the *Southern Quarterly Review* argued, "[Athenian women] were treated nearly as chattels, and regarded with but little more consideration than the slave ... while [the husband] indulged in guilty pleasures with concubines.... To her all intellectual education and amusements were alike denied."[53]

The push for southern independence and the optimism associated with the onset of the Confederacy only heightened the sense that southerners were in the midst of an age of progress and advancement. As a contributor to *De Bow's Review* proclaimed in late 1861, "The beginning of our career as an independent nation, a career destined, we believe, to be prosperous beyond all comparison in the annals of history, ought to be signalized by the beginning of a nobler, loftier career for women." Envisioning a new government that embraced the intellectual abilities of women, this author linked the drive for southern independence with a similar drive for the recognition of women's intellectual independence from men.[54] Although the Confederacy was defeated, this author's claim that future southern women would benefit from

[50] J. B. S., "Female Education," *Southern Lady's Companion* 3 (September 1849), 133.

[51] Une Femme [pseud.], "Professor Sassnett's 'Theory of Female Education," *Southern Lady's Companion* 7 (February 1854), 344.

[52] Anna Willa, "Female Education," *Ladies' Pearl* 3 (July 1855), 280.

[53] "Athens and the Athenians," *Southern Quarterly Review* 11 (April 1847), 307. See also J. L. M., "The Women of France," *Southern Literary Messenger* 5 (May 1839), 297.

[54] "Education of Southern Women," *De Bow's Review* n.s. 6 (October/November 1861), 390.

more enlightened perspectives on their intellectual abilities was eventually borne out.

After the Civil War, the notion that the sexes were intellectually comparable was widely accepted, but in the minds of many southerners the movement for women's rights was closely aligned with the radicalism of northern reformers, the same reformers who had brought the South to its knees over slavery and secession. Thus, in some ways the immediate postwar years were even more reactionary on matters of gender than were the antebellum decades. For example, in an 1869 essay in the prominent Baltimore magazine the *Southern Review*, a commentator posited that "everyone will concede" that there were women who had legitimate claims to genius. "We were quite sensible," the author claimed, "that man has been unjust to woman, and has wantonly excluded her from many pursuits." However, having stated this caveat, the essayist then went on to assert the fundamental differences between men and women that were supposedly rooted in biology rather than custom. In the final analysis, the conclusion to be drawn was "that there is an essential and material difference between the sexes in respect of mental and moral development."[55] In reaction against such prejudice, southern women often complained about male bias in newspapers and magazines. They read such attacks on female intellect and sometimes wrote to editors to register their opposing views.

Thus, there were strong-minded women who viewed the postwar South as a chance to remake society. Women like Sarah Morgan were outspoken proponents of women's intellectual abilities and called on like-minded women to contravene traditional notions of feminine weaknesses. Traditional notions of women's sphere, Morgan asserted, did not allow women to be strong and intelligent independent beings. "Bless their weakness!" Morgan sarcastically proclaimed in a Charleston newspaper in 1873, "We like them better for that, or for anything which proves their inferiority.... Mental flaccidity is a potent charm in woman. It fascinates the wise. Only flabby-minded men can tolerate a strong-minded woman."[56] As Morgan complained, "Knowledge, shown or suggested, is slavery for a woman.... The woman who would be friends with the average mankind, must reduce herself to a state of semi-imbecility. If she has sense, she must conceal it.... A learned pig is more respected and admired." Morgan must have felt the sting of being belittled as an intellectual woman, for the editorials she wrote evince an anger that is borne of personal experience. Similarly, Eliza Francis Andrews remarked in June 1865 that she, her father, and some acquaintances had stayed up until midnight discussing a range of topics. "It was not politics, this time," Andrews wrote in her diary, "either, but the relative merits of Dickens and Thackeray, and I think it would be much better if we would stick to peaceful encounters of this sort instead

[55] "Women Artists," *Southern Review* 5 (April 1869), 299, 301, 311.

[56] Sarah Morgan, "The Natural History of Woman," reprinted in Roberts, *The Correspondence of Sarah Morgan and Francis Warrington Dawson*, 68.

of the furious political battles we have, which always end in fireworks, especially when Henry and I cross swords with father – two hot-heads against one."[57] Blanche Butler Ames wrote in 1871 that she "betook myself manfully, or womanfully, to the newspapers, reading steadily until it was time to go to bed."[58] Most importantly, postwar southern women turned to reading politics in the papers. Ella Gertrude Thomas noted in her postwar diary that "I have been reading of late the proceedings of the political world with a great deal of interest."[59] Like Thomas, southern women were more politically aware after the war, and that new awareness of the political would lay the groundwork for the broader exploration of women's rights in the late nineteenth and early twentieth centuries.

As southerners debated the meaning of gender difference, they engaged in a parallel discussion of the impact of race on intellect. However, although many male southerners granted freely and openly that there were few if any distinctions in the mental capacities between men and women, nearly all white southerners embraced the notion of white intellectual superiority. As Michael O'Brien has shown, southern thinkers like Alabama's Josiah Nott and South Carolina's Stephen Elliot were actively involved in the classification of the natural world, particularly racial classification. As an integral component of the region's defense of slavery, which became more elaborate as the proslavery argument developed over the course of the early nineteenth century, studies of race began with the assumption that whites were superior. As Winthrop Jordan and many other scholars have argued, the analysis of racial difference, and in particular the placing of white over black, had a long history in Western civilization. Yet, as O'Brien points out, even by the late antebellum period, terms like "race" were still contentious and ill-defined, despite efforts by men like Nott and Elliot to use skin color to justify slavery.[60]

When white southern thinkers and politicians searched for ways to justify human bondage, they turned to a wide array of sources and arguments, all of which supposedly demonstrated that Africans and their descendants were destined by nature and by God for slavery. From the Bible they culled stories that seemed to support the separation of the races, and they argued that Jesus never spoke out directly against slavery. From classical history southerners gleaned that two of the world's greatest past civilizations, the Greeks and Romans, were both slave societies. Southern apologists pulled information from natural history, philosophy, and even science to prove that blacks were

[57] Entry for June 1865, in Spencer Bidwell King, ed., *Eliza Frances Andrews: The War-Time Journal of a Georgia Girl, 1864–1865* (New York, 1908), 284.

[58] Blanche Butler Ames to Adelbert Ames, April 24, 1871, in *Chronicles from the Nineteenth Century: Family Letters of Blanche Butler and Adelbert Ames* (Clinton, MA, 1935), 84.

[59] Entry for September 1866, Diary of Ella Gertrude Thomas, in Virginia Ingraham Burr, ed., *The Secret Eye: The Journal of Ella Gertrude Clanton Thomas, 1848–1889* (Chapel Hill, 1990), 233.

[60] O'Brien, *Conjectures of Order*, 250.

best suited for their lives as slaves. It was commonly believed, indeed almost universally accepted, that slave men and women were intellectually inferior to whites. Routinely described as carefree, childlike, lazy, and prone to short-sighted behavior that emphasized pleasure-seeking over planning, slaves were thought to be biologically incapable of higher order thinking.

The debate over black intellect in the antebellum period often focused on human origins. Of course the Biblical story of Genesis told the story of one creation, of Adam and Eve as the progenitors of mankind. But remarkably, as powerful as religious beliefs were in the Old South, the need to defend bondage even sometimes trumped faith. The most prominent scientific southern thinker on matters of race and intellect, Josiah Nott of Mobile, not only denied the accuracy of Genesis, but he actually reveled in ridiculing what his fellow southerners considered Biblical truths. His iconoclastic views on religion were combined with a fierce and visceral belief in a racial hierarchy that placed whites above blacks. In fact, in arguing for the notion of multiple creations (or polygenesis), Nott maintained that blacks and whites were a "distinct species."[61] Building on Nott's work and that of others with a "scientific" perspective, including Charles Caldwell's popular 1830 pamphlet, the theory of separate origins for blacks and whites gained widespread acceptance in the Western world by the 1840s.[62]

Nott's racial theorizing was buttressed, he believed, by his argument that as "hybrids" of black and white parents, mulattoes were tainted by inferior African blood and thus inferior to whites. This was especially true of mulatto women, whom Nott called "sickly."[63] In his widely cited 1854 study *Types of Mankind*, Nott held that mulatto women were marked by their "want of chastity," a trait supposedly inherited from their pleasure-seeking black parent.[64] Nott's views on race were broadly accepted in the South by the 1850s, and he traveled the region delivering well-attended lectures to spread his theories. Despite his radical views on religion, fellow southerners embraced his arguments about the biological distinctiveness of the races.

Of course, this would not be the first time or the last pseudoscience justified a social custom or aided a political agenda. By the mid-nineteenth century the study of phrenology, or the so-called science of examining bumps of the head to identify abilities and tendencies, was embraced by a number of northerners and southerners.[65] Abolitionists seized on observations by phrenologists that seemed to indicate greater promise for the intellectual abilities of African Americans, an argument that southerners rejected. Thus both the North and South used current scientific theories in their volleys in the debate over slavery.

61 See Reginald Horsman's excellent biography, *Josiah Nott of Mobile* (Baton Rouge, 1987), 87.

62 *Ibid.*, 84.

63 *Ibid.*, 87.

64 *Ibid.*, 196.

65 Stephen Tomlinson, *Head Masters: Phrenology, Secular Education, and Nineteenth-Century Social Thought* (Tuscaloosa, 2005).

Southern thinkers like Nott did not spend much time dealing with the issue of gender difference. It was enough in his mind to argue for the separateness of the races, and to this central argument he devoted his energies. Black women were lumped with black men as intellectually inferior. However, black women bore the additional burden of their femaleness, which not only purportedly rendered them racially inferior, but also made them victims of assumptions about gender. This "double inferiority" placed black women at the bottom of the racial and gender hierarchy, an unfortunate status that only justified and rationalized in the minds of many brutal masters the raping of their female slaves. Indeed, as scholar Frances Smith Foster has argued, slave narratives were often written by men who depicted slave women as the "inevitable" victim of white sexual depravity. However, as Foster notes, "Slave women saw themselves as far more than victims of rape and seduction."[66] They viewed their suffering and physical and emotional abuse as character-building trials. White audiences refused to grant black women such agency, however. Foster rightly concludes that white readers and popular magazines such as the *Southern Literary Messenger* and the *Southern Quarterly Review* deliberately ignored black women such as Phyllis Wheatley who exhibited talent and intellect. Such avoidance smoothed the potentially troublesome path toward justifying slavery on the grounds that Africans were an inferior race.[67]

Despite whites' deliberate obtuseness on the question of black achievement, black slave women stole opportunities to learn to read, free black women sometimes attended schools, and African Americans in the antebellum North even formed literary societies. Elizabeth McHenry has found a lively literary culture among northern black women both before and after the Civil War in which female readers established associations at rates higher than men.[68] Groups such as Philadelphia's Colored Reading Society and Washington's Bethel Historical and Literary Association demonstrated that given the chance, African Americans not only enjoyed reading but relished discussing literature as well.[69] Moreover, black literary societies demonstrate that free blacks in the North and Upper South readily realized the importance of literacy, reading, and intellectual engagement as vital tools for racial advancement.

It is hard to overestimate the importance of reading and literature to black and white southern women. Many of them, newly informed as a result of the movement for female education that swept the nation in the middle of the nineteenth century, were bolder in their pursuit of a more public vehicle for the discussion of politics, gender roles, culture, and many other issues.

[66] Frances Smith Foster, *Witnessing Slavery: The Development of Ante-Bellum Slave Narratives* (second ed., Madison, 1994), xxxiii.

[67] Frances Smith Foster, *Written by Herself: Literary Production by African American Women, 1746–1892* (Bloomington, 1993).

[68] Elizabeth McHenry, *Forgotten Readers: Recovering the Lost History of African American Literary Societies* (Durham, 2002), 57.

[69] *Ibid.*, 51, 151.

Magazines for women would become this public vehicle. Given their importance to the evolution of the movement for women's rights, and given the paucity of attention paid to them by historians, magazines and newspapers warrant an even greater analysis. For, not only did northern magazines such as *Harper's* and *Graham's* emerge to encourage female subscribers to add to the already available male readership, but periodicals designed solely for southern women also flourished in the South. Magazines aimed at primarily a female audience offer insight into the intellectual life of southern women and also add further weight to the argument that cultural ties united the nation even as slavery threatened to divide it.

The level of education for women seemed inadequate to the task, however. The haphazard nature of education, even for middle-class and elite white women, remained a substantial barrier to advancing careers as writers and journalists. Ironically, nineteenth-century southerners would help advance women's intellectual and political expression via the conservative trumpeting of her domestic duties. For, as we will see in Chapter 2, the movement to provide women with a broad and substantive education emanated not from any progressive desire to champion gender equality but was instead rooted in the ideology of motherhood.

2

Education, Gender, and Community in the Nineteenth-Century South

"The old times have passed away," an observer wrote in *De Bow's Review* in 1868, "when Betsey was content to learn reading, writing and arithmetic at the parish school house in order that John might enjoy the advantage of a college education. Now-a-days, Betsey wants a college education too, and it is very probable she will make a far better use of it when once acquired than John ever will. In fact, if it can be accorded but to one, Betsey should have it."[1] Typical of nineteenth-century calls for greater educational opportunities for white women, this passage from one of the South's leading magazines is evidence of the commonplace paeans made to a substantive education. As scholars such as Mary Kelley and Christie Anne Farnham have pointed out, southerners increased the length of schooling and the sophistication of the curriculum for girls and young women in the decades leading up to the Civil War.

Research in this chapter generally confirms the findings of Farnham and Kelley. Farnham argues that the subjects taught at schools, academies, and colleges for girls and young women were quite comprehensive.[2] Far from an education limited to art or music, women learned about history, mathematics, science, and philosophy. More recently, Kelley has shown that southern girls and young women not only studied subjects traditionally considered to be for men only, but also that these same female students often found themselves in public circumstances, delivering a poetry reading or demonstrating knowledge during school exams.[3] The necessity of educating young women to fulfill their sober duties as the teacher of their young children, an essential component of southern middle-class ideology, began as a conservative ethos that emphasized the role of women in the domestic sphere. However, the tradition-bound ideology that underlay the movement to educate white women ended up expanding the mind of those women who began searching for opportunities to use their

[1] "Our Boys and Girls," *De Bow's Review* 5 (September 1868), 855.

[2] Farnham, *The Education of the Southern Belle.*

[3] Kelley, *Learning to Stand and Speak.*

knowledge. Many women sought those opportunities in careers as writers, journalists, and editors.

Analyzing the movement for female education also holds implications for a fresh perspective on southern society and the history of education more broadly. Scholars who study the history of American education often highlight the paucity of public schools in the South in the 1800s. David Tyack and Elisabeth Hansot argue in *Managers of Virtue* that "the antebellum South was barren ground for promoters of the common school."[4] Southerners expended merely intermittent efforts to establish public schools systems in the South, which met with little success until the late nineteenth century. However, the line that modern scholars have drawn between public and private institutions holds little meaning for the mid-nineteenth-century South. Indeed, as Margaret A. Nash has recently pointed out, southern education was "quasi-public, quasi-private."[5] While public schools in the modern sense were slow to develop in the South, and private academies and seminaries were the norm, the word "private" is misleading. For even though such schools were not supported with state monies, they received broad community support and were the recipient of community funds, energy, and attention. Indeed, the public exhibits by female students at commencements became community-oriented, festive events that drew strangers from far and wide. Ordinary southerners were involved deeply in their communities' schools.

For African American women, the support for education was not to be found in the same lectures and periodicals that trumpeted the cause for white women. Because the main push for white women's education derived from the need to prepare them for their roles as mothers or teachers, roles in which slave women could not fully participate, there was no need for such a formal education. Whites believed that black men and women were not designed by God for higher-order thinking; they were designed for work. Still, one finds in the writings and recollections of female slaves a remarkable desire to learn, even as their ambitions were often frustrated by racism and the bonds of slavery. What little education they were exposed to came from the Bible. As former slave Louisa Picquet recalled, "When I was a little girl in Georgia the madame, Mrs. Cook, used to read the Bible, and explain it to us."[6] Through religion, white and black women shared a common experience even if white women chose not to use that shared experience to form close bonds with their slaves. Women of both races were shaped by their listening to, reading of, and thinking about the Bible.

Many antebellum black women learned to read and write surreptitiously. After the war, many black women published memoirs that evince a greater

[4] David B. Tyack and Elisabeth Hansot, *Managers of Virtue: Public School Leadership in America, 1820–1980* (New York, 1982), 84.

[5] Margaret A. Nash, *Women's Education in the United States, 1780–1840* (New York, 2005), 11.

[6] Louisa Picquet, *Inside Views of Southern Domestic Life* (New York, 1861), 20.

understanding of vocabulary, sentence structure, and other writing basics that one could pick up only with some kind of training. As in the case of the black family, which sometimes managed to provide a stable and loving environment for many children despite the repression of slavery, the story of the struggle to obtain a modicum of education under difficult circumstances is inspiring.

As southerners in the mid-nineteenth century began to accept the possibility that men and women were intellectually equal, calls for female education had greater resonance and a broader following after 1820. If white women were capable of a thorough and substantive education, as southerners like Virginia's James Garnett claimed, then it behooved the region to provide them greater opportunities to learn. Girls and young women from wealthy families commonly benefited from at least some private tutoring throughout the eighteenth and early nineteenth centuries, often in subjects that would facilitate their transition into polite society. "In general," one observer wrote, "the system may be described as one for *show* and not for use.... The knowledge imparted is a mere smattering; the accomplishments mere tinsel gloss."[7] Furthermore, such education might only last a short period; Louisiana diarist Sarah Morgan wept at the age of twenty when she recalled that she had only "ten short months at school where you learned nothing except Arithmetic."[8] The push for an education that would not only equip women for genteel society but also allow them to expand their minds, follow intellectual pursuits, and develop individual talents and even careers was one of the most powerful in America after 1820 and a movement in which southerners participated with enthusiasm.[9]

Although the speeches and essays on female education flowed liberally throughout the Old South, by the 1840s the subject was so hackneyed that even southerners themselves grew tired of writing about it. Professor J. Darby, a chemistry and philosophy instructor at Georgia Female College, complained in the *Family Companion and Ladies' Mirror*, a Macon, Georgia, monthly that "a subject that has become more stale, by being constantly harped upon, could hardly be proposed. It has been the theme of the popular orator. It has had champions of every grade, from the school-girl, to the accomplished writer."[10] Few topics were as widely discussed in the early nineteenth-century South as women's education.

Almost universally, the calls for expanded schooling for women were based on the notion that woman's responsibilities as mother demanded a broad

[7] "Education of Southern Women," *De Bow's Review* 6 (October/November 1861), 383.

[8] Charles East, ed. *Sarah Morgan: The Civil War Dairy of Southern Woman* (New York, 1992), entry for October 2, 1862, 290.

[9] Farnham, *The Education of the Southern Belle.*

[10] J. Darby, "Education," *Family Companion and Ladies' Mirror* 1 (October 15, 1841), 51. Another author, "J.B.S." of Russellville, Alabama, even apologized for his "venture upon this oft explored field." J. B. S. [pseud.], "Female Education," *Southern Lady's Companion* 3 (June 1849), 50. "J.B.S." published another essay on the subject in *Southern Lady's Companion* 3 (September 1849), 133–5.

and substantive education. "Republican motherhood," the understanding of women's primary function in society as the conveyor of knowledge and virtue to her children, underlay the increase in interest in female education in the South before the Civil War. "Who is it," asked a writer in 1824 in the *Ladies' Garland*, a magazine published in Harpers Ferry, West Virginia, "that molds and directs the character of our boys for the first ten or twelve years of their life? ... How then ought she to be accomplished for this important office! How wide and diversified her reading and information!"[11] To be able to fulfill these duties, southern society required white women to be "renaissance women," to be well-versed in many different subjects so that they would be able to impart that knowledge to their sons and daughters. The southern woman was "expected to be a living encyclopedia of human endowments."[12] As one Georgian put it in 1840, "Woman's varied relations – her influence early, constant, unfailing – demand that she should have every facility for acquiring knowledge – that her mind should be stored with varied information, thus fitting her for the honorable discharge of her high and multiplied responsibilities."[13]

The ubiquity of support for female education was not mere rhetoric; elite planters, merchants, and middle-class professionals evinced great interest in the schooling of girls and young women. In their correspondence, southern families commented often on the education of their daughters, sisters, and cousins. Parents advised their daughters to keep focused on the goal of education and to avoid distractions. B. T. Williams of Smallwood, Alabama, told his daughter, "You are about to enter the Intellectual Machine Shop. My advice is to throw off every thought or reflection that is calculated to dissipate the mind. ... If you give way to sympathy and homesick reflections, it will be very difficult to bring your mind to a vigorous effort in the accomplishment of your studies."[14] The ritual exchange of letters comforted parents worried about the health and safety of daughters who often traveled across the country to attend school, and shared news about life back home.

Fathers seemed particularly interested in the welfare of their daughters, and the letters reveal a paternalistic commitment to their daughters' educational success and shed light on father-daughter relationships. Abram Maury of Tennessee was pleased that his daughter Sarah wrote to him from school, but apparently her letter was unsatisfactory: "You should have informed me what you are studying at school, what progress you are making, and how you are pleased with your new teachers."[15] Fathers saw correspondence with their daughters as a way to exercise paternalism and to remind girls and young

[11] "Importance of Female Education," *Ladies' Garland* 1 (April 24, 1824), 43.

[12] W. B. S., "The Claims of Woman," *Southern Lady's Companion* 3 (November 1849), 169.

[13] Philip C. Pendleton and George F. Pierce, "Introduction," *Southern Ladies' Book* 1 (January 1840), 2.

[14] B. T. Williams to Helen Williams, September 9, 1853, B. T. Williams Letters, Alabama Department of Archives and History, Montgomery.

[15] Abram P. Maury to Sarah Maury, February 6, 1839, Maury Papers, Clements Library, University of Michigan.

women of the importance of education.[16] Pressure to succeed from fathers back home probably generated anxiety in southern girls and young women, but the admonishments and reminders to study were important ways for fathers to attempt to exercise some control over the lives and direction of their daughters despite great distances.

Brothers, sisters, and friends also reminded schoolgirls that their loved ones expected students to become accomplished and learned.[17] Caroline Gordon, who was studying in Salem, North Carolina, probably at the Salem Female Academy, received encouragement from her older siblings back home in Wilkesboro. In 1842, her sister advised her, "Now that you have commenced, your ascent up the steep and rugged hill of science, I hope you will not stop short, but pursue your course, with vigor and perseverance."[18] Southern families expected their female relatives to keep them informed about their studies, teachers, and progress.[19] The word "scholars" was often employed by southern women to describe themselves and other students, and it reflected the seriousness and dedication with which many approached their schooling.[20] Letters home about schoolwork were often specific, mentioning favorite areas of study, books, and teaching methods.

Southern families expected academic rigor from female family members who were studying at school, and in letters they made those high expectations clear. "Whenever you feel lazy," Ella Noland MacKenzie's cousin wrote her in Virginia, "you must think how much disappointed your dear Father, Mother, and all your friends at home, will be if you do not make a great deal of improvements while you are at school."[21] Such pressure was also meant to be encouraging. In addition to letters from her brother, Caroline Gordon also received more uplifting guidance from her sister Anna, who reminded Caroline that "if you will only make use of the proper application and industry, which I am disposed to think you will, you can accomplish anything you undertake."[22] Intellectual growth, not just the learning of manners for polite society, was key to parents who sent their children to school. However, elite and middle-class parents clearly understood that polite society expected refinement from their women. Education was by no means open to all southern white women who desired to learn, and women who lacked the opportunities to pursue education felt the inadequacy acutely.

[16] Lloyd Noland to Emma Noland, Ella Noland MacKenzie Papers, Southern Historical Collection, University of North Carolina.

[17] William Lewis to Emma Lewis, March 10, 1838, John Francis Speight Papers, Southern Historical Collection, University of North Carolina.

[18] M. L. Gordon to Caroline L. Gordon, December 18, 1842, Gordon-Hackett Family Papers, Southern Historical Collection, University of North Carolina.

[19] Mary Webb to Ann Eliza Thompson, January 27, 1838, Webb Family Papers, Southern Historical Collection, University of North Carolina.

[20] For another example, Rebecca Magill of Middletown, Virginia, referred to her students as her "scholars." Rebecca Magill to Sarah Magill, August 30, 1845, Sarah Magill Papers, Perkins Library, Duke University.

[21] M. L. Berkeley to Ella Nolland MacKenzie, May 2, 1844, Ella Nolland MacKenzie Papers, Southern Historical Collection, University of North Carolina.

[22] Anna Gordon to Caroline Gordon, February 4, 1844, *ibid.*

Southerners blamed women's educational deficiencies on tradition and customs rather than inadequate access to schooling. Much of the blame for shortcomings in female education, southerners claimed, lay with the institution of marriage. "Young ladies," one southerner argued, "should not only be educated for wives – which they all expect to be; but also to be widows – which they all are liable to become."[23] Other southerners questioned the actions of parents who were consumed with providing material wealth for their daughters to prepare them for marriage but who failed to provide equal attention to the education. As one observer from Russellville, Tennessee, put it in 1849: "Strange indeed is the infatuation that possesses the minds of parents, when every exertion is expended in the accumulation of a little property for their daughters, while the mind is left in its rude uncultivated state." This author suggested that an educated young woman would make a more suitable wife than a wealthy one.[24] The effort to expand women's education therefore confronted some of the most cherished practices in the South, confrontations from which supporters did not shrink.

Once at school, girls and young women often boasted about enriching experience in learning history, literature, and science. Research has confirmed the findings of Farnham and Kelley that the subjects taught at women's schools reflect the belief that women could learn and understand the same subjects as men. Farnham demonstrates clearly that women were taught languages (especially Latin and Greek), philosophy, history, and mathematics. At Livingston Female Academy in Alabama, for example, students were exposed to algebra, geometry, history, chemistry, logic, ethics, classic literature, rhetoric, and modern and classical languages.[25] Science was particularly important, and astronomy, physics, chemistry, botany, and anatomy were offered at female schools.[26] For Farnham, the movement to promote education for women represented an extension of the conservative hegemony of the planter class, instead of the questioning of that hegemony.

The fact that women were taught subjects such as logic, math, and science shows that southerners believed women were capable of understanding complex topics. By no means was female education in the South limited to the teaching of music, art, etiquette, and other traditionally "feminine" subjects. In fact, southerners often stressed that their schools for women should not focus solely on such learning. As Tennessee's H. S. Porter argued in 1854, "Life

[23] "Practical Female Education," *Southern Lady's Companion* 6 (September 1852), 191.

[24] J. B. S., "Female Education," *Southern Lady's Companion* 3 (September 1849), 134. He added, "Perhaps if the parent had given his daughter an education, a man of a high sense of intellectual and moral honor would have sought a lifetime alliance with her – a man who would have known how to appreciate her worth in altogether a different way from computing it by dollars and sense."

[25] Ralph M. Lyon, "The Early Years of Livingston Female Academy," *Alabama Historical Quarterly* 37 (Fall 1975), 201.

[26] Farnham, *The Education of the Southern Belle*, especially chapter 3.

is not a toy, it is not a May-day festivity, it is not a comic song, it is not a laughing comedy; it is something real, sincere, positive, and serious."[27] Over time, the course offerings became even more rigorous. By 1861, at Salem College in North Carolina, algebra, geometry, and trigonometry were considered "regular branches of study."[28] In fact, more traditional feminine subjects such as music and art were considered "extra studies" at the Judson Female Institute in Marion, Alabama.[29] Religious rivalries helped to spark the rapid growth of female colleges in the South. Even small communities sometimes possessed two schools for women opened by different denominations. In 1848, Baptists in Murfreesboro, North Carolina, a small town, established Chowan Female College. Not to be outdone, the area's Methodists in 1855 set up Wesleyan Female College. The two schools competed for students, qualified faculty, and even the beauty of flowers on the grounds.[30]

Advertisements for women's schools, which are frequently found in the pages of southern magazines and newspapers, often boasted of an ability to teach science, math, and other disciplines.[31] An ad for the Somerville Female Institute of Leasburg, North Carolina, that appeared in the Greensboro *Weekly Message* noted, "The Institute has a very good chemical, and Philosophical Apparatus, and experiments are exhibited during the session."[32] A notice of the Carolina Female College listed the faculty and claimed, "A set of highly valuable apparatus [sic] has been provided for the illustration of experiments in Chemistry, Natural Philosophy, and Astronomy; and it is in contemplation to furnish, at an early day, a library of choice works for the use of the young ladies."[33] Teaching periodicals, such as the *North-Carolina Journal of Education*, printed many ads for female schools and schoolbooks.[34] Southern schools thus had a firm notion of what constituted a proper education for girls and young women, and these institutions made clear that learning was a serious, sober business.

Although numerous scholars have shown that young women valued highly the education they received at southern schools, until Mary Kelley's *Learning to Stand and Speak*, few pointed out how important these institutions were to the communities that harbored them. As Kelley argues, towns that could

27 H. S. Porter, "Female Education," *Ladies' Pearl* 3 (November 1854), 1.

28 Elizabeth Barber Young, *A Study of the Curricula of Seven Selected Women's Colleges*, (New York, 1932),14.

29 *Ibid.*, 29.

30 Stephenson, "The Davises," 257–61.

31 Catherine Clinton, "Equally Their Due: The Education of the Planter Daughter in the Early Republic," *Journal of the Early Republic* 2 (Spring 1982), 39–60. On the education of southern women in the sciences, see Deborah Jean Warner, "Science Education for Women in Antebellum America," *Isis* 69 (March 1978), 58–67.

32 *Weekly Message* 4 (March 15, 1855). The *Weekly Message* newspaper was started by Sidney D. Bumpass, whose wife assumed the duties of editorship upon his death sometime in 1852.

33 *Weekly Message* 1 (June 17, 1852).

34 For example, see *North-Carolina Journal of Education* 4 (January 1861).

boast of a female academy were proud of their institutions and exhibited a sustained interest in their welfare. The schools returned the commitment and became important contributors to the intellectual culture of their communities. Each school conducted commencement ceremonies that often became community festivals that ran for two or three days. During these exhibitions, southern young women performed before the public, reading essays, solving math problems, and playing music, among other activities. Finally, female schools contributed to the intellectual and cultural vitality of southern communities by publishing their own literary journals that became important links to the broader community.

Examinations for women's schools, frequently held twice a year in June or July and in December, were open to the public and became community events, a source of pride for parents, and no doubt the cause of much angst and nervousness for southern girls. Often in front of a large audience of both sexes, many of whom were not parents but merely spectators, female students read compositions, delivered speeches, and were tested orally on questions about science, history, mathematics, and other subjects. It was an unusual and exciting period that provided young women with probably their first, and perhaps last, opportunity to appear in a public forum. Consequently, many girls and young women viewed the examinations as a chance to please family and friends by demonstrating their knowledge.

Along with presentations by students during the day, commencements included lectures at night by regionally recognized speakers. Often the subject of these lectures focused on the place of women in society or the importance of fostering women's intellectual abilities. At one school, Professor Labode of South Carolina College came to speak on "the position of woman" in southern society.[35] Similarly, Rev. Charles Force Deems was often called on to deliver a speech on the vital importance of female education or to elucidate a passage in the Bible. Indeed, because many women's colleges were affiliated with a Protestant denomination, religious themes were ubiquitous in the speeches given by students and invited speakers. Deems, a leader in the Methodist church, actively promoted the establishment of Methodist schools, and Baptist leaders responded with equal fervor in pushing for the erection of their own educational institutions. Thus, a kind of competition developed in which Protestant churches worked to outdo one another in the number and quality of their affiliated schools, a competition that only encouraged communities and their citizens to support such institutions as actively as they could.

Girls and young women devoted considerable time and effort to studying for these examinations, aware that they would be put on the spot in the public eye. As pressure built, students became increasingly concerned with making a good impression because the potential for public embarrassment was great.

[35] Carrie and Adeline Dogan to Caroline L. Gordon, July 29, 1852, Gordon-Hackett Family Papers, Southern Historical Collection, University of North Carolina.

As C. A. Shaw wrote to her brother, "I don't know whether we will have an interesting examination or not; we have commenced preparing for it some. I don't know whether we will have composition or not, but I hope we will not. I dread them more than anything else except measles."[36] Humiliation was an ever-present possibility in the minds of students, particularly if they were insufficiently prepared. Caroline Nicholson of Tennessee recalled with still-powerful emotions many years later her experience at her schools. "At one of our public examinations," she remembered, "when numbers of young men and other visitors crowded to hear us, Mr. Martin requested the members of his highest class, Rhetoric, to change places in rank that he might prove our thoroughness. Horrors: we had numbered and memorized our paragraphs," not the entire recitation as they were apparently supposed to commit to memory. "Such utter discomfiture," Nicholson called to mind, "befell the class as I have not forgotten in all these years."[37]

The presence of young men no doubt added to the stress. Writing as an older woman, Nicholson remembered back to her school days. "At one of our public examinations," she recalled, "... numbers of young men and other visitors, crowded to hear us."[38] The possibility of embarrassment in front of potential suitors meant that girls and young women felt the public's gaze even more acutely. Robert McKay attended the examinations of the Greenville Female Academy in South Carolina for the sole purpose of admiring one Octavia Atwood. As "she took her position at the blackboard," McKay recalled, "oh how I watched her every movement, and troubled, lest she might fail in her task!"[39] When they succeeded in their task, young women became quite proud. Margaret Ulmer, a student at the Tuskegee Female Academy, boasted in her diary, "I demonstrated a theorem that none of the girls could do."[40] Therefore, despite the potential for embarrassment, young women could also gain confidence from public exams.

Periodicals often reported detailed accounts of the commencements, including the titles of student essays. At the exercises of the Greensboro Female College, young women delivered speeches titled "Knowledge is Power," "Modern Belles," and "Visions of the Future for the Old North State."[41] At the Buckingham Female Collegiate Institute in Virginia, students read essays titled "The Proper Sphere of Woman" and "The Influence of Educated Females on our National Character."[42] Even controversial subjects might be addressed in

[36] C. A. Shaw to D. A. Shaw, April 30, 1858. Mrs. Scott R. Newton Papers, North Carolina State Archives, Raleigh.

[37] Caroline O'Reilly Nicholson Reminiscences, Southern Historical Collection, University of North Carolina.

[38] *Ibid.*

[39] "Notes on the Life of Octavia Atwood after her death," manuscript in private collection of Samuel R. Zimmerman, Jr., quoted by Judith T. Bainbridge, "A 'Nursery of Knowledge': The Greenville Female Academy," *South Carolina Historical Magazine* 99 (January 1998), 23.

[40] Diary entry for June 3, 1858, Margaret A. Ulmer Diary, Southern Historical Collection, University of North Carolina.

[41] "Colleges and Schools," in Charles Force Deems, *The Annals of Southern Methodism* (New York, 1956), 163.

[42] *Ibid.*, 170.

these speeches, as one woman who read an essay on "Capital Punishment" at the Bascom Female Institute in Huntsville, Alabama, demonstrated.[43] Students also demonstrated knowledge of history, philosophy, literature, mathematics, and science by responding to questions submitted by their teacher. Exhibitions were also interspersed with piano concerts, singing, and presentations of artwork, which is why they often attracted the public.

Southerners remarked in their private letters about having attended examinations at female schools. Orville B. Martin, writing to Mary E. Claiborne in Kentucky in 1824, remarked that he found an examination at a female academy in Lexington to be "highly interesting." "The compositions," Martin wrote, "read by the young ladies, were written in a chaste & elegant style, indicating an elevation of sentiment seldom found in young men of a much more advanced age."[44] Martin went on to praise the heartfelt farewell address delivered by one student apparently emotional at the notion of leaving friends and teachers. Frequent allusions to these events in the public and private writings of southerners testify to their importance to the intellectual life of southern communities.

In addition to being examined in both "solid" and "ornamental" subjects, the young women provided entertainment with a concert. "So popular," boasted the report, "have these concerts become that it is impossible for all who attend them to be comfortably seated in the large Schoolroom in which they are given."[45] Southern communities showed much interest in their female schools, and schools repaid towns by providing cultural entertainment. Students at Wesleyan Female College in Murfreesboro, North Carolina, offered a number of public concerts each year. Anne Beale Davis, wife of the college's president, remarked in 1856 that a concert had drawn considerable interest from the community: "The weather being very auspicious we had a very full attendance. ... The rostrum was large enough to have placed on it four pianos, as well as seat all the teachers. There were some 3 or 400 persons present."[46] Given the number of people in the audience, residents from a wide range of economic status must have attended, providing an important event around which southern communities could cohere. The rural nature of the South hindered frequent personal contact, so southerners took advantage of opportunities for social engagement and cultural entertainment when offered. Thus, the public examinations and concerts at female schools and colleges were considered by friends and family to be important events. They

[43] *Ibid.*, 175.

[44] Orville B. Martin to Mary E. Claiborne, August 1, 1824, Maury Family Papers, Clements Library, University of Michigan.

[45] *Southern Weekly Post* 2 (June 11, 1853), 111. A report on the exams later that year praised the "promptness of their replies, the brevity yet lucid clearness of their explanations and the decided merits of some of their original essays." *Southern Weekly Post* 2 (December 11, 1852), 6.

[46] Anne Beale Davis to Wilbur Davis, February 27, 1856, Beale-Davis Papers, Southern Historical Collection, University of North Carolina. Quoted in Stephenson, "The Davises," 262–3.

were taken seriously by all involved, particularly the students. These popular events tell a rich story of community commitment to women's institutions that sprung up in towns and cities.

Female schools contributed to the intellectual life of their communities in still other ways. Newspapers and magazines that were closely allied with female schools were important links between the institutions and their communities. Indeed, the devotion and pride that southerners felt for female schools is especially evident in newspaper reports of school events and activities. Even advertisements were important ways for schools and their communities to connect. Raleigh's *Southern Weekly Post* published in one issue ads for Belford Female Academy, the Hillsborough Female School, the Bloomfield Female Seminary, and the Warrenton Female Institute.[47] The Greensboro *Weekly Message* supported schools for girls and young women by publishing news of exams and fund-raising efforts. In the 1850s, Greensboro possessed two female colleges (Edgeworth and Greensborough), and the interest that the local newspaper took in these institutions is evidence of the ties between the schools and the community. The *Weekly Message* also frequently printed news about other North Carolina schools, such as the Carolina Female College, the Buckingham Female Institute, and Somerville Female Institute, and reprinted lectures given before the literary societies of those schools.

Female schools frequently published literary magazines that contained light poetry, brief essays, and short stories written by students and teachers. Corona Female College, established in Corinth, Mississippi, in 1857 on land donated by community residents, had its own lyceum society and library. The students and faculty of the school also published a monthly literary magazine, the *Corona Wreath*.[48] Similarly, the *Guardian*, a monthly journal published in Columbia, Tennessee, from 1841 to 1847, was edited by F. G. Smith and his wife who were teachers at Columbia Female Institute. The first number of the magazine appeared in January 1841 and contained many pieces on female education, a short story in four chapters titled "Uncle Matthew's Tales," a notice of new books donated to the library, two poems (one by a student and one by a teacher), a student's composition, and an address to the graduating class by Rev. James H. Otey advising the young women not to act rashly or hastily in marriage.[49] In fact, the first issue was devoted almost entirely to female education.

One of the most important southern periodicals closely aligned with a female college was the *Southern Ladies' Book*, which began in Macon, Georgia, as the literary companion to the Georgia Female College. (The name of the journal was later changed to the *Magnolia*, and it moved from Macon to Savannah

[47] *Southern Weekly Post* 1 (January 31, 1852), 36.

[48] Ricky Harold Gray, "Corona Female College (1857–1864)," *Journal of Mississippi History* (May 1980), 130.

[49] *Guardian* 1 (January, 1841).

and finally to Charleston).[50] Edited initially by Philip C. Pendleton and George F. Pierce, the latter editor also the president of the Georgia Female College and later president of Emory, the *Southern Ladies' Book* (like the female college) was affiliated with the Methodist church. In its first issue, the magazine identified its chief purpose: "Our convictions of woman's mind and worth compel us to believe that we can furnish a more agreeable entertainment by providing a magazine of sterling periodical literature."[51] The articles and essays in the journal promoted the idea of a broad education for women: "Let ladies be educated well in all those branches which are useful and of social value to the thinking and reasoning powers of the mind."[52] The *Southern Ladies' Book* fulfilled its promise to link the Georgia Female College with the broader community. Its first article was a reprint of Pierce's speech before the college's Board of Visitors on the importance of female education. Other essays kept readers abreast of the progress of the college, and speeches delivered at commencements and other public events were often reprinted in the pages of the *Southern Ladies' Book*.

That female schools, colleges, and academies brought communities together in united, socially leveling events was further demonstrated by an ideology that emphasized plain dress and the seriousness of education. Indeed, within the culture surrounding female education one finds rejections of ostentatious display. Guidelines for dress at southern schools made this clear. For example, a pamphlet at St. Mary's School in Raleigh intended "to prevent rivalry and extravagance" by requiring students to wear "a simple uniform" consisting of "a plain white dress, with straw bonnet trimmed with blue ribbon." "Jewels," the rules stated flatly, "are prohibited."[53] The Judson Female Institute in Marion, Alabama, required that "all dresses must be made *perfectly plain*; without inserting edgings, or any trimming whatever."[54]

When middle-class southerners spoke out on the issue of women's education, they often attacked the "fashionable" schooling associated with women of the upper class. "There is nothing more *demoralizing*" for young women, wrote a Kentuckian, "than the constant round of balls and parties where young ladies are content to be miserable for the sake of fashion."[55] As an outgrowth of the evangelical sentiments that stressed rejecting luxury and embracing hard work, this ideology was central to southern culture in general

50 David Spencer, "The Magnolia; or, the Southern Appalachian," in Kathleen L. Enders and Therese L. Lueck, eds., *Women's Periodicals in the United States: Social and Political Issues* (Westport, CT, 1996), 209.

51 "Introduction," *Southern Ladies' Book* 1 (January 1840), 2.

52 L. Pierce, "Female Education," *Southern Ladies' Book* 1 (March 1840), 133.

53 Pamphlet for St. Mary's School, John Lancaster Bailey Papers, Southern Historical Collection.

54 Judson Catalogue, 1851, quoted in Elizabeth A. Taylor, "Regulations Governing Student Life at the Judson Female Institute During the Decade Preceeding the Civil War" *Alabama Historical Quarterly* 3 (Spring 1941), 27.

55 Alexander Crittenden to Clara Crittenden, October 12, 1837, Crittenden Papers, Clements Library, University of Michigan.

and to the impetus for female education in particular. As many clergymen railed against "Mammonism" in sermons to their congregations, and as early nineteenth-century evangelical rhetoric scorned elite learning in favor of simplicity, the denunciation of the values of the upper class became fodder for those who believed that Christianity and the pursuit of luxury were fundamentally at odds. "Females have no less responsible position in society than males," argued one Tennessee author. "There are two extremes in reference to female character to be condemned. The one in savage life, among barbarous nations, which reduces her to the lowest condition of slavery. The other in a pretended condition of refinement of society, where she is made a superb toy, a magnificent doll."[56] Plain girls and young women were urged to reject the latest trends emanating from the shops of New York or Paris. The *Southern Ladies' Book* reprinted a lengthy essay by Timothy Dwight titled "The Evils of Fashionable Education."[57] There are undertones of class resentment in antebellum southern writings, suggesting that fashions, refined manners, and luxury of aristocratic circles were corrupting and dangerous to southern society in general and women in particular.[58] Young men were supposed to be wise to these "fashionable" women and to avoid them at all cost.

Southern advocates of female education often lamented the bodily contortions that fashion required of young women. A writer on the subject of corsets similarly opposed the focus on the body and fashion rather than on the mind: "It shows to what ridiculous excess *fashion* will carry its giddy votaries; and it points to the American female the impropriety of torturing the lovely form which nature has given her, to make it appear what it really is not ... unnatural contortions of body and gaudiness of decoration can excite only contempt and derision."[59] Even the vaunted belle was not immune to criticism for her superficiality: "Extravagance and finery in dress," a southern author opined in 1825, "I would censure and condemn. A fop, or a belle, I would hold in steady contempt.... Against the splendor, gaiety and fickleness of fashion, the pure and unassuming influence of Christian piety is naturally arrayed."[60] Southerners recognized that gender conventions required irrational concessions to fashion. Advocates of education for white women not only promoted broader learning for female students, they also attacked traditional gender ideology regarding marriage, domestic duties, and fashion.

[56] H. S. Porter, "Female Education," *Ladies' Pearl* 3 (November 1854), 1–2.

[57] Timothy Dwight, "The Evils of Fashionable Education," *Southern Ladies' Book* 1 (May 1840), 260–2.

[58] L. Pierce, "The Education of the Poor," *Southern Ladies' Book* 1 (April 1840), 222.

[59] "Singular Female Beauties," *Ladies' Garland* 1 (May 22, 1824), 78. For similar sentiments, see "The Corset," *Southern Planter* 7 (September 1847), 269.

[60] "Female Character," *Ladies' Garland* 2 (September 24, 1825), 129. Other essays on women's education appeared in all of the antebellum southern magazines but with particular frequency in the *Ladies' Garland* and the *Messenger*. See, for example, the *Ladies' Garland* 1 (February 14, 1824), 3; 1 (April 24, 1824), 43; 2 (February 12, 1825), 2; 2 (February 19, 1825), 7–8; 3 (August 19, 1826), 109–10; 3 (September 2, 1826), 117–8; 3 (September 9, 1826), 121 and the *Messenger* 1 (December 1834), 169–70.

Although significant gains were made in the education of white women, free African Americans in the South had a difficult time securing a modicum of schooling. As Suzanne Lebsock has found in Petersburg, Virginia, free black boys and girls were prohibited from attending school in the wake of Nat Turner's Rebellion in 1831.[61] The repression brought on by the fears of slave rebellions affected not just blacks in Virginia but those in other southern states as well. After the early 1830s, if a free or slave black woman was to learn to read, then she would have to do it furtively. Some were secretly taught by kind mistresses on the plantation, whereas others had to learn on their own. George Moses Horton, a slave who lived on a plantation near Chapel Hill, North Carolina, learned to read and write by scrounging after scraps of paper found lying about on the plantation and by trying to read Bible verses.[62] No doubt slave girls and young women engaged in similar attempts; the remarkable aspect of these attempts to learn is that they were successful. Slaves were sometimes educated by fellow slaves who had learned to read and write. We have precious few reports of this activity, but we know that slave boys were sometimes taught furtively, at least as best their slave parents could accomplish. In his slave narrative, Noah Davis recalled that his "father could read a little, and make figures, but could scarcely write at all. His custom, on those Sabbaths when we remained at home, was to spend his time in instructing his children, or the neighboring servants, out of a New Testament. … I fancy I see him now, sitting under his brush arbor, reading that precious book to many attentive hearers around him."[63] Davis's experience reflects perhaps the most structured education a southern slave could receive: that of one literate slave (or master or mistress) teaching another to read and write. Throughout the South it was customary for slaves to have all or most of Sunday to themselves, to work in their gardens, to worship, or to engage in other activities, including listening to a literate slave read the Bible.

The chief defining characteristic for slaves' education was, therefore, its haphazard nature. Whereas white children often learned in structured environments under the guidance of a teacher or tutor, slave children were fortunate if their plantation or household harbored a slave who could read or write and provide even a facile level of instruction. Thus, the experience that Davis relates, the catch-as-catch-can approach to reading, listening, and writing, was the most common one for southern African Americans. As historian Elizabeth Fox-Genovese has argued in *Within the Plantation Household*, "Slave codes rigorously prohibited teaching slaves to read and write, and well over 90 percent of the slaves remained illiterate."[64] The proximity of house

[61] Suzanne Lebsock, *The Free Women of Petersburg: Status and Culture in a Southern Town, 1784–1860* (New York, 1984), 34.

[62] Joan R. Sherman, *The Black Bard of North Carolina George Moses Horton and His Poetry* (Chapel Hill, 1997).

[63] Davis quoted in Foster, *Witnessing Slavery*, 135.

[64] Fox-Genovese, *Within the Plantation Household*, 156.

slaves to their masters' family might facilitate instruction. "As the white girls began to learn to read and write from their mothers," Fox-Genovese explains, "they in turn might try to teach their favorite slaves ... [and] many mistresses as well as their daughters frequently avowed their commitment to teaching the female house slaves religious principles and read to them from the Bible or tried to draw them into family prayers."[65] However, as Fox-Genovese argues, southern learning was a privilege of whiteness.

Despite advances in education for white women, career options for educated white women were still severely limited in the Old South outside of teaching and writing. Yet these two professions provided some women with the ability to articulate their needs and desires, ultimately helping to weaken the strict division of work and home. Writing, particularly for publication, was the antithesis of private; women authors were public women with recognition, reputation, and even some power in southern communities. Thus was the ideology of separate spheres, so powerful and prominent in the thinking of antebellum Americans, pregnant with notions that ultimately weakened and redefined it. Once women were given agency as republican mothers, as vital components in the survival of the republic, they needed an education; and education brought with it greater self-awareness, knowledge about the larger world, and the ability to question the way things were.

Given that southern schools for girls and young women taught a wide range of disciplines, and given the community's interest in seeing that these disciplines were taught well, how did education affect the students themselves? How did exposure to history, science, literature, philosophy, mathematics, and other fields of study shape the identity of girls and women? Whether that education culminated in graduation or ended after a brief period of limited schooling, it shaped not only their lives as wives and mothers but also their identities as individuals. Given the level of involvement of southerners in building and maintaining female schools, the sharp distinction that historians have drawn between public and private institutions may be a false dichotomy. Even before the schools were constructed, interested parties solicited donations and subscriptions from ordinary citizens. Denominations that supported schools for women were actively engaged in overseeing these institutions and were proud when the institutions flourished. The hiring of teachers was of great interest to southern communities as well, and local newspapers boasted of the quality of instruction, the diversity of subjects taught, and the excellence of the pupils. Public examinations during commencements became festive public events that attracted not just parents and relatives but strangers as well. Thus, although the Old South could point to only a few efforts to establish state-run public school systems, efforts that met with little success before the Civil War, it cannot also be said that private institutions were so private that they were unconnected to their communities. Indeed, at the local level even nominally

[65] *Ibid.*

private schools and colleges for girls and women were really public institutions in practical operation.

Without appreciating the new educational experiences of southern women, the success of female editors and journalists in the later antebellum period and the post-Civil War South is difficult to explain. However, when we understand advances in schooling and literacy as well as the extent to which southern communities were committed to female education, we shed considerable light on the rise of women as literary consumers and producers. Over the course of the nineteenth century, white southern women and later their African American counterparts used their abilities as writers and journalists to promote the cause of women's rights.

PART TWO

WOMEN JOURNALISTS AND WRITERS IN THE OLD SOUTH

Forty years after Sarah Cooper dreamed of becoming an editor and created her homemade magazine in Virginia, Nannie Grant and Paulina Warinner, two friends also from Virginia, handwrote their own periodical. Like Cooper, Grant and Warinner fashioned themselves important editors, taking care to pen by hand not one but four different magazines, entitled "The Ark," "The Lone Star," "The Casket," and "The Wreath." Each magazine included a hand-drawn masthead and incorporated handwritten short stories, editorials, advertisements, biographies, and poems. "The Ark" was available for "$5.00 Confederate."[1] While momentous events had passed in the four decades between the time Cooper rendered her journal and the years in which Grant and Warinner made theirs, including the Civil War and the end of slavery, young women still dreamed of lives as authors and editors.

With advances in education and literature, and a growing sentiment that women were the intellectual equals of men, a path opened for women interested in writing poetry and prose for the South's periodicals. Due to improvements in the postal service, the transportation of goods via railroads, and the printing business, the number of magazines and newspapers published in the region rose significantly between 1820 and the Civil War. White southern women actively participated in the growth of this industry, initially by contributing poems, short fiction, translations of European works, and serialized novels in periodicals such as *The Ladies' Magazine* and *The Southern Literary Messenger*. However, white women (for even free black southern women were largely excluded from this emerging periodical culture), quickly moved from contributors to associate editors and editors. As associate editors, they often headed a special "woman's column" or "woman's section" inserted in periodicals to attract female subscribers. But such separate sections, often focusing on motherhood, recipes, or fashion, could not contain women readers' interests. Although southern women had been involved in printing in the 1700s,

[1] Handwritten periodicals located in the Nannie A. S. Grant Papers, Virginia Historical Society.

the early nineteenth century witnessed the expansion of women's involvement into the burgeoning periodical business. Women's expansive interests, too broad to be constrained and isolated in sections supposedly designed for female readers, led to roles in editing and publishing.

As writers and editors, white women offered a range of views, and their periodicals expressed their individual tastes, interests, and ideologies. Some offered traditional works that focused on childrearing, household tips, and other hallmarks of domesticity. Other writers and editors, though, indulged in partisan politics, criticized political leaders, offered views on issues like the Bank of the United States and cabinet appointments, and commented on funding for railroads, the treatment of Native Americans, and religion. Almost no condemnations of slavery are to be found in the pages of antebellum periodicals, either those edited by women or those edited by men but designed for female readers. The role of women in society, however, was often discussed, debated, and commented on. Women's active participation in the periodical culture of the Old South, in fact, should be viewed as vital to the origins of the southern movement for women's rights. Although there was no southern Seneca Falls, the emergence of women editors like Anne Royall, Mary Chase Barney, and Rebecca Hicks helped generate calls for the expansion of women's roles and responsibilities.

3

Periodicals and Literary Culture

Southern white women read a wide range of fiction and nonfiction, welcoming books and periodicals as both a diversion from everyday life and as a source of erudition. Magazines in particular attracted significant readerships across the region. As Sarah Lois Wadley proclaimed after reading two periodicals, "I received them with gratitude and read them with gravity; and after the perusal was finished, felt about as much edified as if I had been reading over the long columns of words in Webster's spelling book."[1] Thus, whereas southern women may have found few outlets for exploring their intellectual attainments, they nonetheless cherished the pursuit of knowledge through printed material, including literary periodicals.

Magazines and newspapers were ubiquitous in the nineteenth-century South. They were affordable, easily circulated, and could be perused quickly or at length. Nineteenth-century observers noted that periodical literature seemed to suit the needs of women educated in many different subjects but lacking expertise in any one field. The diverse character of magazines and newspapers, in which recipes and housekeeping hints appeared alongside essays on Shakespeare or commentary on political issues, fit well with the emphasis on the breadth of learning expected of the "Renaissance woman." "Time and again," scholar Amy Beth Aronson has noted, "contributors and printers called for the consistent reading of a wide range of text types, regulated by short exposure and episodic attention.... [Such] consistent but episodic reading constructed the popular woman reader as the ideal reader of the women's magazine, with its miscellaneous contents and serial format."[2] The establishment of a more advanced postal system, the increasing efforts to educate American women, the emphasis on the importance of "Renaissance women" in teaching their children, and the concerted effort to appeal to women readers with gender-specific content all combined to create a culture

[1] Sarah Lois Wadley Diary, volume 2, June 25, 1861, Southern Historical Collection, University of North Carolina.

[2] Amy Beth Aronson, *Taking Liberties: Early American Women's Magazines and their Readers* (Westport, 2002), 57.

conducive to the spread of women's periodicals and ultimately to enhanced opportunities for female members of the press.

In general, southern women read the same authors and works as their northern counterparts. Historians have long considered the importance of national institutions such as the Democratic or Whig parties or the large religious denominations that spanned the North and South. The collapse of these national institutions played a significant part in facilitating the onset of disunion and civil war. Literature also formed an important element of the culture shared by all Americans, and the sectional schism in American literary culture parallels the role played by other national institutions in contributing to the division of the Union. In reading northern books and periodicals, southerners were exposed to a wide range of ideas about literature, society, and economy. Southerners also thought carefully about the ideas they read, including those that emanated from New England culture, such as transcendentalism. Therefore, in examining the reading in which southern women engaged, the modern observer can see the ways in which a truly national literary culture was already forming by the early nineteenth century. Although fundamental differences between the sections existed, throughout much of the nineteenth century those differences were in part smoothed over by the literary interests that bridged the sectional gap.

Southerners, particularly in the early 1800s, often debated the virtues and vices of reading book-length works of fiction. A commonly held notion was that reading novels posed a danger to the sensibilities of southern women. Numerous essays and countless speakers denounced the writing and reading of novels for a variety of reasons. First, the imaginative depictions of plots and characters were deemed a frivolous indulgence for wives and mothers who had more serious tasks to comprehend, reflecting the evangelical distaste for luxury and self-indulgence. Just as women were supposed to be educated for the sober duties that awaited them in marriage and just as they were to avoid instruction in superficial subjects and ostentatious clothing, so too should women's reading befit their roles as wives and mothers. Thus, periodical literature was acceptable because many magazines and newspapers contained helpful hints on cooking, gardening, childrearing, and housekeeping even as they offered women short stories and poetry. In addition, most women's magazines published essays on various historical or even scientific topics, knowledge that would help to fill the minds of the mother-teacher. However, the perusal of novels filled no practical need, contained no recipes, or useful religious instruction. As Mary Kelley has shown, women "looked to books to spark flights of fancy, relieve solitude, provoke laughter, and furnish refuge."[3]

Closely aligned with this powerful sentiment was the belief, percolating just under the surface of many encomiums against novel reading, that because such reading provided only escape and extravagance, young women might

[3] Kelley, "Reading Women/Women Reading," 402–3.

be distracted by the pursuit of pleasure. Pleasure, many antebellum northern and southern writers argued, was not something in which the female gender was to partake. Indeed, women were often depicted as balancing the whims and passions of man by providing sound, grounded advice to her "helpmate." This was the southern woman as counselor and friend, the wife whose primary purpose was to offer sober thoughts on matters confronting the family. Passions and pleasures were always to be kept in check.

Despite the power of this rhetoric, novels proved popular in the South among women, and over time opposition to them withered. As Isaac Baker of St. Martinsville, Louisiana, wrote to a female relative, "Novels are by many considered a dangerous sort of reading for you ladies but I think those lately published, ascribed to Walter Scott, are of a class you may read not only for recreation and amusement but for profit and advantage."[4] By the later antebellum period, when it was clear that reading novels had not in fact ruined generations of women, the attacks on novel reading eased. In fact, southern women read novels of all kinds, from historical fiction to romances to humorous sketches, from the pens of all kinds of authors. "Read no trash," James Harris of Port Gibson, Mississippi, advised. "If you read novels at all, let them be the works of the great masters, of Scott, of Cooper, of Miss Edgeworth."[5]

Reading, especially of novels, could be a powerful distraction from a rural existence that most southerners led before the Civil War. As Caledonia Brown of Tennessee wrote to her girlfriend: "But why should I speak thus of Franklin [Tennessee]? I assure you it is a New Orleans compared to Sommerville; language fails when I attempt to describe its miserable dullness, monotony, and perfect want of interest to me. Suffice it to say I am buried alive."[6] Thus, literature could be an important escape. Lucy Ruggles, who came to South Carolina from the Troy Female Seminary in New York, delighted in reading Augustus Baldwin Longstreet's comedic *Georgia Scenes*. She recorded in her diary that she "laughed until I cried" and expressed remorse when the book was finished. "I am really sorry that the rich treat is over, for I know not what I shall do for fun. It is the most amusing thing that I ever read."[7]

Women often expressed their views on their reading in diaries or letters, offering reflections on works they read. Amy Morris Bradley of Wilmington, for example, wrote in her diary her views after reading "Tennyson's last work, 'In Memoriam.'" Bradley identified with the work: "I think I appreciate this little volume [as] there are so many passages expressing my own feelings at the present time.... I have seen some almost go wild with ecstasy on perusing

[4] Isaac Baker to Mary Eliza Claiborne, April 23, 1822, Maury Family Papers, Clements Library, University of Michigan.

[5] James Harris to Cary A. Harris, March 15, 1852, Maury Family Papers, Clements Library, University of Michigan.

[6] Caledonia Brown to Sally C. Maury, March 12, 1846, Maury Family Papers, Clements Library, University of Michigan.

[7] Lucy Spooner Ruggles Diary, April 2, 1845, Perkins Library, Duke University.

a poem by T. But for my own part I would prefer Bryant's or Longfellow's" poetry.[8] Among the most popular authors in antebellum America was Sir Walter Scott, and southerners relished his works with a fervor equal to that of other readers on both sides of the Atlantic. "Novel reading," Alexander Crittenden wrote to his seventeen-year-old wife, "... has a beneficial effect, where a proper selection is made and where it is nor carried to excess ... Scott's novels can never be too much read, to be conversant with them should be considered an indispensable part of a ladies [sic] education."[9] Rachael Mordecai Lazarus agreed. Lazarus, a teacher from Warrenton, North Carolina, conducted a remarkable correspondence with the famous educator and novelist Maria Edgeworth, who resided in Ireland, from 1815 until Lazarus' death in 1838. Lazarus, who was Jewish, originally wrote Edgeworth to complain strongly but respectfully of the negative portrayal of a Jewish character in one of Edgeworth's novels. Edgeworth thanked her American correspondent for the lesson, and the two women exchanged views on numerous authors, including Lord Byron, James Fennimore Cooper, Washington Irving, and Catherine M. Sedgwick. However, their literary friendship was primarily based on a mutual admiration for the writings of Scott. The two women exchanged long letters that analyzed in detail the stories penned by Scott, and they frequently devoted particular attention to female characters. For example, Lazarus remarked that one of Scott's fictional women, Rebecca, "appears to me the most finished female character that Scott has drawn. Her mind, her principles, her feelings, all highly wrought, are still under the control of reason, of discretion and of true feminine dignity."[10]

Southern women read the same authors that were highly regarded in the North. Even as sectional animosities grew in the 1850s, southerners continued to subscribe to northern publications. "If the angel Gabriel [entered] into the very heart of the South," editor George Bagby angrily declared, "if he had taken his seat on the top of the *Charleston Mercury* and there proclaimed the immediate approach of the day of Judgment, that would not have hindered the hottest secessionist from buying the *New York Herald* and subscribing for *Harper's Magazine*."[11] Indeed, Cooper, Irving, Dickens, Sedgwick, Byron, Shakespeare, Pope, and others were as widely read in the slave states as elsewhere. South Carolinian Carey North read poems by Thomas Moore and Longfellow, histories by Voltaire and Macaulay, and novels by Dickens and Thackeray.[12]

[8] Diary entry for January 19, 1851, Amy Morris Bradley Papers, Perkins Library, Duke University.

[9] Alexander Crittenden to Clara Crittenden, May 14, 1837, Crittenden Papers, Clements Library, University of Michigan.

[10] Rachael Mordecai Lazarus to Maria Edgeworth, June 17, 1824, in Edgar E. MacDonald, ed., *The Education of the Heart: The Correspondence of Rachael Mordecai Lazarus and Maria Edgeworth* (Chapel Hill, 1977), 64.

[11] Bagby quoted in Ray Morris Atchison, "Southern Literary Magazines, 1865–1887," (Ph.D. diss., Duke University, 1956), 53.

[12] Michael O'Brien, ed., *An Evening When Alone: Four Journals of Single Women in the South, 1827–67* (Charlottesville, VA, 1993), 27.

Despite her unease about women venturing into the masculine world of political debate, North herself read a wide variety of nonfiction. European authors like Dickens remained popular with southern women throughout the nineteenth century. Even after the publication, in 1842, of his biting critique of the United States, *American Notes*, in which Dickens disparaged American manners and politics and was particularly critical of southern slavery, he remained a widely read author in the South. Harriet Vance remarked in 1852 that she was "much more pleased with Dickens' last work ... than I was with David Copperfield."[13] Exposure to authors such as Dickens could come not only from bookstore purchases but also from the many lending institutions that existed in the South in the 1800s. For example, the libraries at southern women's academies were often considerable. The Columbia Female Institute held more than seven hundred volumes by January 1841, including recently donated titles such as *The Works of Washington Irving* (twelve volumes), *Comstock's Physiology*, Sir Walter Scott's *History of Scotland* (two volumes), and *Silliman's Travels* (three volumes).[14]

Southern women read avidly on political and economic questions and had no problem procuring volumes on these topics, though finding time to read while also fulfilling domestic responsibilities was often trying. Lazarus was no defender of slavery; she wrote repeatedly that she prayed for its demise. Yet, like many southern men and women, she took umbrage at Harriet Martineau's criticism of America, and especially of the South. "As to Miss M's opinion that marriage is the sole object of an American woman," Lazarus bristled in a letter to Edgeworth in 1838, "I can only say that we do not understand the meaning of her assertion.... We thank her for her commiserations, tho' in fact until informed by her, we were scarcely aware of our imbecility."[15] Still, Lazarus admitted that her domestic responsibilities sometimes seemed overwhelming; most bothersome, domestic duties took time away from her reading. In 1821, she married a widower who already had seven children. Though she filled her new role as mother ably and happily, she lamented the passing of earlier days when she had more time for herself. Lazarus wrote to Edgeworth in 1828: "My reading hours are now very limited. The care and education of my children, with domestick duties, engross almost my whole time – not unprofitably, nor undelightfully; yet do I often wish that my hours could be lengthened, or that some of those which hang heavily on the idle could be transferred to me."[16]

Despite the difficulty that parents faced in finding time to read, women in the South balanced their reading of fiction with works on history, politics, and travel. Although women were generally barred from participating actively in politics or government, they still kept abreast of contemporary issues. One

[13] Harriet Newell Espy Vance to Zebulon Vance, May 22, 1852, in *My Beloved Zebulon*, 91.

[14] *Guardian* 1 (January, 1841), 9.

[15] Rachael Mordecai Lazarus to Maria Edgeworth, March 18, 1838, in MacDonald, *Education of the Heart*, 303.

[16] Lazarus to Edgeworth, November 3, 1828, in MacDonald, *Education of the Heart*, 178.

Charleston governess, a native of Massachusetts, was determined to read essays and speeches on politics and slavery. She read works on the annexation of Texas, slavery, and abolitionism. Having read remarks by John Jay, Jr., son of the Supreme Court Justice, this woman recorded in her diary that "he has gone mad with abolitionism, and is ranting for the dissolution of the Union.... I myself wonder that my northern brethren cannot mind their own affairs."[17] For those residing in remote rural regions, accounts of faraway lands were as entertaining as novels. Anna C. Lesesne recorded in her diary her pleasure at reading Nathaniel Parker Willis' descriptions of travel to Italy and Switzerland. She even attended two lectures on Greece by a Mr. Perdicuris.[18]

Reading political works, even politically charged novels such as *Uncle Tom's Cabin*, strongly affected southern women and helped to set the stage for the broader questioning of society. Georgia's Ella Gertrude Thomas, for example, was a sensitive reader who thought carefully about the political implications of her reading. As she put down in her diary: "But as to the doctrine of slavery altho I have read very few abolition books (*Uncle Tom's Cabin* making the most impression) nor have I read many pro slavery books – yet the idea has gradually become more and more fixed in my mind that the institution of slavery is not right." Thomas searched for works that would confirm slavery's legitimacy but she had her doubts: "I am reading a new book, *Nellie Norton*, by the Rev E. W. Warren which I hope will convince me that it is right – Owing a large number of slaves as we do I might be asked why do I not free them?"[19] However, the most common reading material for southern women like Thomas was not novels but magazines.

Planter families like Thomas's could afford to subscribe to as many as six or seven magazines, but the wealthy were not the only southern patrons of periodical literature. As one scholar has found, consumers from a single southern town "included women, planters, small farmers and at least one farm laborer, a seamstress, a harness maker, a jeweler, one or two carpenters, a clerk in a cotton store, a possible mechanic, and two 'servants.'"[20] Postal records demonstrate clearly that men and women in the South subscribed in surprisingly large numbers to periodicals from the North. Even as sectional hostilities waxed and waned over the later antebellum period, southerners continued to purchase northern periodicals. At Fort Defiance, North Carolina, for example, periodical records from the 1850s mention subscriptions to Philadelphia's *Banner of the Cross*, *Arthur's Home Magazine*, *Saturday Evening Post*,

[17] Lucy Spooner Ruggles Diary, volume 1, March 6, 1845; January 17, 1846. Quotation appears in volume 1, April 28, 1845.

[18] See entries for January 16, 1836, January 18, 1836, and March 31, 1836, Diary of Anna C. Lesesne, South Carolina Historical Society, Charleston.

[19] Entry for September 1864, Diary of Ella Gertrude Thomas, in Burr, ed., *Secret Eye*, 238.

[20] Helen R. Watson, "A Journalistic Medley: Newspapers and Periodicals in a Small North Carolina Community, 1859–1860," *North Carolina Historical Review* 60 (October 1983), 466.

Sartain's Magazine, and *Graham's Magazine*, as well as New York's *American Messenger*, *Christian Advocate Journal*, and *Cultivator*.[21] Small towns and cities helped to funnel national publications to southern farms. Through such reading materials, southern women could compare the ideas that circulated within their own local areas with those discussed in northern periodicals. Through such periodical reading, southerners learned about the same ideas about gender roles and separate spheres that scholars have presumed could only have existed in the industrializing North.

Even in the late antebellum period, southerners continued to subscribe in great numbers to northern newspapers and magazines. William Reavis, a postmaster in the Piedmont town of Henderson, North Carolina, kept records from 1849 to 1863.[22] The records generally list a citizen's name, followed by the magazines and newspapers to which he or she subscribed and the postage owed. Residing in an unusually productive and wealthy town surrounded by rich farmland, Henderson's citizens probably had more to spend on printed matter than some of their less fortunate neighbors in North Carolina and the South.[23] Records left behind by the postmaster of Rocky Mount, North Carolina, show that more than 175 residents subscribed to several dozen different periodicals in 1859 and 1860. Interestingly, the most subscriptions (twenty-nine) were for New York's *Banner of Liberty*. Supporting historian Michael O'Brien's conclusions about the active participation of the South in the broader world of ideas, Rocky Mount citizens bought *Harper's*, *Godey's Lady's Book*, *Peterson's Magazine*, the *Edinburgh Review*, and numerous others. More than thirty women subscribed to periodicals by themselves, including many New York publications, such as the *New York Day Book* and the *New York Ledger*.[24]

Northern magazines popular among southern readers such as *Graham's* and the *Knickerbocker* were hardly bastions of northern radicalism; on the contrary, these journals were important vehicles for the dissemination of middle-class Victorian values. Here ideas about women and the family found full expression. The "cult of true womanhood" and the "cult of domesticity" are apparent in nearly every issue, as short stories and poems related tales of women's responsibilities as wives and mothers.[25] Like *Graham's*, the *Knickerbocker* contained numerous stories and poems on women's roles in family and society.[26]

[21] Wells, *The Origins of the Southern Middle Class*, 46.

[22] Amy M. Thomas' dissertation "Who Makes the Text?" offers much insight into the Reavis papers and the subscription lists he left behind. See especially chapter 3.

[23] *Ibid*, 107–8.

[24] Watson, "A Journalistic Medley," 463–4, 479, 485; Wells, *The Origins of the Southern Middle Class*, 248.

[25] For evidence of this tendency in *Graham's*, see E. C. Kinney, "The Young Mother's Lament," 37 (July 1850), 14; Alice B. Neal, "'What Can Woman Do?' or the Influence of an Example," 37 (September 1850), 158–62.

[26] J. A. S., "The Mother's Last Prayer," *The Knickerbocker* 29 (March 1847), 213.

Southerners were exposed to northern culture through northern books and periodicals, but often they could read the same authors in southern newspapers and magazines. Works by northern writers appeared frequently in the pages of southern periodicals, either in the form of essays, short stories, and poems reprinted from northern journals or as original contributions. Authors like the Maine native John Neal penned numerous poems and short stories for southern magazines.[27] Until the early 1850s, the authors most popular in the North were also the ones most admired by southerners. Irving's prose and poetry, for example, dot the pages of southern journals.[28] Lowell's poem "A Parable" appeared in Greensboro, North Carolina's *Weekly Message* newspaper.[29] Even works by northern women appeared with great frequency in the pages of southern periodicals. Northern women writers like Sigourney, Frances Sargent Osgood, Mrs. Seba Smith, and hundreds of lesser-known authors can be found in the pages of southern magazines.[30] The *Bouquet*, a weekly literary newspaper published in Charleston, featured a short story titled "Truth" by Osgood in one of its 1843 numbers.[31] Sigourney's works appear often, mostly in the form of sentimental poems reprinted from northern journals. The Connecticut native seems to have been widely popular with southern readers and was often discussed as one of the nation's premier authors.[32] "The Friend," an instructional essay by Sigourney, appeared in the *Young Ladies' Journal of Literature and Science*, the Baltimore monthly edited by Almira Spencer, in 1831; and her sonnet "To Miss Edgeworth" appeared in the *Orion*, a literary periodical published in Athens and Penfield, Georgia, in 1842.[33] As ideal forums for the exchange of literature and ideas between the North and South, periodicals helped to unite the sections even as other differences, particularly the debate over the extension of slavery, drove them apart.

[27] Neal published in many different southern periodicals, but he seems to have contributed with particular frequency to a journal edited by Sarah Lawrence Griffin in Macon, Georgia. See "Sketches From Life," (biography of Sarah Austin) *Family Companion and Ladies' Mirror* 1 (January 1842), 242–3; "The Ins and the Outs," *Family Companion and Ladies' Mirror* 1 (October 1841), 13–23.

[28] See, for example, Washington Irving, "Abderrahman: The Washington of Spain," *Southern Ladies' Book* 1 (June 1840), 292–302; "The Widow and her Son," *Southern Lady's Companion* 3 (September 1849), 142–3. Whittier's short works also appeared often in southern magazines. His poem "The Crucifixion" was reprinted in the *Southern Lady's Companion* 3 (October 1849), 152.

[29] James Russell Lowell, "A Parable," Greensboro *Weekly Message*, 1 (November 8, 1851).

[30] Osgood published prose and poetry in both northern and southern journals. Poems include "Song: 'He Bade Made Me Happy,'" *Family Companion and Ladies' Mirror* 1 (October 1841), 43; and "To Little Carnally," *Family Companion and Ladies' Mirror* 1 (January 1842), 242.

[31] Frances Sargent Osgood, "Truth," *Bouquet* 2 (February 25, 1843), 33–4.

[32] "The Literary Women of America," Greensboro *Weekly Message* 4 (March 22, 1855), 1.

[33] Lydia Huntley Sigourney, "The Friend," *Young Ladies' Journal of Literature and Science* 2 (February 1831), 162–4; and "To Miss Edgeworth," *Orion* 2 (November 1842), 4. For other works by Sigourney, see "The Intemperate: A Thrilling Story of the West," *Mistletoe* 1 (February 1849), 25–9 and (March 1849), 49–52.

With foundations laid for improved literacy rates and a broader education, the rise of a female reading public helped to spur a remarkable growth of periodicals published in the South beginning in the 1820s. Examining this world of newspapers and magazines opens a new and enlightening perspective on women and the mind of the South. Women eagerly devoured the latest novels by their favorite female writers and often borrowed copies from their girlfriends, school roommates, and libraries.[34] In focusing on novels and novelists, however, scholars have missed a significant portion of the reading and writing accomplished by southern women. In fact, women eagerly subscribed to periodicals, especially monthly magazines, and it is within these yellowed pages that one can delve into nineteenth-century women's literary experiences.[35] Indeed, as nineteenth-century southern thinker Thomas Dew remarked, the "periodical press is now the organ of communication, and the potent engine that controls the popular will."[36]

The number of titles, as well as the sophistication and diversity of magazines, increased dramatically after about 1820 nationwide. One chief reason for their expansion was the improvement of the postal delivery system. As documented by historian Richard John, the postal system benefited greatly from railroads, canals, and other transportation improvements that facilitated the movement of cargo.[37] Every major southern town and city had at least one periodical, and often several could be purchased through subscriptions or through local bookstores. Agents for magazines drummed up subscribers, and nearly all magazines published in the North or South had agents stationed in important cities. Ads for publications, often in the form of a prospectus if the magazine was new, provided further opportunities for potential subscribers to learn about a given periodical. Advertisements appeared in newspapers, journals, and fliers distributed in bookstores. Most southern periodicals were written and edited by southerners and printed by southern presses. As Table 3.1 shows, beginning in the 1820s the region harbored many native periodicals that clamored for the attention of the reading public. Subscribers could choose from dozens of southern publications, in addition to the hundreds offered by northern editors. In fact, many southerners bought northern subscriptions to magazines like *Godey's* and also purchased journals printed locally. A typical middle-class or planter family might well subscribe to five or six periodicals, including a local newspaper, a financial journal from the North, a periodical

[34] Kelley, *Learning to Stand and Speak.*

[35] Limited but important work has been done on female editors outside the South. See, for example, Sharon M. Harris, ed., *Blue Pencils and Hidden Hands: Women Editing Periodicals, 1830–1910* (Boston, 2004); Sherilyn Cox Bennion, *Equal to the Occasion: Women Editors of the Nineteenth-Century West* (Reno, 1990); and Patricia Okker, *Our Sister Editors: Sarah J. Hale and the Tradition of Nineteenth-Century American Women Editors* (Athens, 1995).

[36] Thomas R. Dew, *A Digest of the Laws, Customs, Manners, and Institutions of the Ancient and Modern Nations* (New York, 1853), quoted in O'Brien, *Conjectures of Order*, 529.

[37] Richard John, *Spreading the News: The American Postal System from Franklin to Morse* (Cambridge, 1995).

TABLE 3.1. *Increase in the numbers of antebellum magazines started in southern states, by decade*

Decade	Number of Magazines Started
1800–1809	22
1810–1819	36
1820–1829	63
1830–1839	120
1840–1849	179
1850–1859	214

Source: Gilmer, *Checklist of Southern Periodicals*, Section III. Southern states included in these tabulations: Alabama, Arkansas, Florida, Georgia, Kentucky, Louisiana, Maryland, Mississippi, North Carolina, South Carolina, Tennessee, Texas, and Virginia.

for women, a humorous magazine, and at least one general literary monthly like *Harper's* or *Atlantic Monthly*, published in the North, or the *Southern Literary Messenger* or *Southern Quarterly Review*. In addition, families might subscribe to religious and agricultural periodicals. As a result of this competitive environment, many journals lasted for only a short period. If the content was bland, if they failed to provide entertainment and information enjoyable and interesting to a broad audience of readers, they were likely to fold. Indeed, many magazines failed to endure longer than a single issue, and some folded after a promising prospectus and advertisements failed to secure a readership for the first number.

Whether they lasted one issue, one year, or one decade, these magazines provide windows into the literary culture of the South, without which the diversity and nuance of southern intellectual life can hardly be appreciated. With a sufficient subscriber list and financial means, any white man or woman could start a periodical. In fact, many widowed southern women used their precarious financial position to justify the launching of a new literary magazine. Other southerners so moved could advertise, edit, and publish literary, agricultural, or religious magazines at will. Thus, periodicals were a democratic venue through which white nineteenth-century southerners, including women, could seek financial reward, regional reputation, and creative expression. Particularly in southern cities where a vigorous intellectual culture thrived, in urban areas such as Richmond, Charleston, and New Orleans, women writers became well-known figures in literary circles and among the educated citizenry.

In the Old South, as in the North, magazines often led very brief existences. Many earnest but inexperienced would-be editors began publishing magazines with very little idea of how to do so successfully. The labors of meeting subscriber expectations, the editing of poems and short stories, and the solicitation of quality contributions proved difficult. Even the most respected editors had to contend with the painful task of reading and evaluating poems written

TABLE 3.2. *Numbers of magazines published in southern states, 1764–1861*

State	Number of Magazines
Alabama	28
Arkansas	3
Florida	1
Georgia	86
Kentucky	100
Louisiana	58
Maryland	118
Mississippi	8
North Carolina	30
South Carolina	75
Tennessee	100
Texas	5
Virginia	78

Source: Gilmer, *Checklist of Southern Periodicals*, Section I.

by aspiring amateurs, and due to their sheer volume many undeserving poems found their way into southern magazines. Poems of all kinds, including many apparently addressed to flowers (such as the poem "To a Rhododendron," which somehow found its way into print), were sent to editors faced with the burden of tactfully letting an anxious author know that his or her prized work was in fact rubbish.[38]

The literary culture of the North and South was a graveyard for small magazines with brief lives, but the proliferation of even short-lived periodicals is testimony to the very diversity of intellectual life in antebellum America. Dozens are no doubt permanently lost, but southern archives preserve some of the smaller literary ventures on which aspiring editors optimistically toiled. Some magazines, like *The New Orleans Miscellany* (1847), were begun in the larger cities of the South, but others tried to take root among the smaller towns of the region, such as the *Southron* of Gallatin, Tennessee, the *Southern Eclectic* of Augusta, Georgia, and the *Southern Light* of Edgefield, South Carolina. As one scholar has shown, there were more than 700 magazines published in southern towns between 1764 and 1861.[39] As Table 3.2 shows, these magazines were published throughout the region, in the Gulf South as well as the Upper South.

Out of such vast numbers a few magazines emerged as more important and enduring. The *Southern Literary Messenger*, a monthly published in Richmond between 1834 and 1864, was the region's leading literary periodical. Edited

38 Author listed only as Kate, "To a Rhododendron," *Southern Literary Messenger* 11 (February 1845), 82–3.

39 Gertrude Gilmer, *Checklist of Southern Periodicals to 1861*, (Boston, 1934).

for a time by Poe, the *Messenger* was valued by both northerners and southerners, as evidenced by the number of northern authors who contributed to its pages. The first issue contained letters from well-wishers across the country, including the New York author and statesman James Kirke Paulding, former president John Quincy Adams, James Fennimore Cooper, and Washington Irving.[40] The *Messenger* lasted far longer than any other literary magazine in the Old South. In addition to this important journal, the *Southern Quarterly Review*, published first in New Orleans, but in itinerant fashion moved to Charleston and later Baltimore and Columbia, South Carolina, was also an important literary magazine that also delved more deeply than the *Messenger* into politics and the defense of slavery. The *Southern Quarterly Review*, edited for a time by William Gilmore Simms, who had a hand in many southern periodicals, lasted from 1842 until 1857. The leading financial magazine in the antebellum South was *De Bow's Review*, immodestly taking its name from its editor, New Orleans' booster of manufacturing, James D. B. De Bow. Starting in 1846, *De Bow's Review* provided readers with articles on financial developments across the nation, essays on the progress of manufacturing and industry in the South, and biographies of southern businessmen. Until it ended in 1880, *De Bow's* also included literary reviews in its monthly offerings, including comments on important northern works, such as Herman Melville's novels *Omoo* and *Typee*.[41]

For women authors and readers, these inexpensive periodicals were a welcome forum in which to feed their interest in literature and an important link to the wider intellectual world beyond their local experiences. The *Southern Rose* and the *Southern Ladies' Book* welcomed female contributors to their pages and published dozens of essays, poems, and short stories by well-known women authors like Mary Elizabeth Lee, Elizabeth Ellet, and Louisa S. McCord, and scores of lesser-known women.[42] Single women appear frequently in the magazines but particularly in the *Southern Ladies' Book*, which encouraged students of neighboring Georgia Female College to submit poems. Even northern women were welcomed into the pages of southern journals, as the frequent contributions by Lydia H. Sigourney of Hartford and Frances Sargent Osgood of Boston in the pages of southern magazines attest. The prominence of women writers in both general periodicals and in periodicals designed for female subscribers demonstrates that women authors were taken seriously in the South.

As in northern magazines, southern literary periodicals for women display a wide range of diverse interests, including essays on philosophy, law, math,

[40] "Southern Literature," *Southern Literary Messenger* 1 (August 1834), 1.

[41] For brief reviews of these two novels, see *De Bow's Review* 3 (June 1847), 586, and 4 (September 1847), 141.

[42] For example, in August of 1826, the *Ladies' Garland*, a magazine published in Harpers Ferry, held a contest for the best written short story that was won by Mary Seleg of Jefferson County, West Virginia. See 3 (August 26, 1826): 112–3.

history, and such scientific fields as medicine and astronomy.[43] In the pages of the *Southern Ladies' Book* can be found discussions of the property rights of married women, mineralogy in northern Georgia, education for the poor, commercialization, and speeches by members of Congress. In the *Southern Rose*, Caroline Gilman printed book reviews and discussions of American literature, such as the issue on Emerson in 1838. She regularly combed the pages of British journals and compiled interesting selections in a column called "The Pruning Knife."[44] The *Southern Quarterly Review* printed numerous pieces aimed at a female audience, such as "The Condition of Woman" and "The Enfranchisement of Woman."[45]

One early periodical that gave voice to the gendered ideology of the early nineteenth-century was the *Ladies' Magazine*, a weekly journal published in Savannah in 1819 by William C. Barton and Richard Edes. A mixture of poems, short stories, and light essays, the *Ladies' Magazine* linked reading and literature to women's domestic nature. Like other early southern magazines for women, the *Ladies' Magazine* reprinted many pieces on women and gender from northern and European periodicals. One scholar has estimated in his study of Georgia periodicals that approximately three-fourths of the selected articles originated in northern periodicals.[46] Thus, southern women learned about and became familiar with northern ideas about women without even leaving their communities. The *Ladies' Magazine* drew selections of poetry and prose from the New York *Advertiser*, an essay on the "Impolicy of Severe Punishment" from the Boston *Gazette*, an essay on "Domestic Economy" from the New York *National Advocate*, and excerpts from more than two dozen other periodicals from Philadelphia, Baltimore, Saratoga, Utica, Providence, and other cities.[47] Often the essays in the magazine reflected concerns that were seen as the province of women, such as aiding the poor, opposition to dueling, education, sympathy for criminals, and ethics.[48]

[43] According to one scholar's estimate of the contents of the *Messenger* and the *Magnolia*, about twenty-five percent of the content was poetry, short stories, and serials, and about seventy-five percent essays and editorials on political, commercial, or social matters. See John C. Guilds, "Simms as Editor and Prophet: The Flowering and Early Death of the Southern *Magnolia*," *Southern Literary Journal* 4 (Spring 1972), 205–12.

[44] Cindy A. Stiles, "Windows into Antebellum Charleston: Caroline Gilman and the 'Southern Rose' Magazine," (Ph.D. Dissertation, University of South Carolina, 1994), 30–7. For examples of book reviews in the *Southern Rose*, see the review of Simms's *The Yemassee* in volume 3 (May 16, 1835): 151.

[45] Louisa S. McCord, "The Enfranchisement of Woman," *Southern Quarterly Review* 21 (April 1852): 322–41, "The Condition of Woman," 10 (July 1846): 148–73. See also Simms' essay "Fanny Kemble," 12 (July 1847): 191–236.

[46] Bertram Holland Flanders, *Early Georgia Magazines: Literary Periodicals to 1865* (Athens, 1944), 17.

[47] *Ladies' Magazine* 1 (March 13, 1819), 38; 1 (April 3, 1819), 61. For a list of these periodicals, see Flanders, 16.

[48] *Ladies' Magazine* 1 (March 6, 1819), 28; 1 (April 3, 1819), 61; 1 (May 22, 1819), 117–9; 1 (June 12, 1819), 138–9.

The eclectic content of southern women's magazines is quickly observed in the *Ladies' Magazine*. An antislavery poem titled "The Negro Boy," an excerpt from a book on women in the American Revolution, an extract from a British magazine titled "Extraordinary Women," and an unfavorable review of Lord Byron's work were just some of the items that appeared in the journal. The *Ladies' Magazine* also noted that Robert Mitchell had donated his books to the Savannah Library Society and in return received "membership for life."[49] An account of President James Monroe's visit to Savannah in May 1819 reported that "the streets through which the procession passed were literally filled with people; and the windows, porches and balustrades crowded with Ladies, all anxious to have a view of the distinguished visitor."[50]

Thus, whereas much of the content of early women's magazines was composed of sentimental, even maudlin, poetry and prose on flowers and romance, periodicals like the *Ladies' Magazine* provided a window into literature, criticism, politics, and local news for southern women. However, the *Ladies' Magazine* could not survive the financial disaster wrought by the economic panic that struck the nation in 1819, and a poem printed in the penultimate issue by a Charleston contributor conveyed the frustration:

> Oh! curse upon the banks;
> No credit's there.
> They issue naught but blanks;
> No cash is there,
> *Hard times*, the men do cry,
> *Hard times*, the women sigh,
> Ruin and mis-e-ry!
> No cash is here![51]

Like the *Ladies' Magazine*, the *Ladies' Garland* sought to provide southern women with models from history, news about science, literature, and the community while also providing light entertainment. The *Garland*, a weekly magazine published in Harpers Ferry, West Virginia, by John S. Gallaher from 1824 to 1828, consisted largely of poetry and extracts reprinted from northern and British magazines. Editor Gallaher stated that his magazine had a dual purpose: It was to be entertaining and provide amusement for its female readership, but it aimed also to "spread before them precepts of their government, examples for their imitation, and models for their improvement."[52] To this end, he included humorous anecdotes about marriage, tales of romantic love, and stories about distant travel in his weekly magazine, but he also printed biographies of historical figures, examples of female patriotism, and

[49] *Ladies' Magazine* 1 (April 10, 1819), 72; 1 (March 6, 1819), 28–9; 1 (March 27, 1819), 52–3; 1 (May 15, 1819), 108–10; 1 (July 3, 1819), 168. The reviewer remarked: "The Vampyre posses no merit, unless it be meritorious to frighten young ladies out of their wits."

[50] *Ladies' Magazine* 1 (May 15, 1819), 108. The journal also printed the addresses of both Monroe and the mayor of Savannah.

[51] *Ladies Magazine* 1 (July 31, 1819), reprinted in Flanders, 18.

[52] Gallaher, "Introduction," *Ladies' Garland*, 1 (February 14, 1824), 1.

even essays on science.[53] As with most early magazines aimed at a female audience published in the North or South, politics or sectarian religious controversies were studiously avoided. However, the focus on literature rather than the public world of politics was not meant to exclude men. On the contrary, in the first issue of the journal, Gallaher declared that "although this work is particularly devoted to the ladies, it must not be inferred that gentleman are to be excluded from a participation with them in its edification … [in fact] we hope to render it acceptable to all who relish the beauties of literature and the production of genius. We therefore invite the aid of literary friends, male and female – to write, to read, and to patronize."[54]

Despite this plea, it is likely that male readers found little to interest them. Whereas the magazine published reviews of books, such as James Fennimore Cooper's *The Pilot*, and notices against dueling, the journal relied heavily on traditional feminine literary fare. Works reminding readers that women were "angels of humanity" or "the purest abstract of Deity that can be found in all his works" were commonplace in the *Ladies' Garland*. "Man is destined to shine in the legislative or martial field," wrote one contributor, "while woman is calculated to polish society, to add luster to the social circle, and to impart happiness around the domestic hearth."[55] In the eyes of editors like Gallaher, women's periodicals, including the *Ladies' Garland*, were important tributes to the ability of women to improve themselves intellectually. The *Garland* printed numerous essays on the importance of female education and insisted that womanhood did not at all preclude mental progress.

Occasionally, even traditional magazines like the *Garland* presented a revealing debate over gender differences. Responding to Gallaher's admonitions against gossip and the loquaciousness of women, a reader angrily called the editor to task for "nothing short of a libel upon the sex." Frustrated with Gallaher's satirical take on gossiping women, this reader (whom Gallaher labeled "Bridget Bitternut") warned: "It might do for some crusty old bachelor to vent his feelings against the ladies and avenge himself of the slights received from the slights of some captious old maid," but Gallaher should know better.[56] In the next issue, a male reader responded to these complaints. "The truth is," a self-described "old bachelor" replied, "your sex have been so often saluted with the dulcet sounds of flattery, that any thing else is considered little short of treason." "Thus have you been toasted and praised and honored," he continued, "until you fancy that you only lack wings to make you angels."[57]

53 Examples of love and marriage stories abound. For an essay on "Female Patriotism," see *Ladies' Garland* 2 (February 19, 1825), 5, and for an example of an essay on ornithology, see "Description of the Hummingbird," 1 (January 15, 1825), 194–5.

54 John S. Gallaher, "Introduction," *Ladies' Garland* 1 (February 14, 1824), 1.

55 "Providence," *Ladies' Garland* 2 (August 27, 1825), 114.

56 "Bridget Bitternut," "Letter to the Editor," *Ladies' Garland* 3 (July 8, 1826), 87.

57 Tim Twist [pseud.], "Letter to the Editor," *Ladies' Garland* 3 (July 15, 1826), 90.

After 1820, when the numbers of newspapers and magazines published nationwide rose rapidly in number, magazines included "lady" or "ladies" in their titles to indicate their targeted audience. Although the 1830s saw the publication of many magazines, the economic hard times caused by the Panic of 1837 made survival for periodicals even more challenging. Once the panic passed, however, magazines once again increased in number. The decade of the 1840s witnessed an explosion of women's magazines in the South. The *Orion*, a monthly published in Athens and Penfield, Georgia, in the early 1840s, is one of the most underappreciated periodicals produced in the antebellum South. Long forgotten even by southern historians and literary scholars, the *Orion* has been deemed one of the South's most important magazines.[58] Edited by William C. Richards, the journal presented readers with an eclectic mix of essays, short stories, and poetry that reflected a more sophisticated and demanding female readership than the *Ladies' Garland*. To be sure the *Orion* printed its share of mawkish bows to womanly virtue and beauty, but it also published short stories and nonfiction pieces that were not necessarily gender specific. An essay by Simms, for example, discussed "The Moral Character of Hamlet," and literary reviews covered northern works such as Theodore Sedgwick Fay's *Hoboken*.[59] The magazine even conducted literary debates with the prominent New York magazine the *Knickerbocker*. The poetry printed in the *Orion* included contributions from well-known female authors such as the ubiquitous Sigourney.[60] Southern female poets were also well-represented. Charleston's reclusive author Mary Elizabeth Lee wrote many poems that found their way into the *Orion*'s pages.[61] The *Orion* thus signaled the emergence of more diverse magazines for women readers that incorporated literary criticism and a more sophisticated approach to the prose and poetry printed between its covers, while at the same time continuing to appeal to conservative readers with nods to traditional depictions of femininity.

The magazines of the 1840s exhibited a new sense of their self-importance as forums for women's learning. The *Floral Wreath, and Ladies' Monthly Magazine*, published in Charleston in 1844 by Edwin Heriot, demonstrated this sense of mission in educating women. "The magazines of our own and other countries," the *Floral Wreath* declared, "embody the concentrated talent and acquirements of a numerous and powerful array of living contributors among the sex to the advancement of education and mental refinement."[62] The content of the monthly lived up to this promise by including many southern young women among its authors. Indeed, as the *Charleston Courier* wrote in review of the magazine, "Among other names not unknown to fame, who contribute to its attractions, we find those of Mrs. [Elizabeth] Ellet, Miss [Penina]

[58] Flanders, *Early Georgia Magazines*, 68–88.

[59] William Gilmore Simms, "The Moral Character of Hamlet," *Orion* 4 (May 1844), 105–19.

[60] Sigourney, "To Miss Edgeworth," *Orion* 2 (November 1842), 4.

[61] Mary Elizabeth Lee, "The Rainy Day," *Orion* 2 (November 1842), 10, and "Lay Me Not in Some Darksome Spot!" 4 (May 1844), 145.

[62] "Sketches of My Native City," *Floral Wreath* 1 (June 1844), 22.

Moise, Mrs. [Caroline] Gilman, and Miss [Mary Elizabeth] Lee, whose lyrical tones, full of melody and richness, are familiar to us as household echoes."[63] In addition, the *Floral Wreath* printed works by Simms, essays opposing dueling, and even delved into literary criticism with reviews such as that of Dickens' *Martin Chuzzlewit*.[64]

At the end of the 1840s, the sophistication and diversity of southern women's magazines took an important leap forward with the publication of the *Mistletoe*. Begun in 1849 by Thomas A. Burke and printed in Athens, Georgia, the *Mistletoe* did not endure long but nonetheless represents an advancement in periodicals for women. This magazine included fewer sentimental tributes to feminine beauty and virtues and instead offered a wider range of content than most of the earlier women's magazines. In its literary content, the *Mistletoe* included northern authors in addition to local ones. Added to the work of prominent northern women authors like Sigourney were works by well-known male authors such as John G. Whittier.[65] But the real progress in the *Mistletoe* came in its offering essays on science and history. In fact, the first issue included an original engraving of the Smithsonian Institution that may have appealed to many readers.[66] The journal also openly advocated the temperance cause, reflecting the entry of southern women into reform movements by the 1840s. Numerous poems, short stories, and essays promoting temperance appeared in its pages.

The *Mistletoe* also opened its columns to some interesting views on women, views that contrast with the devotions to traditional femininity depicted in early magazines such as the *Ladies' Garland*. A short essay on the virtues of the "real lady" appeared in the second number of the *Mistletoe*. "Commend to us to the girl of whom it is sneeringly said, 'she works for a living,' in her we are always sure to find the elements of a true woman." The author appealed directly to young men to choose wives who possessed practical knowledge. "You who are looking for wives and companions, turn from the fashionable, lazy, haughty girls, and select one from any of those who work for a living. You want a substantial friend, and not a doll … a counselor, and not a simpleton.… We know many a foolish man, who, instead of choosing the industrious and prudent woman for a wife, took one from the fashionable walks, and is now lamenting his folly in dust and ashes."[67] With undertones of class resentment, essays such as these mirrored the Protestant evangelical jeremiads against fashion, luxury, and impracticality.

[63] *Charleston Courier* quoted in the *Floral Wreath*, 1 (August 1844), 64.

[64] On dueling see, *Floral Wreath* 1 (June 1844), 24–6, for the review of *Martin Chuzzlewit*, see 1 (September 1844), 79, and for a poem by Simms, see "The Exile from Home," 1 (September 1844), 77.

[65] Sigourney published a short story titled "The Intemperate: A Thrilling Story of the West" in the *Mistletoe* 1 (February 1849), 25–9, and Whittier published a poem in the magazine's first issue published in January 1849.

[66] "The Science, Arts and Mechanics of the Ancients," *Mistletoe* 1 (February 1849), 32–4.

[67] "She Works for a Living," *Mistletoe* 1 (February 1849), 43.

The content and diversity of southern magazines for women did not necessarily become more sophisticated as time went by. Many magazines retained the earlier style of periodicals in which politics, the questioning of established gender roles, or essays on science were anathema. Into the 1850s, magazines for women paid homage to traditional notions of virtuous womanhood. Even those magazines that adhered to conservative ideas of gender roles, however, often presented discussions of current topics. The *Southern Lady's Companion*, published in Nashville beginning in 1847, retained an overall traditional, even conservative, tone, but it also explored topics earlier nineteenth-century magazines tended to avoid. The *Southern Lady's Companion* welcomed not only female authors like Caroline Hentz but male authors as well, including many from the North such as Whittier and Irving. The magazine published reviews of works by Alexander von Humboldt, essays on Lord Byron, and articles criticizing the movement for woman's rights in the North.[68] Demonstrating the eclectic nature of women's magazines, the *Companion* printed advice on making potato cheese and pressed beef! Even more noteworthy was the journal's willingness to delve into political discussions. Reflecting a decidedly Whiggish cast, the *Companion* praised Henry Clay and Daniel Webster for their political service. Upon Clay's death, the *Companion* published a lengthy tribute to his career, and any new biographies of Clay and Webster were sure to be reviewed in the magazine.[69] Interestingly, the *Companion* ventured into discussions of slavery, though only to denounce abolitionism. *Uncle Tom's Cabin* received a lengthy, highly negative review. Author Harriet Beecher Stowe, the magazine declared, "has been guilty of doing violence to the laws of truth and propriety." Indeed, like "a common slander, or an attack of infidelity on religion," the book was full of false depictions of the lives of slaves, the laws of southern states, and the cruelty of masters.[70] Like other newspapers and magazines, the *Companion* championed the right of the South to counter attacks by abolitionists like Stowe, thus hastening the dissolution of the Union by dividing American writers, journalists, and intellectuals.

The emergence in the early nineteenth century of periodicals expressly designed for women readers, rather than merely isolated "women's columns," helped to legitimize the role of southern women in the public sphere of literature, journalism, and printing. As the next chapter suggestions, southern women were not shy to use these new roles as a wedge to expand their influence in society. Women's magazines offered opportunities for female authors, even

[68] See the review of Humboldt's *Cosmos* as well as *Life and Letters of Barthold Georg Niebuhr* in *Southern Lady's Companion* 6 (July 1852), 128. On Byron, see "Byron and His Wife," *Southern Lady's Companion* 7 (June 1853), 77–9. On the women's rights movement, see "The Claims of Woman," *Southern Lady's Companion* 3 (November 1849), 169–73.

[69] On Clay, see "Henry Clay," *Southern Lady's Companion* 6 (September 1852), 178–80. For reviews of books on Webster, see "Webster," *Southern Lady's Companion* 6 (February 1853), 352.

[70] "Uncle Tom's Cabin," *Southern Lady's Companion* 7 (August 1853), 157–8.

when those magazines were edited by men. Through prose and poetry contributions, women authors fashioned themselves as professionals on a par with the leading male writers of the period. Indeed, many southern women became literary celebrities whose work was highly sought after by male editors and whose writings were eagerly anticipated by loyal readers. Most importantly for our purposes, women's elevated status in the literary world opened opportunities in editing and publishing that significantly advanced the cause of women's rights.

4

Female Authors and Magazine Writing

The world of southern periodicals, though limited to a white upper- and middle-class readership, was one of the most open of southern institutions. Copyright laws, still ill-defined even by the late antebellum period, were rarely enforced, and the postal service permitted the mailing of periodicals between editors free of charge. This exchange system almost guaranteed that columns and entire works would be reprinted, with or without granting original publication credit.[1] Some papers, often with the word "eclectic" in the title, were composed entirely of selections from other periodicals. Male and female authors alike were angered and frustrated by the haphazard nature of copyright, for they were well aware that they lost royalties to unscrupulous editors. Fanny Fern, a well-known northern writer, complained in 1857 about Europeans who dipped "their forefinger and thumb into my pocket."[2] The lack of copyright enforcement, however, had the beneficial effect of widening the availability of reading material. This is significant because even small publications were rarely the product of purely local efforts; southerners reading an "eclectic" magazine were exposed to writers, poetry, and essays that might have originated in New York, Paris, London, or some other city.

The eclectic nature of American newspapers and magazines, and even the open exchange of literature with little regard for copyright protection, helped to make periodicals affordable and broadened readership. As scholar Melissa J. Homestead has noted, "At a time when literary proprietorship was seldom secure ... a woman whose legal status similarly oscillated between possession and dispossession in marriage, between being a property owning subject and being the property of her husband, was particularly suited to the role of author in America."[3] The notion of writing for the public was undoubtedly fraught with a range of mixed emotions for southern women. Although northern

[1] Melissa J. Homestead, *American Women Authors and Literary Property, 1822–1869* (Cambridge, 2005), 155.

[2] Fanny Fern quoted in *ibid.*, 190.

[3] *Ibid.*, 191.

female writers, such as the exceedingly popular Lydia Huntley Sigourney, provided models to follow, many southern women were reluctant to embark on the kind of career embraced by women like Sigourney. To be sure, many women writers struggled with the notion of revealing their identity in public and resorted to pseudonyms. Some women recoiled from public recognition; Mary Elizabeth Lee was known as a recluse who shied away from the lecture halls, literary clubs, and intellectual societies of her native Charleston, activities that so occupied male authors like Simms. Kate C. Wakelee, an important Georgia poet during the Civil War, was a "shrinking and modest" woman. As one observer wrote, "For twelve years she has written constantly, but, mimosa-like, has shrunk from the ordeal of publication."[4]

Celebrity was unwelcome for many, though Sigourney herself was widely admired in the South. Known as the "Sweet Signer of Hartford," Sigourney hailed from Connecticut yet was welcomed into southern parlors. Throughout the antebellum period, she published hundreds of poems and dozens of books and corresponded with leading authors. She was perhaps the most famous female writer of the prewar period, and her fame as an author was certainly envied by southern women. Limestone Springs High School for girls in Gaffney, South Carolina, harbored a Sigourney Club, which functioned as a discussion group, reading circle, and lending library. The members even wrote to Sigourney and declared her an honorary affiliate, an honor that the gracious writer welcomed. Similarly, the Greensboro Female College in North Carolina possessed a Sigourney Society of its own.[5] So even if southern women sometimes shied away from the glare of publishing, they certainly admired the ability of those like Sigourney who were known not only for their literary talents but for their business acumen and poise in the public eye as well.

Scholars such as Michael Warner argue that concepts such as the "public," particularly the "reading public," are not as straightforward as we often believe. "What is a public?" Warner asks. "It is a curiously obscure question, considering that few things have been more important in the development of modernity." This lack of clarity becomes even more acute in the realm of a reading public, for texts may be circulated and recirculated indefinitely. Indeed, we know that literary and debating societies in the Old South, including the Sigourney Club in South Carolina, bought one subscription for a magazine like *Graham's* or *Godey's* and then passed the material on to fellow students. Often in the evening hours, men and women sat together in wallpapered parlors to hear one another read from novels and periodicals. Although subscription lists suggest the existence of large numbers of readers of nineteenth-century periodicals, we also have considerable evidence that reading did not end with the subscriber but rather continued in an ever-widening circle, as friends, relatives, and colleagues passed on reading materials to the expanding reading public. "Publics," Warner reminds us, "have an ongoing life: one

[4] Ida Raymond, ed., *Southland Writers, vol. 1* (Philadelphia, 1870), 459.

[5] Wells, *The Origins of the Southern Middle Class*, 102–4.

doesn't publish to them once for all (as one does, say, to a scholarly archive). It is the way texts circulate, and become the basis for further representations, that convinces us that publics have activity and duration."[6]

Women authors in the Old South believed that their published works would be timeless, to be poured over not only by readers of their own age but perused for decades. Female writers often fretted over how their works would be received, and such fear often drove them to remove their names from published works. To be noticed or even reviewed more substantially with a lengthy critique was too much scrutiny for some, despite the fact that most notices were positive. Skeptics even referred to the "puffery press" when they remarked about how journals praised one another with hyperbole or when mediocre works collected facile reviews proclaiming the "genius" of a writer. Moreover, magazines and newspapers rarely criticized female novelists or poets with any trenchant attacks, seeking instead to stroke their literary egos with favorable and polite praise. Perhaps this relatively gentle literary climate is one reason why southern women often chose to have their names as authors (and often the name of their town or plantation residence) printed alongside their works.

Although historians and literary scholars have resurrected the lives and careers of many northern nineteenth-century female journalists and authors, such as Sigourney and Sarah Josepha Hale, historians have only reluctantly hinted at the connection between these women's writings and the broader push for equality. Yet, in the essays, poems, and fiction penned by hundreds of women who published in periodicals between 1820 and 1900, one can discover evidence of assertiveness and boldness of expression that can be found nowhere else in southern public culture. Because it was acceptable for women to engage in literary pursuits, even as editors of magazines or newspapers, women wisely and deliberately used literature as a vehicle to express opinions on politics and society that were not acceptable in other contexts. So in the search for the cultural roots of southern feminism, one must examine the underutilized magazines that survive from the nineteenth century. In the files of these long-forgotten periodicals, the forward-thinking and even audacious writings of women demand greater attention from historians and literary scholars.

The willingness of women to publish their fiction and nonfiction in public places, where they were judged by their (often male) readers, may seem surprising given what we know about the southern woman. Many welcomed the chance to win public esteem. They viewed publishing prose or poetry as perhaps their only opportunity to earn local and regional acclaim, and they particularly enjoyed the respect of fellow writers and intellectuals. Octavia LeVert, Susan Petigru King, Mary Bayard Clarke, Margaret Junkin Preston, Sarah Morgan, and many other southern women writers won regional and

[6] Michael Warner, "Publics and Counterpublics," 88 *Quarterly Journal of Speech* (November 2002), 413–25.

even national fame for their literary contributions. Even the reclusive Lee published numerous poems with her name or initials. The intellectual culture of the Old South was enlivened with the writings of women who, lacking other means of earning fame, employed their literary talents to become prominent and highly visible members of their communities. Even more importantly, these literary women helped to create a dialogue about gender equality and the place of women in society that was not possible in the political realm. By their very example as independent-minded women, female journalists and authors provided a foundation for later discussions in the late nineteenth and early twentieth centuries about women's rights.

Many male writers complained of the influence on American literature of "scribbling women," to use the words of Nathaniel Hawthorne, words with which South Carolinian William Gilmore Simms would have agreed. Hawthorne's lament reflected the popularity of women writers in the nineteenth century, and no matter how much Hawthorne or Simms might disapprove, the reading consumer made celebrities out of women writers like Caroline Lee Hentz, Augusta Jane Evans, and Sarah Josepha Hale. By the middle of the nineteenth century, women were commonly found in the pages of literary magazines, sometimes even at the helm of such periodicals, as well as among best-selling novelists and poets. For, as independent actors, as individuals with talents, opinions, and the ability to articulate themselves in a public forum, such women provided powerful models. The literary world, as the one acceptable venue for women's intellectual and creative expression, was the incubator for the women's rights movement, particularly in the South. In the case of literary popularity, society's assumptions about the "emotional woman" aided the cause of female authors.

Americans also depicted women, somewhat contradictorily, as the voice of reason and, in a commonly used contemporary phrase, the "counselor" of men. Whereas women were believed to be more emotional, men were more easily swayed by their passions, including lust, anger, and jealousy. In fact, much of nineteenth-century literature gives play to the battle between emotion and reason, and fiction and nonfiction alike warned of the "dangers of passion." Women, many southern observers claimed, were perfectly designed by God as a counterweight to the passionate nature of men. Wives and mothers were more patient and calm, whereas men were quick-tempered; women abhorred violence, whereas men were often guilty of fighting on a whim; women were more pious and pure, men more secular and tainted by zeal. Such notions of gender difference seemed to Americans North and South to have been divinely sanctioned, a harmonious balance created by the union of man and woman, thus bolstering traditional values like marriage and monogamy.

When race was added to the mix, however, gender differences became even more complicated. The need to defend slavery against abolitionist attacks beginning in the 1830s meant that southerners devoted considerable resources to the meaning of race, the origins of racial differences, and the justifications for the separation of white and black into owners and slaves. Although concepts of race remained contested, this did not prevent white southerners from conjecturing about inherent traits that distinguished white men from black men. African American men were believed to be even more susceptible to passion and even less apt to follow reason than their white counterparts. Indeed, their supposed predisposition to give in to the amusements of life, the supposed propensity to be licentious, pleasure seeking, and undisciplined, can be seen as an exaggeration of white male foibles. Such characteristics made African Americans unsuitable for civilized existence, many white defenders of slavery claimed, and so justified their bondage much like a child's inability to reason warranted parental control. White southerners commented less frequently on the innate qualities of black women, but the accepted wisdom on African American women's personalities were exaggerations of some of the features attributed to white women. Like their white counterparts, black women were seen as sexual beings but without the balance and ability to reason often attributed to white women. Such rationalizations made it easier for white masters to take sexual advantage of their female slaves, for such women possessed a powerful and alluring sexuality without the more elevated characteristics of rationality, or so racist ideology held.

Gender ideology in both regions held that men belonged in the rough-and-tumble public world of work and politics, whereas women were meant to occupy the private sphere of domestic responsibilities, particularly if married. The reality, as many historians have shown, was more complicated than this Manichean dichotomy would suggest, and women (particularly young single women) often worked in textile mills or other industries that contradicted the notion of distinct spheres for men and women, and men rarely surrendered their power in the domestic sphere to their wives.[7] The ideology held firm nonetheless throughout the nineteenth century: Women were better suited to the quiet demands of the home. Even after the Civil War, southerners reinforced long-held notions about the origins of gender difference. In an article on boys in *De Bow's Review* in 1866, an observer maintained that "in early infancy girls and boys develop opposite traits of character. The girl is kind, merciful, gentle and humane, whilst her brother, of the same blood and with the same training, begins to betray opposite moral qualities even from the cradle. Woman was sent into the world on a mission of mercy – to help and comfort man."[8]

The celebrity of southern women authors is a topic seldom explored but one that illuminates a great deal about gender dynamics in the nineteenth century. Because many women signed their name and often their place of residence to their literary contributions, subscribers to magazines could follow the careers of their favorite authors. In turn, female authors could attract

[7] See Susanna Delfino and Michele Gillespie, *Neither Lady Nor Slave: Working Women of the Old South* (Chapel Hill, 2002).

[8] "Boys," *De Bow's Review* n.s. 1 (April 1866), 369.

quite a following, not just among girls and other women, but among male readers as well. As Susan Coultrap notes in *Doing Literary Business*, women like Ann S. Stephens used popular notions about literature being a feminine pursuit to carve out professional literary careers.[9] The dramatic expansion of the American publishing industry in the antebellum era opened new avenues for women interested in literary careers. "Between 1820 and 1850," Coultrap points out, "the publishing industry expanded tenfold in response to increasing national levels of literacy, people's growing interest in reading as cheap entertainment, and an expanding railroad system making national distribution of books possible."[10] Whereas scholars have pointed out that women writers and even a few editors and printers operated in the colonial period, before the nineteenth century the nation lacked the transportation network and postal system to distribute periodicals widely. So, although journalism as a career for southern women would not become a profession until the later nineteenth century, when hundreds of female editors and members of the press would form press associations, the Early Republican and antebellum periods witnessed the emergence of self-conscious literary women who not only wrote for periodicals but also managed them as editors. As authors and contributors, these women hardly remained nameless or faceless in the culture of the Old South. On the contrary, although some shrunk from public exposure, others openly embraced the visibility and reputation that came with being a female writer or journalist.

One of the best examples of women earning such celebrity in the Old South was Caroline Gilman. Gilman, a native of Massachusetts who had moved to Charleston with her minister husband Samuel, responded to a request from a male fan for her autograph in 1853. Although she was happy to send her signature to Clifton Bolton, he must have intimated in his letter that he was interested in more than just Gilman's autograph. For, as a postscript to her reply, she noted, "My address is *Mrs.* Carolina Gilman."[11] Interestingly, in this one exchange of letters, one can see the limits and the possibilities for southern literary women. Even as Gilman obviously did not shy away from her status as a literary celebrity, she asserted to a male reader her role as wife and mother.

Even with such elevated status, however, publishers often took advantage of their authors. Gilman often complained about not seeing profits from her books and magazine contributions, even though she knew they sold many copies. Samuel Gilman was not shy about uttering complaints on behalf of his author-wife, particularly when hard times made family income an acute concern. "The disaster of the last two or three years in Charleston ...," Samuel Gilman complained in the aftermath of the Panic of 1837, "have taken from us the revenue which we had reason to expect.... The Harpers paid Mrs. G

[9] Susan Coultrap, *Doing Literary Business: American Women Writers in the Nineteenth Century* (Chapel Hill, 1990), xii.

[10] *Ibid.*, 30.

[11] Caroline Gilman to Clifton Bolton, March 4, 1853, Caroline Howard Gilman Papers, South Caroliniana Library, Columbia.

only $200 for the first edition of the *Matron* though 2000 were entirely sold in six months! It has been stereotyped, and they put 2000 more to press, for which nothing has yet been received."[12] Clearly, Gilman was in part dependent on Caroline's literary earnings, and the lack of income was not only an affront but a financial hardship. Caroline, however, did not always rely on her husband to perform the necessary business tasks. She also complained about the financial difficulties of the 1837 Panic. In the summer of 1838, she complained that her "literary affairs are singly *at a stand*. Mr. Burger, the publisher of the *Rose* [Gilman's magazine] was fearful of failing, & asked us to take back the papers.... Thus, although no salary comes in to us from that quarter as we hoped, yet we have only the literary trouble."[13] As Gilman's protests indicate, literary careers were not mere expressions of gentility, carried out by elite women of leisure. Women authors and early journalists like Gilman wrote because they wished to earn fame as authors and because they benefitted financially from their endeavors. Although there were certainly wealthy women from prominent planter families who saw literary pursuits as an extension of their other interests as members of a leisure class, middle-class authors and editors such as Gilman expected financial rewards from their efforts, and when those rewards were not to be found they experienced financial distress.

Gilman penned many poems even though she primarily served as an editor and writer of longer works. Poetry was for southern women a powerful path for literary fame, for poetry was believed to be a genre particularly well suited to women's mind and temperament. In addition, nearly all literary periodicals published poetry, if only to fill the spaces left by longer works. Nineteenth-century readers expected to see poetry in their magazines and newspapers, but much of the poetry penned by male and female authors alike makes for difficult reading today. Maudlin tributes to women's beauty, saccharine veneration for nature (especially flowers), and mawkish accounts of lost love are ubiquitous themes in northern and southern poetry. Such overly sentimental writings are a hallmark of the Victorian era and strain the patience of modern readers. At the time, however, such writings were considered to be well suited to women's emotional disposition. Indeed, such poetry was the embodiment of feminine self-control, for the organized and structured presentation of sentiment represented female passion kept in check. Female emotions out of control were seen as a sickness and labeled "hysteria." As historian Carroll Smith-Rosenberg has noted, "For centuries hysteria has been seen as characteristically female – the hysterical woman the embodiment of a perverse or hyper-femininity."[14] Because women were supposed to provide an outpouring

[12] Samuel Gilman to Ellis Gray Loring, November 8, 1838, Samuel Gilman Papers, South Caroliniana Library, Columbia.

[13] Caroline Gilman to Harriet Fay, June 28, 1838, Gilman Family Papers, American Antiquarian Society, Worcester.

[14] Carroll Smith-Rosenberg, *Disorderly Conduct: Visions of Gender in Victorian America* (New York, 1985), 198.

of love for her husband and children, so too were women assumed to be able to express these emotions in writing. Consequently, the pages of many an antebellum northern and southern magazine are filled with syrupy accounts of love, beautiful flora, and Christian devotion.

It would be a mistake, however, to dismiss these women poets and their works because they do not suit the tastes of current readers. Indeed, to nineteenth-century readers, such literature accomplished its goal of generating strong emotional reactions that might trigger a painful memory. There are many sad poems devoted to the memories of children who perished in a world where death was ever-present. A cold or fever, which modern medicine treats with ease, could at any time mushroom into an infection that would result in death. Poems were sometimes written and published decades after the death of a child, reflecting the lifelong suffering of their parents. Nineteenth-century poetry became an emotional outlet, and even a catharsis, for writers. Within this context, the works of antebellum southern women poets deserve the respect and sympathetic reading of twenty-first-century readers.

Mary E. Lee, despite her hermit-like existence, was one of the best-known authors in Charleston. In fact, when Simms published a collection of works by local authors titled *The Charleston Book* in 1845, a work that included prominent authors such as Washington Allston, Hugh Swinton Legaré, James L. Petigru, Daniel Whitaker, Joel Poinsett, and Charles Fraser, he printed four of her poems; no author had more than four. Although her name was readily recognized in the South, Lee was mysteriously withdrawn and private. In the open literary world of Charleston, in which authors and intellectuals knew one another well on a personal basis, Lee was an anomaly. Born in 1813 in Charleston to a prominent family (her father William Lee was a lawyer and state legislator and her uncle Thomas Lee a judge), Lee would have had ample opportunity for social activity. But according to the writer and preacher Samuel Gilman, who befriended Lee and wrote a short biography for a collection of her poems, Lee from her earliest years "shrank, almost morbidly, from personal distinction and notoriety, even while seeming to affect them by the willing publication of her compositions."[15] Part of the explanation for Lee's reticence to appear in public was that she was disabled by an unknown disease at about the age of thirty that caused her considerable pain and numbness in her hands. Paradoxically, despite her reticence to appear in public, Lee, like many southern women writers, almost always signed her full name to her poems, short stories, and translations, ensuring that her name would be widely recognized.

A sensitive child, Lee disliked being away from home for schooling and managed to teach herself French, German, and Italian. As she reached the age of ten, Lee was provided one of the leading tutors of Charleston.[16] Her

[15] Samuel Gilman, *The Poetical Remains of the Late Mary Elizabeth Lee* (Charleston, 1851), xii.

[16] John S. Hart, *Female Prose Writers of America* (Philadelphia, 1852), 458.

first publication appeared in Caroline Gilman's *Rose Bud* magazine in 1833. Throughout the 1840s, Lee penned numerous translations of foreign short stories, particularly those from Germany, and she also wrote a collection of moral tales titled *Social Evenings; or, Historical Tales for Youth* (1840). Lee earned her literary reputation almost completely through her periodical work, as she did not venture to parties or balls to meet other South Carolina intellectuals. According to one scholar, in 1845 alone Lee's work appeared in the *Southern Literary Messenger*, *The Orion*, *Whitaker's Journal*, *The New Orleans Miscellany*, *Graham's*, *Godey's Lady's Book*, *The Token*, and *The Philadelphia Courier*, among others.[17] "She sought few pleasures," recalled a fellow author, "save those of letters, home and friends – and these she loved most dearly – and received in return the meed of literary fame, and the responsive love of all around her."[18]

Lee's poems often dealt with death, disability, or other unhappy subjects, and she usually shunned the traditional fare of southern women's poetry such as flowers and love. Of the dozens of poems Lee published, two in particular earned her a national following: "The Lone Star" and "The Blind Negro Communicant." Given Lee's reclusive nature, the title of the poem became her moniker and she was referred to as the "lone star" more than once in newspapers and magazines.[19] "The Blind Negro Communicant," apparently drawn from Lee's experience watching a black preacher, is interesting because of its unusual subject matter. Lee expressed a passion, even a reverence, for an elderly blind man who seemed to be in direct contact with God:

> The symbols were disclosed, and soon there rose
> The sweet tones of the shepherd of the flock,
> Telling once more the story of the Cross;
> And as he spoke, in sympathy I gazed
> Upon the blind old pilgrim by my side.[20]

Interestingly, Lee makes no reference other than the title to the fact that the man is black or a slave; she sees him only as another human. Perhaps because she too was disabled, Lee sympathized with him:

> My heart yearned for him – and I longed for power
> To say, as the disciples said of old,
> "Blind man! receive thy sight," – and in the might
> Of strong compassion, I could even, methought,
> Have entered his dark prison-house awhile,
> And let him gaze, in turn, on the blue skies
> And the glad sunshine, and the laughing earth.[21]

[17] Caroline Zilboorg, "Mary Elizabeth Lee," *American Women Writers* (v.2., New York, 1980), 543.

[18] "Miss Lee's Poems," *Southern Quarterly Review* 3 (April 1851), 519.

[19] See Gilman, *Poetical Remains*.

[20] Reprinted in *ibid.*, 90.

[21] *Ibid.*, 91.

The "dark prison-house" and the man's lack of sight could have been a metaphor for slavery; he was blind to freedom and unable to see the gaiety of life as she could. Lee concluded the poem with the comforting thought that in heaven, bodily discomfort vanished and all were equal before God:

> And though thou art
> A creature lonely and unprized by *men*,
> Yet thou mayst stand a Prince 'mongst Princes, when
> The King makes up his jewels!"[22]

"The Blind Negro Communicant" attracted national attention and appeared in literary and religious periodicals throughout the country.[23]

Lee died young at only thirty-six years in 1849. "Her decline [die to disease]," Gilman remembered, "was gradual from day to day, and almost imperceptible."[24] Lee's death received prominent notices in the *Southern Literary Messenger* and the *Southern Quarterly Review*, but in the Charleston papers, her passing was noticed with particular urgency.[25] "Mary E. Lee is no more! The '*lone* star' of the South has hastened to her setting," reported the *Southern Quarterly Review*.[26] Despite avoiding the public arena, she was able to acquire a local reputation. Even the reclusive Lee could earn respect and stature in southern communities, and in such cities as Charleston where a crowded field of authors and intellectuals competed for the public's attention.

Whereas women like Lee could earn respect among their fellow southerners, authors who were alienated in some way from southern society often became the most incisive critics of custom as well as important advocates of new ideas. There was no paucity of nineteenth-century southern intellectuals, authors, and scholars, but there was a paucity of those sufficiently distanced from the norms of southern politics and culture to be able to critique the region in any consistent manner. When W. J. Cash complained in *The Mind of the South* about the lack of southern authors to match the quality of northerners such as Emerson, Thoreau, Melville, and others, Cash was really pointing to the difficulty of identifying southern writers or thinkers who managed to step outside the conservative regional ideology on issues like slavery that surrounded them. Yet when one turns to the women authors of the mid-nineteenth century, anger, disgust, and disapproval over elements of southern society emerge, particularly on questions of traditional gender boundaries. Female writers through fiction as well as nonfiction expressed feelings of disaffection from southern society that seem scarce in other quarters of the region.

Newspapers and magazines of the Old South are replete with poems, short stories, essays, and translated works. Although much basic biographical work

[22] *Ibid.*, 92.
[23] *Ibid.*, xvi.
[24] *Ibid.*, xxxii.
[25] For notices of Lee's death and reviews of her works, see the *Southern Literary Messenger* 15 (December 1849), 760, and *Southern Quarterly Review* 3 (April 1851), 518–23.
[26] "Miss Lee's Poems," *Southern Quarterly Review* 3 (April 1851), 518.

needs to be done to fill in the details for these women, some limited work has been accomplished to help us understand the hundreds of little-known female authors whose names appear prominently in southern periodicals. Penina Moise, for example, has received some attention from intellectual historians.[27] Moise's family fled Haiti during the 1791 revolution and lost significant land and wealth in slaves as a result. Moise was born in Charleston in 1797 where she lived and wrote until her death in 1880. Like many Jewish residents, the Moise family found the South to be generally tolerant, and she earned wide acclaim for her literary talents. In addition to writing "the first Reform Jewish hymnal published in the United States," Moise wrote dozens of poems for periodicals, including *Godey's*, the *Southern Patriot*, and the Charleston *Courier*.[28] It was also common for women in the antebellum period to collect their poems into volumes, and in 1833 Moise's *Fancy's Sketch Book* was published, the first book of poems by an American Jewish woman. For all the tolerance that Moise experienced in Charleston, however, she was certainly sensitive to the plight of immigrants. In 1820, she wrote a poem for the *Southern Patriot* that welcomed foreigners to America and the South:

> If thou are one of that oppressed race,
> Whose name's a proverb, and whose lot's disgrace,
> Brave the Atlantic – Hope's broad anchor weigh,
> A Western Sun will gild your future day.

The number of southern women who, like Lee and Moise, published poems and other short pieces in the periodicals of the nineteenth century runs into the several hundreds. Most of these authors remain completely obscured today but nonetheless were well known to antebellum southern readers. Both Carrie Bell Sinclair and Annie R. Blount, for example, earned recognition in books such as Ida Raymond's *Southland Writers* (1870) and later in works like Mildred Lewis Rutherford's *The South in History and Literature* (1906). Sinclair was born in 1839 in Milledgeville, Georgia, to a Methodist minister and his wife; she wrote numerous popular poems such as "Georgia, My Georgia" and "The Homespun Dress."[29] Blount, born in Virginia in the same year as Sinclair, attended the Methodist Female College in Madison, Georgia, and published books of poems, including *The Sisters*, beginning in 1859.

One of the underappreciated aspects of the careers of southern literary women was the number of daughters who took up the pen by following in the footsteps of their mothers. For example, Caroline Hentz is well known for her antebellum publications, including *The Planter's Northern Bride* (1854), a retort to *Uncle Tom's Cabin*. Her daughter, Julia Louisa Hentz Keyes, also acquired a prominent reputation throughout the South for the poems and

[27] O'Brien, *Conjectures of Order*, 720–22.

[28] Janet Gray, *She Wields a Pen: American Women Poets of the Nineteenth Century* (Iowa City, 1997), 26.

[29] Mildred Lewis Rutherford, *The South in History and Literature* (Athens, 1906), 272.

short pieces she published in periodicals. Residing in Montgomery, Alabama, with her dentist husband, John Washington Keyes, she won a prize for a poem about an academy run by her parents in Florence. During the war, she earned praise throughout the Confederacy for her poems "Soldier in the Rain" and "Only One Killed," both of which were published in Simms' vaunted *War Poetry of the South*.[30]

Women like Lee, Moise, and Hentz earned considerable regional reputations, but they were relatively unknown outside the South. Other southern women gained the attention of national as well as local readers. Susan Petigru King, like Lee a South Carolina native, exhibits in her writing the sense of estrangement from societal norms that seems to characterize many southern women's work. Born in Charleston in 1824 into a wealthy family that fell on hard economic times, King married in 1843, a union encouraged by her mother who insisted King marry for reasons other than affection. Much of King's alienation from southern society's expectations of women derived from her unhappy marriage and her belief that women were subjected to demands that conflicted with their pursuit of individual happiness. Known in Charleston for her outspokenness and her disdain for those who denied her the right to express herself verbally or in writing, King published her first book, *Busy Moments of an Idle Woman* in 1854. A series of essays on issues women faced such as marriage, widowhood, and fashion, King made clear her skeptical view of nuptials in a chapter titled "Old Maidism versus Marriage." A fictional collection of letters from married women, this chapter reports the horrors and sacrifice of one's soul that marriage required from women. *Busy Moments*, like all stories of alienation, met with much criticism in Charleston, but King seems not to have backed down from her attacks on marriage and the customs bound up within it. Further alienating herself from the society in which she grew up, King included thinly veiled representations of real Charleston residents in her work.[31]

King's later writings continued to condemn the institution of marriage and its ill effects on women. In *Lily* (1855), King highlighted the low expectations for even the brightest and most talented women who were seen not as individuals but as fixtures in the social hierarchy, and attacked men who viewed courtship and marriage as a game. In *Sylvia's World* (1859), King dealt with the problems of abusive relationships; and in *Crimes Which the Law Does Not Reach* (1859), she built on the notion that women were often pushed into marriages based on wealth rather than love.[32]

After her husband's death during the war in 1862, King continued to address the themes that underlay her antebellum writings. According to her

[30] Benjamin B. Williams, "Nineteenth Century Montgomery Authors," *Alabama Historical Quarterly* 37 (Summer 1975), 142.

[31] Leslie Petty, "Susan Petigru King," in Amy E. Hudock and Katherine Rodier, eds., *American Women Prose Writers* (Detroit, 2001), 175–7.

[32] Petty, "Susan Petigru King," 177–8; Mary Louise Weaks and Carolyn Perry, eds., *Southern Women's Writing: Colonial to Contemporary* (Gainesville, FL, 1995), 55.

biographer, Leslie Petty, King published *Gerald Gray's Wife* (1864) "to mine the familiar territories of Charleston upper-class society, false men and foolish women, and unhappy, money-motivated marriages."[33] With often acerbic commentary King, through the story's narrator, launched attacks on the superficiality and pretentiousness of elite culture. In one of her last works, *My Debut* (1868), King addressed the plight of women laborers who worked as hard as men but did not receive equal pay. Through one of the key characters, King made clear that although she is not calling for a radical overturning of gender relations, her early feminism demands equal respect: "Let me pause to say that I neither wish to vote nor to preach, nor to practice medicine or law, but I should like not to be damned into eternal mediocrity in those few lines where a woman may modestly assert herself."[34]

King's nascent feminist perspective stemmed from her alienation from southern society, particularly from society's compulsion to devalue women. Her estrangement from the South only worsened in later years, as she remarried in 1870 to C. C. Bowen, a Radical Republican carpetbagger. King paid dearly for this "betrayal" because "she was completely shunned both by her former friends and by most of her" surviving family.[35] But upon her death in 1875, King had left behind a potent legacy of criticism of traditional notions of woman's place in the social order and especially in the institution of marriage.

There were other female authors for whom marriage and men's treatment of women formed central themes in works of fiction. Like King, Eliza Ann Dupuy used these themes as common tropes in the approximately twenty-five novels she wrote between 1845 and 1881. Although not as biting as King, Dupuy similarly critiqued traditional gender relations. Born in Virginia, Dupuy's family, much like King's, suffered from financial setbacks, and they moved to Kentucky when she was still relatively young. Upon her father's death, Dupuy worked as a tutor for the Natchez, Mississippi, family led by Thomas G. Ellis.[36] Her second novel, *The Conspirators* (1850), sold over 20,000 copies and earned Dupuy recognition as an author. In this popular novel, she depicted women in much the same way as they were in the King's works: as sufferers at the hands of men. In subsequent novels, Dupuy ventured boldly into seldom-explored topics and themes, such as the place of mulatto women in southern society, sexual aggression, and female villains.[37] In *The Planter's Daughter: A Tale of Louisiana* (1857), she confronted, in the words of one scholar, "the dangers of male greed and ambition, the silent suffering of unrequited love, the frenzies of male lust, and the victimization of women at the hands of unscrupulous fathers and lovers."[38]

[33] Petty, "Susan Petigru King," 179.

[34] *Ibid.*, 180–1.

[35] *Ibid.*, 181.

[36] Dorri R. Beam, "Eliza Ann Dupuy," in Kent Ljungquist, ed., *Dictionary of Literary Biography: Antebellum Writers in the South* (Detroit, 2001), 104–6.

[37] *Ibid.*, 106.

[38] *Ibid.*, 107.

Dupuy was linked to another mid-nineteenth-century female author, Catherine Ann Warfield. Thomas Ellis, for whom Dupuy worked as a governess, was Warfield's step-brother. Warfield herself was born in Natchez in 1816 into a wealthy family who was hit by hard times because of her mother's mental illness. The author of two antebellum collections of poetry and eleven novels, Warfield rapidly acquired literary admirers. Her first novel, *The Household of Bouverie, or The Elixir of Gold* (1860), earned her praise in *Harper's* as "a female novel-writer who displays the unmistakable fire of genius, however terrific its brightness."[39] Much like King, she addressed in this novel, and in later ones such as *The Romance of the Green Seal* (1866), issues like the often abusive relationships women faced, the lack of individuality for married women, and mental illness. In her postbellum works, Warfield, as one observer has noted, drew female characters who "gradually become more assertive, taking greater control over their own lives and the lives of others around them … [and] are shown rejecting the social conventions for women in the antebellum South."[40]

Whereas King, Dupuy, and Warfield were primarily novelists, Mary Bayard Clarke of North Carolina viewed poetry as a path to publishing prominence. Clarke, however, lived a much longer and in many ways more interesting life. Born in Raleigh in 1827 to one of the wealthiest planter families in the state, Clarke flourished even though her mother died when she was but a child. Her father, Thomas P. Devereux, ensured that Clarke received an excellent education based on a traditionally rigorous university-level program of study. Thus educated, Clarke employed her literary talents in a long career until her death in 1886. Throughout her long tenure as a poet and author of short fiction, Clarke demonstrated that southern women did assume highly visible roles in the literary culture of the region, and in turn earned fame and respect.

Even as a young adult, Mary Clarke sought her father's approval. A stern Whig who was strongly pro-Union, Thomas Devereux did not easily express approval. When she wanted to marry William J. Clarke, a veteran of the Mexican War whom Mary had known for some time, her father withheld his support. As the editor of Clarke's letters suggests, the motive behind this lack of support for the marriage is unclear, but Thomas Devereux had many reasons to question the union. Whereas Devereux was staunchly Whig, William Clarke was a Democrat; whereas Devereux prided himself on the tight fiscal management of his plantation, Clarke seemed to be always on the verge of insolvency; whereas Devereux could point to a prominent lineage based on land ownership and political leadership, Clarke's father was a merchant. Mary Clarke's father must have felt that he had more than enough cause to refuse to grant his consent to the marriage. As a result, Mary and William

[39] Larry W. Gibbs, "Catherine Ann Warfield," in *Dictionary of Literary Biography: Antebellum Writers in the South*406, 408.

[40] *Ibid.*, 409.

were wed in Louisiana in 1848 but did not receive her father's blessing until well into the marriage.[41]

Mary's interest in writing poetry formed at an early age, but her father disapproved of seeing his daughter's name in print. She and William had moved to the barren frontier town of San Antonio in 1855, and Mary wrote several essays for newspapers, including the *New York Herald*, about life in Texas. However, her father made clear that although women could be intellectuals, the public world of publishing was reserved for men. Adhering to the traditional notion of a woman's place, Devereux appreciated Mary's intellect but not her desire for public recognition. Conforming to her father's wishes, Mary used a nom de plume for her early publications. In an 1860 letter to *Southern Literary Messenger* editor George Bagby, Mary Clarke explained that she wished to publish under the name "Tenella." She implored Bagby to "say what you like about Tenella but nothing at all about Mrs. Clarke.... This feeling is so strong that I will give up writing rather than appear out of my social circle except as Tenella."[42] Indeed, although Clarke published numerous pieces for the *Southern Literary Messenger*, she always signed her works as Tenella. As she wrote to Bagby in 1861, "My incognito I only endeavor to preserve in print, [as] my social circle extends from Boston to Brownsville one way, and from Cuba to Chicago the other; in it I am as well known by the name of Tenella as of Mrs. Clarke, but the newspapers and public generally, have nothing to do with the later personage." At this early stage of her career, she viewed her name in print as a violation of her privacy. "Every gentleman, and rowdy too, is at liberty to look at Mrs. Clarke as she dashes by the hotel on horseback, but that does not give them the right to look through her parlor window and watch her kiss her husband or pet her children."[43] In addition to her desire to refrain from offending her father and protecting her privacy, Clarke seems to have used her nom de plume as a way to isolate herself from potentially harmful criticism: "Mounted on my Pegasus, I soar along as Tenella and never think of the public, or if I do, don't regard their remarks as applying to me individually and consequently am neither embarrassed or annoyed by them."[44]

Clarke did not have to worry much about criticism because her early publications were well received. Like many southern women authors, Clarke sent her poems to the literary magazines that provided the chief forum for women's literary expression. She published at least sixteen poems and essays in the *Messenger* alone between 1853 and 1861 and received in return acclaim from readers. After the appearance of her poem "The Triumph of Spring" in the

[41] Crow and Barden, eds., *Live Your Own Life*, xxxiii.

[42] Clarke to George Bagby, December 16, 1860, in Crow and Barden, eds., *Live Your Own Life*, 57. Mary's choice of "Tenella" as a nom de plume remains a mystery.

[43] Clarke to George Bagby, April 8, 1861, in Crow and Barden, eds., *Live Your Own Life*, 66–7.

[44] *Ibid.*, 67.

June 1853 issue of the *Messenger*, a reviewer praised the piece as evidence of "poetic genius" and its author as "rarely gifted."[45] Such positive responses probably emboldened her to take on a task that few women assumed in the antebellum South: She edited a two-volume collection of poetry by North Carolina writers titled *Wood-Notes; or, Carolina Carols* (1854). Published in Raleigh under "Tenella" and comprising nearly 500 pages, the collection included poems by both male and female authors. In order to orchestrate such an anthology, Clarke must have been well known to her fellow North Carolina authors, and yet she still used "Tenella" in her role as editor. Like her own contributions to the magazines, Clarke's compilation was praised by reviewers.[46]

During the Civil War, Clarke continued to write poems and short essays despite the many hardships she and her family faced. Living in Texas, both Mary and her husband were strong supporters of the Confederacy. In fact, Mary penned a lengthy report of the rebel activities in Texas for the *New York Herald*. "Our city [San Antonio]," Clarke wrote in February 1861, "has been regarded as the black spot in Texas; but I think we have now wiped out the disgrace cast on us by the so-called Union party, whose leaders and spokesmen, many of them, are Northern men, or fresh from an Ohio hot-bed of abolitionism."[47] Such strong pro-secessionist sentiment was characteristic of Clarke's views despite her own father's unionist leanings. Mary's husband William, as a Democrat and veteran, stood to gain much in a southern confederacy, and Mary undoubtedly counted on a prominent role for her husband in a new southern government.

Still, like many women writers during the war, Clarke found carrying on her literary career difficult. Writing to Macfarlane and Fergusson, publishers of Richmond's *Southern Literary Messenger*, Clarke explained why she had not sent them any contributions recently. "I have not deserted the *Messenger*," she promised, "but my time and strength are now devoted to the sick soldiers of our army generally, and my husband's regiment particularly." No doubt in need of additional income, however, Clarke offered to help edit the monthly literary magazine. As she wrote the publishers, "I am considered a pretty good proof reader, and if you need assistance in that or any other way while your corps of the office is reduced by the war, it will give me great pleasure to do anything in my power to aid you."[48]

While William secured an appointment in the Confederate army, Mary did her part for the war effort by turning her literary talents to propaganda. She moved back to North Carolina with her four children as William's regiment

[45] Anonymous review of "The Triumph of Spring," *Southern Literary Messenger* 19 (July 1853), 445.

[46] See, for example, the review in *Southern Literary Messenger* 21 (January 1855), 63.

[47] Mary Clarke, "Interesting from Texas," *New York Herald*, reprinted in Crow and Barden, eds., *Live Your Own Life*, 60.

[48] Mary Bayard Clarke to Macfarlane and Fergusson, September 21 (no year), Macfarlane and Fergusson Papers, Virginia Historical Society.

engaged in fighting in Virginia. She remarked that one of her poems "was composed in the cars while on my way to the encampment of the 14th at Weldon," but before she "had time to do more than copy it out fairly" she was diverted by an officer of the 2nd North Carolina.[49] Eventually, however, she made it to Weldon; and "The Battle of Manassas," though hastily penned, was read to the soldiers, who responded with cheers.[50] Between 1861 and 1863, Clarke contributed a number of works to magazines such as the *Messenger* and the *Southern Illustrated News*, but like many southern women she grew weary of the war and her husband's absence. As she wrote in early 1863 while sewing the uniform of a tall officer who was a "treat to the eyes," she longed for her husband even though he was "a wiry little fellow ... all beard and moustache and not flesh enough on his bones to get a flesh wound." Such yearning made her sick of the war and even of writing. "Oh dear me! How tired I am of this war, and everything pertaining to it – especially the poetry."[51] Making matters even more frustrating was the fact that by April 1863 Clarke was finding it difficult to locate good paper on which to write.[52]

In June 1864, William was wounded badly, which further tested Clarke's support for the Confederate war effort. Although she welcomed his return home to Raleigh, Clarke realized that as soon as he was healed William would return to the battlefield. But for William the fighting ended early because he was captured by Union forces in Virginia in February 1865 and held at Fort Delaware for the remainder of the war.[53] While William suffered the wrath of the enemy, Mary kept her anger in check. In fact, she was harshly criticized by family members, especially her sister, for conversing with Union soldiers when they occupied North Carolina in 1865. Mary's willingness to engage men in conversation, even men she did not know, and the fact that she counted many men among her friends, had attracted the scorn of her father and sister well before the war. But the notion of Mary talking openly and in a friendly manner with the northern troops was more than her sister Frances Miller could countenance. An incident in June 1865 that took place in Miller's home sparked a passionate letter to Mary. "Do not take what I say as a threat," Miller explained to her sister, "... for you know how much pleasure it would give to a large number of our family if they could say 'they have parted in anger.'" The incident that compelled Miller to write involved Mary conversing with and treating as a welcome guest a member of the Union army. "I know we must receive them some times & be decently polite," Miller admitted, but "I can not & will not permit the recurrence of yesterday's incident. It is against my taste an outrage to my children & above all in my view it is an insult to Bro

[49] *Ibid.*

[50] Clarke to Macfarlane and Ferguson, September 21, 1861, in Crow and Barden, eds., *Live Your Own Life*, 90.

[51] Clarke to George Bagby, January 7, 1863, in Crow and Barden, eds., *Live Your Own Life*, 130.

[52] Clarke to George Bagby, April 1, 1863, in Crow and Barden, eds., *Live Your Own Life*, 140.

[53] Crow and Barden, eds., *Live Your Own Life*, 169, 178.

William while he is in a northern prison to have his wife entertain for 4 hours one of his jailors."[54] The rift between Mary and Frances permanently damaged their relationship, and Mary soon moved out of Frances' home where she had been staying during the latter part of the war.

After the war, Mary continued her writing and assumed some limited editorial duties. She became the literary editor of *Southern Field and Fireside* in 1865, but her writing and her interests were beginning to focus more on politics rather than literature. She continued to write poetry and published an epic narrative poem in 1871 titled *Clytie and Zenobia*. She wrote reviews for magazines such as *The Land We Love*, and many publishers sent her books to review. Shortly after the war, Mary turned more often to writing political essays. For example, she wrote about Sherman's presence in Raleigh for the New York periodical *The Old Guard*, explaining to northern readers that the South was ready to move on after slavery. She also authored contributions to the New York *Daily News* and other northern papers.[55] Despite her readiness to write for northerners, Clarke did not retreat from earlier conservative opinions about the faults she saw in black Americans, nor did she argue that the South was wrong to pursue independence. As she became more political, however, Clarke also opened up to the cause of women's equality by the 1870s, and her willingness to forgive northerners for her family's suffering during the war also generated more opportunities to work for northern publishers. She became a journalist for a Chicago paper in 1877, reflecting a new level of political engagement in contemporary issues.[56]

White southern women who wrote for periodicals before and during the Civil War made significant inroads into public life. Although prohibited from voting or holding office, these women influenced society through their contributions to newspapers and magazines. In so doing, they not only took advantage of literary careers to engage politically, they also opened paths to careers as professional journalists. Not content to be merely contributors, white southern women took control of their own periodicals. Even with limited means, educated women could line up printers, authors, and subscribers to start their own journals. Chapter 5 illuminates the largely forgotten lives and careers of these early journalists, not simply to rediscover their individual biographies, as important as that task might be, but more importantly to appreciate the myriad ways in which they contributed directly and actively to the intellectual life of the region and to an emerging sense that women might be political as well as intellectual equals to men.

54 Frances Miller to Mary Clarke, June 1865, in Crow and Barden, eds., *Live Your Own Life*, 182–3.

55 Crow and Barden, eds., *Live Your Own Life*, 180, 185–6, 205, 241–2.

56 *Ibid.*, 344–5.

5

Antebellum Women Editors and Journalists

Most southern women writers, like those in the North, did not challenge traditional gender roles and wrote poetry and prose on subjects that were considered appropriately feminine topics. Women writers on these subjects, like Charleston's Mary Elizabeth Lee and the Florida native Mary Edwards Bryan, were received warmly by the southern reading public. But women who became editors fashioned themselves as public figures with some authority and thus challenged traditional notions of separate spheres. As arbiters of taste and quality, these editors served a public function: They decided which contributions by both men and women merited inclusion within the pages of their magazines. Even women who did not utilize their periodicals explicitly to challenge gender roles were acutely aware of their unusual position as public women. Some, like the dozen or so women who edited antebellum southern magazines and newspapers, supported their families and earned a public audience and regional reputation. Unable to vote or hold office, southern women editors like Anne Royall, Mary Chase Barney, and Rebecca Hicks would find ways to participate directly and actively in a broad set of political discussions, from railroad funding to cabinet appointments.

Women editors have attracted the interest of historians recently as scholars seek to understand the ways in which antebellum Americans constructed ideas about gender and femininity. Periodicals, it has been argued, were particularly important to the northern suffrage movement because they provided women with both a platform for new ideas and a way to disseminate those ideas. The *Lily* and the *Una* before the Civil War, and the *Woman's Journal* and the *Revolution* in the late nineteenth century, were just a few of the northern periodicals that advocated greater rights and equality for women.[1] Important work, such as Sylvia D. Hoffert's biography of Jane Grey Swisshelm, who edited the *Pittsburgh Saturday Visiter* [sic] between 1847 and 1857, and

[1] Martha Solomon, ed., *A Voice of Their Own: The Woman Suffrage Press, 1840–1910* (Tuscaloosa, 1991); William E. Huntzicker, *The Popular Press, 1833–1865* (Westport, CT, 1999), 86.

Patricia Okker's work on northern editors, has already begun.[2] Despite the importance of these contributions to understanding the lives and careers of women editors, southern women have been almost completely neglected.[3] Yet, southern women, like women across America, were part of a nineteenth-century explosion of interest in women's periodicals and female editors in North America and Europe. Women journalists could be found in Canada and Britain as well as New York and New England.[4] The emergence in the South of a periodical literature aimed at female audiences as well as the growing number and importance of women members of the press were part of a broader phenomenon emerging across the English-speaking world.

Women edited newspapers and magazines in all regions of the Old South. Some of them were native southerners; others moved from the North to teach or write. Wives of ministers transferred to the South were part of a wave of antebellum northerners who saw in the South professional opportunities for literature and teaching, a group that included people of diverse interests. Often the duties of editorship were thrust on women by the death of a husband or other family misfortune. Under such dire circumstances, rigid notions of gender distinctiveness weakened and the idea of separate spheres became more flexible. Southern women who became editors as the result of a family tragedy were often the most outspoken, as if their experience allowed them greater leeway in expressing their own views. Southern society sanctioned considerable latitude in gender roles for those women who, through no fault of their own, needed to support a family. Interestingly, women editors received the support of southern communities and contributed to the vitality of intellectual life in the nineteenth-century South. By serving as examples of bold and independent women, female editors demonstrated that southern women could participate in political discussions, contribute to important debates about culture and literature, and manage a business.

In the earliest period of women editors and printers, between 1700 and 1820, women often assumed the editorship of a periodical upon the death of their husbands. Such was the case with one of the earliest and most successful of female editors in the Old South, Sarah Hillhouse, a Connecticut native who came south around 1790 with her husband and settled in the northeastern Georgia town of Washington. David Hillhouse started a four-page weekly newspaper called the *Monitor* in 1801, a periodical that brought together

[2] Sylvia D. Hoffert, *Jane Grey Swisshelm: An Unconventional Life 1815–1884* (Chapel Hill, 2004). See also Okker, *Our Sister Editors* and Bennion, *Equal to the Occasion*.

[3] For recent works on women editors outside the South, see David Dary, *Red Blood & Black Ink: Journalism in the Old West* (New York, 1998) and Okker, *Our Sister Editors*.

[4] Barbara Onslow, *Women of the Press in Nineteenth-Century Britain* (New York, 2000), 103; David Reed, *The Popular Magazine in Britain and the United States* (Toronto, 1997), 27; Hilary Fraser, et al., *Gender and the Victorian Periodical* (Cambridge, 2003), especially Chapter 3; Marjory Lang, *Women Who Made the News: Female Journalists in Canada, 1880–1945* (Montreal, 1999).

articles and brief news stories from papers across the country and provided the Hillhouse family with financial stability. However, the death of her husband in 1803 shattered that stability. With three children to support, Sarah had no choice but to attempt to keep the paper afloat and, as her son later wrote, she "immediately took the management of the paper and learned and practiced every mechanical service pertaining to that office."[5] Under Sarah Hillhouse, the *Monitor* reached a circulation of 800, appealing to subscribers with selections from a variety of newspapers like the *Connecticut Gazette*, the *National Intelligencer*, and other papers from New York, New Orleans, London, and Paris.[6] Hillhouse achieved even greater renown and probably significant financial rewards when she landed a contract to publish state and federal documents in the *Monitor*, making her Georgia's first and perhaps only female state printer.[7]

Hillhouse was hardly alone. More than sixty-five women edited periodicals or worked as printers in the period before 1820; one scholar has identified eighteen in the southern states alone.[8] Elizabeth Roulstone, for example, edited *The Knoxville Gazette* upon the death of her husband from 1804–1807. Roulstone served as the state printer of Tennessee when her husband died in 1804. Roulstone had played an active role in the family printing business, including the Knoxville paper, and thus felt confident in taking it over upon her husband's death. To supplement her income, Roulstone also ran a boarding house to help support her two children.[9] After remarrying, she sold the Knoxville paper and started a new one in Carthage with her new husband. The two newspapers largely shunned controversial topics and raised little ire among subscribers. Like Hillhouse, Roulstone's status as a widow undoubtedly granted her a measure of public sympathy, inoculating her against scorn for stepping outside the feminine sphere.

After 1820, the number of periodicals published, as well as women's active participation in their publication, significantly increased. In this period, women continued to take on novel roles necessitated by the death of a husband. The earlier nineteenth-century trends of widows assuming the operation of a family-run periodical did not disappear, but after 1820 both married and single women became editors not as a consequence of widowhood but as individuals in their own right. Southern society was not as open to women editors acting

[5] Sarah Hillhouse's son quoted in Marion Marzolf, *Up From the Footnote* (New York, 1977), 10.

[6] For examples of the numerous periodicals from which Sarah Hillhouse culled her essays and stories, see *Monitor* 5 (November 23, 1805) and 9 (September 16, 1809). See also Dexter, *Career Women of America*, 103, and Hudak, *Early American Women Printers and Publishers*, 590–9.

[7] Hillhouse printed electoral results for the governor's race in Pennsylvania (5 [November 9, 1805]), Georgia Governor Milledge's Address to the Georgia Assembly in 1805 (5 [November 23, 1805]), state financial news (9 [September 2, 1809]), and James Madison's 1810 message to Congress (10 [December 29, 1810]).

[8] http://www.stockton.edu/~gilmorew/oamnhist/cprojec.htm

[9] Joseph Hamblen Sears, *Tennessee Printers, 1791–1945* (Kingsport, TN, 1946), 9–10.

on their own; widowhood was still the more acceptable means by which traditional gender boundaries might be crossed. Undeterred by societal norms, however, this new generation used two new trends as wedges to open the door of editorships: women's acceptance in the pursuit of literature and the new efforts to increase education and literacy for southern white women.

With at least a modicum of schooling, women could turn to establishing a periodical as a way to explore avenues for intellectual growth. Mary Chase Barney of Baltimore proved to be one of the most outspoken antebellum southern editors, but even she started a monthly magazine because of a hardship experienced by her family: her husband's firing at the hands of President Andrew Jackson. Even before she began editing *National Magazine, or Ladies' Emporium* in 1831, she was well connected to national politics: Her father was Supreme Court Justice Samuel Chase and her father-in-law was the War of 1812 hero Joshua Barney. She married William Barney with whom she had a number of children and lived comfortably until her husband lost his position as a naval officer for the port of Baltimore shortly after Jackson took office. Although no direct correlation appears in the historical record, Barney was convinced that the president had something to do with her husband's firing. She managed to get the United States Senate to consider a resolution that would have required Jackson to provide the reasoning for William Barney's firing, a resolution that was not successful.

However, Mary Barney did not stop there. In retaliation for her husband's humiliation, Barney drafted a lengthy essay condemning Jackson that was trumpeted by rival Whigs as a powerful rejection of the president's usurpation of political power.[10] Ostensibly, the purpose of Barney's letter was to convince Jackson to return her husband to his post, but the vituperative and accusatory tone of the letter made that unlikely. In the lengthy document, Barney immediately attacked the president for "the injury you have inflicted on a meritorious officer and his helpless family." Her anger was directed at Jackson's spoils system, which she characterized as authoritarian. "*Rotation* in office," Barney prodded, "is that magical phrase, so familiar to the demagogues of all nations, and of times, your great and much vaunted principle of *Reform*?" She called his administration "a cancerous excrescence fastened upon the body politic."[11] Such colorful language negated any chance of William Barney reacquiring his job, but the diatribe attracted the notice and widespread approval of Jackson's political opponents. In the early 1830s, the nascent Whig party seized Barney's letter and printed it by the hundreds in pamphlet form. The text was printed on satin in the form of a broadside and distributed widely, attracting notice in newspapers across the country, from the *Connecticut Mirror* and *Vermont*

[10] J. Thomas Scharf writes in *Chronicles of Baltimore* that the "letter was so much thought of at the time, that large editions of it were printed on satin and circulated throughout the United States." Scharf also reprints Barney's letter to Jackson in full. See *The Chronicles of Baltimore*, (Baltimore, 1874), 434–9.

[11] Mary Chase Barney, "Letter from Mary Chase Barney, of Baltimore, to Andrew Jackson," (Washington, 1830), Sevier Collection, Vanderbilt University.

Gazette to the *Richmond Enquirer*. Readers of the *Enquirer* were so dubious as to the notion that a woman could have authored the essay that one writer suggested the author of the anti-Jackson diatribe was really William Wirt.[12]

In publicly unleashing her attack on Jackson, Barney made no attempt to hide her identity or her gender. All of the pamphlets and silk banners that reprinted her vitriol against the president also featured her name prominently as the manifesto's author. Barney recognized, of course, that the drafting of such a letter was unusual for a woman, and in the letter she therefore referred to her role as a mother. "The sickness and debility of my husband, *now call upon me to vindicate* his and his children's wrongs. The natural timidity of my sex vanishes before the necessity of my situation; and a spirit, sir, as proud as yours, although in a female bosom, demands justice." The heart-felt rhetoric continued, as Barney criticized the president for caring little how his policies affected families. "Careless as you are about the effects of your conduct," she complained to Jackson, "it would be idle to inform you of the depth and quality of that misery which you have worked in the bosom of my family."[13]

Barney kept the rhetorical heat on Jackson by starting her *National Magazine*, a forum for discussing politics and for highlighting the evils of the Democratic administration. Given the frequency with which she criticized Jackson and his followers, it is easy to see the entire literary endeavor as an attempt to keep the attacks on the president alive. Barney was also in need of income to help support her eight children. In the first issue of her journal, Barney rejected those who believed such an undertaking was unbecoming for a woman: "I had enjoyed the immunity of many years; I glorified in that immunity, for my family was my world.... Well may I now feel as the doe chased from its covert of years, who, with timid steps measures the wide campaigne, but finds no shelter."[14] She made clear, as had many female editors before her, that familial difficulties erased any reluctance she might have had about taking the helm of her own periodical.

The tenacity and boldness with which she disparaged Jackson makes Barney unusual among nineteenth-century women. But as she engaged in publishing a politically charged magazine, Barney demonstrated that southern women could compete with men in the rough-and-tumble world of American politics, as later advocates of woman's rights would indeed claim. In the first editorial of her magazine in November 1830, she promised that even as a woman, "In the struggle which is now going on between civil liberty and wild anarchy, under the garb of democracy, she will sometimes raise her feeble voice; not as a disputant in the arena of party, but as an advocate for certain great principles which it may become her sex and condition to feel a lively and deep interest

[12] See *Vermont Gazette* (June 1, 1830); *Connecticut Mirror* (June 12, 1830); *Richmond Enquirer* (October 8, 1830).

[13] Mary Chase Barney, "Letter from Mary Chase Barney, of Baltimore, to Andrew Jackson," (Washington, 1830), Sevier Collection, Vanderbilt University.

[14] Barney, "To Patrons," *National Magazine* 1 (November 1830), 1.

in maintaining, in these times of mis-called 'reformation.'"[15] Jackson's lack of intelligence, Barney argued, made him a dupe for ambitious and unscrupulous demagogues and party hacks. She condemned the president, for in her eyes "his whole scheme of administration has been a series of attacks upon the vital interests of our country, its honor, its industry, its prosperity, its public and domestic happiness."[16] By mid-1831, Barney's attacks on Jackson had reached a fever pitch. Using a new tactic, Barney questioned the president's mental fitness for the office, claiming that Jackson was "completely destitute of intellectual ability."[17]

Although it might seem that the sole purpose of the *National Magazine* was to provide a forum for Barney's encomiums, she did venture into discussions about culture, politics, and literature. She unhesitatingly asserted her right to discuss virtually any subject, even topics usually reserved for men, and promised that "such a course will be mine."[18] True to her word, Barney discussed economic policies on railroads and reflected on literature. She delved into essays on the history of Native Americans and the French Revolution.[19] "But why should we deem it necessary," she wrote in "The State of the Union," "to apologize, for taking part in the discussion of questions of such vital importance to all we hold dear upon earth? We ought rather to be entitled to some credit for having so long forbore, than exposed to censure for now uttering our thoughts."[20] "Because we have no voice in the government," Barney asked her male readers, "have we no voice in the nation? Because ye have had the power to stifle one will ye claim the right to smother the other? – But thus it has always been with arbitrary power."[21]

Barney continued her literary assaults on Jackson and the Democrats into 1831 when she abruptly discontinued her magazine. Her husband may have secured employment, or she may have tired of editorial duties; editors complained of subscribers who refused to pay on time, if at all, of authors who demanded too much compensation for their contributions, of the pressures of trying to maintain quality month after month. Barney published a biography of her father-in-law, Commodore Joshua Barney, in 1832.[22] With forthrightness and candid descriptions of her family's plight, Barney expressed herself as a woman and mother who felt wronged by the president.

Barney stood out in the 1830s as perhaps the nation's boldest female critic of President Jackson, but there were other women who embraced the

[15] Barney, "Proposals," *National Magazine* 1 (November 1830), 1.

[16] Barney, "The State of the Union," *National Magazine* 1 (February 1831), 325.

[17] Barney, "General Jackson," *National Magazine* 2 (July 1831), 210.

[18] Barney, "To Patrons," 2.

[19] Barney, "The Late Revolution in France," *National Magazine* 1 (November 1830), 26–39; "The American System," "Daniel Webster," 1 (January 1831), 162–74, 197–8; "The Indians," 1 (February 1831), 293–7; "The Post-Office Department," 2 (May 1831), 26–35.

[20] Barney, "The State of the Union," 323.

[21] Barney, "To Patrons," 2–3.

[22] Barney, *A Biographical Memoir of the Late Commodore Joshua Barney* (Boston, 1832).

public role of activist. Like Barney, Maryland native Anne Newport Royall proved equally tenacious and outspoken. Royall was an important forerunner of later advocates for women's rights because she so freely spoke her mind and expressed her views on religion and culture, because she was active in Washington politics, and because she employed her talents as a writer and an editor to earn a national reputation as a strong-minded woman. Indeed, Royall was one of the most remarkable American women of the nineteenth century. Unlike Barney, however, who was praised by the Whigs for her anti-Jackson diatribes, Royall was to be reprimanded harshly for so freely expressing herself. Whether writing about religious fundamentalism, defending Native Americans, or condemning the corruption of local officials, Royall earned fame as America's first female reporter and professional newswoman. Her rich legacy is all the more extraordinary because her journalistic career began when she was in her mid-50s.[23]

Royall's early life gave little indication of her future success in reporting and editing, though she did exhibit an early fascination with reading. At a young age, Royall lived in Pennsylvania and then West Virginia, but the death of her father and then her step-father left Anne and her mother in search of a home. Her first two decades of life were itinerant, as Anne and her mother, who worked as a housekeeper, moved from one home to the next. The life as a housekeeper's daughter was not one, of course, that afforded either luxury or social inclusion. In fact, as a teenager living near Staunton, Virginia, Anne was snubbed by her more wealthy peers, and her treatment during this period undoubtedly sensitized her to the plight of underdogs of all kinds, a sensitivity that she would employ in her later career as a journalist. Being an outcast, however, provided her with ample time alone to read, and she became an inquisitive learner as a youth. Royall's hunger for knowledge received a boost when at the age of eighteen she and her mother moved once again, this time to keep the home of a planter named William Royall, whose library in Sweet Springs, Virginia, would provide Anne with a wealth of reading material.[24]

Anne's life in the Royall home would prove to be a complicated one, filled with both positive and negative experiences. A planter more interested in history and literature than growing profitable crops, William recognized Anne's brightness and inquisitive nature and took it upon himself to become her teacher. From him she learned to distrust Christian fundamentalism and to embrace the Freemasons. After a decade of living on his plantation, Anne married William when she was twenty-eight years old. Her marriage was haunted by William's lack of interest in conducting the business side of the plantation, responsibilities that fell on Anne. More troublesome was William's propensity to drink. Upon his early death in 1812, Anne was willed a substantial sum

[23] Lynda W. Brown, "Anne Newport Royall," in Lina Mainiero, ed., *American Women Writers* (Detroit, 1982), 509–10; Madelon Golden Schlipp and Sharon M. Murphy, *Great Women of the Press* (Carbondale, IL, 1983), 21–3.

[24] Schlipp and Murphy, *Great Women of the Press*, 23.

that promised a life of relative comfort.[25] The possibility of financial stability, however, was illusory as relatives successfully contested William's will and Anne was left with almost nothing.

Left with little means, Royall had to use her authorial talents to scrape together a living. Her first literary works were travel accounts; she published the first of ten volumes of travel writing, *Sketches of History*, in 1826 after venturing from Alabama to New England. Demonstrating an indomitable spirit, at the age of forty-eight she rode on horseback with a slave and few provisions from Charleston, (then) Virginia, to the Alabama Territory. She richly described the landscape and culture and towns she observed as she passed through Ohio, Kentucky, and Tennessee. At times she demonstrated little concern for her own personal safety, dashing off for example to interview Native Americans by herself while in Tennessee.[26] Yet she honed her already substantial talents as an interviewer, reporter, and author. Her first works of travel writing, *Sketches of History* and *Letters from Alabama*, would prove to be popular, spurring Royall to continue her career as a writer. Still in search of a consistent source of income, however, Royall came to Washington in 1824 to petition the government to receive pay from William's military service, and she hounded every politician she could to hear her plea, including John Quincy Adams. Washington became the base from which she would launch her editorial career and remain most of her long life.

In Washington, Royall became widely known in the highest levels of government. She interviewed every U.S. president from the 1830s through the early 1850s and appeared often in the halls of the capital building to hear a speech by Webster or Clay. Her physical presence failed to impress the wealthy or famous, however. She was a small woman, about five feet tall and slight, and her untidy clothing included a tattered black dress and shawl. The impression she made on those whom she met was significant nonetheless. She earned the respect of men like the younger Adams because of her wit and intelligence, not because of her appearance. And her boldness, which struck many as more masculine than feminine, demanded that people take notice of her. As John Quincy Adams recorded in his diary, "Mrs. Royall continued to make herself vexious to many persons, tolerated by some and feared by others, by her deportment and books; treating all with a familiarity which often passes for impudence, insulting those who treat her with civility, and then lampooning them in her books. Stripped of all her sex's delicacy, but unable to forfeit its privilege of gentle treatment from the other, she goes about like a virago in enchanted armor."[27]

Royall's forthrightness was tolerated when it came to politics, but not in matters of religion. She was acerbically critical of the "holy terror" that

[25] *Ibid.*, 24–5; Alice S. Maxwell and Marion B. Dunlevy, *Virago!: The Story of Anne Newport Royall (1769–1854)* (Jefferson, NC, 1985), 14–5.

[26] Schlipp and Murphy, *Great Women of the Press*, 26–7.

[27] *Ibid.*, 28–31.

fundamentalist Protestants inflicted on those who did not agree with them, and their intolerance for competing views on religious issues made Royall's attachment to the Freemasons suspect. She was ostracized for her unorthodox views, but being an outcast from religious extremism was a point of pride for Royall. As a strong believer in freedom of speech, she refused to keep her views to herself.[28] She openly referred to evangelicals as "Holy Willies," and she made fun of religion in her writings and in her conversations with others.[29] One man pushed her down the stairs to remove her from his home, an act of violence that caused a broken leg from which Royall was a long time recovering.

Tensions between Royall and Christian fundamentalists worsened when a group of evangelicals began to pray loudly outside her home in Washington in 1829. Fed up with the harassment, including their pelting her walls and windows with rocks, she uttered a verbal assault, which according to the mob present, included obscenities. Royall was charged with an antiquated law for being an "uncommon scold," and at the age of sixty she was fined and put on probation. Her fellow reporters, two from the *National Intelligencer* as well as James Gordon Bennett, supported her and paid the fine.[30] If the Washington orthodoxy thought this would finally quiet the seemingly indefatigable Royall, they were mistaken. Instead, she started writing as busily as ever, and in 1831 began a weekly newspaper, *Paul Pry*, which provided the perfect outlet for Royall's desire for self-expression.[31]

Royall's four-page paper was filled with news reports, interviews, literary notices and book reviews, poetry, and her opinions on the issues of the day. As she stated early in the paper's run, "We shall expose all and every species of political evil, and religious fraud, without fear or affection.... We shall advocate liberty of press, the liberty of speech, and the liberty of conscience."[32] She supported the Masons, disparaged local and federal government malfeasance where she saw it, and commented freely on a wide range of issues. She supported the disadvantaged and the downtrodden, particularly white workers and Native Americans, but seems to have been unable to see the injustice of slavery. She also seems to have been skeptical of calls for female suffrage. However, as she herself put it, she was "always in the van of the editorial corps, and attacked the enemies of its country in their strongholds."[33]

Royall published *Paul Pry* for five years and then began a new and more significant periodical, *The Huntress*. The telling title reflected her motives

[28] Maxwell and Dunlevy, *Virago!* 14–5, 55, 59.

[29] Brown, "Anne Newport Royall," 510.

[30] Bessie Rowland James, *Anne Royall's U.S.A.* (New Brunswick, NJ, 1972), Chapter XIII. Schlipp and Murphy, *Great Women of the Press*, 32.

[31] Patricia Bradley, *Women and the Press: The Struggle for Equality* (Evanston, IL, 2005), 60–3.

[32] *Paul Pry* 1 (December 3, 1831), quoted in Schlipp and Murphy, *Great Women of the Press*, 33.

[33] Schlipp and Murphy, *Great Women of the Press*, 34.

and purpose better than the gossipy heading *Paul Pry*.[34] In the pages of *The Huntress*, Royall promised to "expose corruption, hypocrisy and usurpation, without favor or affection in ALL."[35] From the beginning of the periodical in 1836 until it ended in 1854, *The Huntress* carried on weekly attacks on politicians and preachers. In the prospectus to the paper, Royall railed against "the untiring and gigantic strides of the Church and State Party" and its attempts "to dissolve our Republic and establish a religious despotism upon its ruins." In opposition to these attempts she pledged that *The Huntress* would "maintain an unflinching and uncompromising hostility."[36] Like Mary Chase Barney, Royall generally supported the Whigs and opposed the Democrats in her magazine; she used the term "Church and State Party" to describe not just Jacksonians but also evangelicals, abolitionists, and any others who interfered in the affairs of independent men and women.

Her attacks on religion in *The Huntress* were highly unusual for their caustic and unyielding nature. In the second issue of her paper, published in December 1836, Royall unleashed a bold assault on preachers and Christianity. "Why, then, has it happened," Royall asked rhetorically in a lengthy essay, "that the Christians are now, and always have been distinguished above all other religions, for war and a thirst for each others blood? It is because hypocrites and tyrants have used it as a mere cloak to hide their thirst for power."[37] It is unclear whether Royall was an atheist; she often defended Christianity as a peaceful faith but strongly denounced religion being used for political purposes. She saved her harshest criticism for the "tract peddlers" and "pious hypocrites" who constantly asked their flock for money. Indeed, referring to one Washington-area preacher, Royall claimed that "all he cares for is to beguile silly women and children of their money."[38] Particularly skeptical about requests for donations to carry on religious missions, Royall believed that preachers took advantage of "ignorant women" and their money to convert Native Americans to the faith. Royall would have none of it. "So far from converting heathens," Royall said of the missionaries, "they are more criminal than the heathens! They are themselves guilty of crimes which would make the heathen blush."[39] Royall could be especially hard on women when it came to religion, using terms like "silly women" and "ignorant women" to describe those she thought were duped by money-seeking Christians. Though Royall promised to avoid partisanship in *The Huntress*, she carried out unyielding condemnations against Van Buren and the Democrats and generally supported Whig ideas and leaders. The early numbers of *The Huntress* came shortly after Van Buren was elected in 1836, and Royall reveled in the prospect of taking

[34] Brown, "Anne Newport Royall," 510.

[35] Anne Newport Royall, "Prospectus," *The Huntress* 1 (December 2, 1826), 4.

[36] *Ibid.*

[37] Royall, "Church and State," *The Huntress* 1 (December 10, 1836), 2. See also "Church and State – Money – Religion – Tracts," 1 (January 7, 1837), 2.

[38] Royall, "Church and State and the Western States," *The Huntress* 1 (December 2, 1836), 2.

[39] Royall, "Church and State," 2.

on Jackson's successor. "We shall have rare *sport*," she declared, "when the new President takes his seat. The squabbles for the spoils will excite much laughter and amusement."[40] She assailed Democratic newspapers, such as her attack on the *Washington Globe* in 1839 for the "flowerish style in which [the paper] is daubing Mr. Van Buren upon his northern tour."[41] Although an early supporter of Andrew Jackson, she came to appreciate Henry Clay, and she reacted against the criticism he faced from other papers. "What barefaced impudence!" she exclaimed in response to an attack on the Kentucky statesman in the *Globe*. She carried on a lengthy disagreement with the *United States Magazine and Democratic Review* and its editors. The *Democratic Review* was the chief national periodical representing the Jacksonians and thus was a repeated target for Royall's vitriol.[42] She denounced the Democracy, week after week, and she could barely contain her glee at the defeat of Van Buren in 1840.[43] "Thank God," she proclaimed, "the great conspiracy is overthrown and the nation is ONCE MORE FREE!"[44]

Royall published *The Huntress* until she died in 1854 at the age of 85. In her paper she continued to lambaste the fools and knaves she saw around her. Although she remained almost penniless to her final days, and although she relied on the help of others to make ends meet, Royall was throughout her career as a journalist an important proto-feminist whose audacious penchant for self-assertion and political activism would be mirrored by later nineteenth- and early twentieth-century advocates of women's rights.

Whereas Barney and Royall were unusually candid about their political opinions, women editors like Charleston's Caroline Gilman preferred to remain primarily focused on literature in their magazines.[45] Gilman generally shunned politics in the early antebellum era, but the native New Englander later became a strong defender of the South and slavery. Born in Massachusetts in 1794, Gilman moved to South Carolina in about 1819 with her husband Samuel, a minister and Harvard graduate. As the mother of seven, Gilman felt like she had some expertise in child rearing and thus started a youth magazine called the *Rose-Bud* in 1832, one of the earliest periodicals for children published in America. A year later, Gilman broadened the content to reach a wider range of ages, and she ultimately changed the name to the *Southern Rose*, which lasted until 1839. Although the new format still avoided controversial subjects, Gilman, like Barney and Royall, handled all of the business side of running the journal herself. She established relationships with agents for the magazine, collected and kept record of subscriptions, and tried to promote

[40] Royall, "The Party," *The Huntress* 1 (December 10, 1836), 2.

[41] Royall, "Washington City," *The Huntress* 3 (August 10, 1839), 2.

[42] See, for example, Royall, "Comments upon the United States and Democratic Review," *The Huntress* 2 (December 23, 1837), 2.

[43] See in particular Royall, "Amos's Last," *The Huntress* 2 (May 5, 1838), 2.

[44] Royall, "The Presidential Election," *The Huntress* 4 (November 14, 1840), 2.

[45] Baym, *Woman's Fiction*, 67–71.

the periodical as best she could.[46] Like most editors she complained about late payments, unscrupulous agents, as well as the costs of printing. "My printer has risen upon me, ... and charges $500 per year. This, with agencies, postage and contingent expenses, will about exhaust my present subscribers, (720) but I feel very much disposed to continue, as there is no risk, and I may get 1000 in a year."[47]

Gilman seems to have handled all of these business activities with aplomb, though she was often frustrated by problems with the mail: "What with the mailings & carriers etc. etc. this business has been complicated enough."[48] It is telling that Gilman referred to editing the *Rose-Bud* as a "business," for although she viewed writing and editing as literary pursuits, she viewed herself as a businesswoman who expected recompense for her work. Like many small business enterprises in the mid-nineteenth-century South, Gilman's was not a highly organized endeavor, and she relied on the informal help of friends and relatives, including her husband, to carry on her duties as author and editor. "You will congratulate me on my new printer," she wrote in a letter in the 1830s, "He prints 1000 for $400. We do the mailing here, with two or three friends, socially, on Friday evenings, & do not trust the putting up to a printer, so that I hope no more will be misplaced."[49] One of Gilman's most frustrating tasks was to deal with issues lost in the mail, and she constantly sought ways to circumvent the problem. Her husband Samuel helped, but even he was frustrated by the lack of dependability of the postal system.[50]

Her literary successes earned Gilman a regional reputation, and she earned admiration in Charleston despite her northern birth. In large part, Gilman upset few southerners because she rarely questioned the legitimacy of slavery or the virtues of states' rights.[51] She also penned two works, *Recollections of a Housekeeper* (1834) and *Recollections of a Southern Matron* (1838), that gave little reason to offend readers' sensibilities. In the latter work, Gilman described contented slaves working for benevolent masters. She was able to see some injustice in the institution of slavery, but her sympathies clearly lay with other southern whites. She even called for a new southern political journal to counterbalance what she perceived to be the abolitionist bias of the northern press. Such a magazine, she claimed, would present "the true state of affairs in this region."[52] Gilman lived until 1888 and published four books during the 1870s. But her importance lies chiefly in her antebellum work as an editor

46 See the Gilman Papers, South Carolina Historical Society.

47 Caroline Gilman to Mrs. A. M. White, January 15, 1833, Caroline Gilman Papers, South Carolina Historical Society, Charleston.

48 Caroline Gilman to Louisa Loring, March 31 (no date, but likely early 1830s), Gilman Family Papers, American Antiquarian Society, Worcester.

49 *Ibid.*

50 See, for example, Samuel Gilman to Caroline Gilman, October 26 and November 7, 1833, Gilman Family Papers, American Antiquarian Society, Worcester.

51 Stiles, "Windows into Antebellum Charleston, 17.

52 Gilman quoted in Jan Bakker, "Caroline Gilman and the Issue of Slavery," *Southern Studies* 24 (Fall 1985), 283.

and businesswoman who used publishing as a way to earn both income and respect in the South.

The success of literary women like Gilman, whose periodicals and books were read widely in both the North and the South, demonstrates that authors could bridge the sectional divide. That magazines and newspapers joined the intellectual culture of the North and South can be readily seen in the discussion of New England Transcendentalism. The South's response to northern thinkers like Ralph Waldo Emerson and intellectual movements such as New England Transcendentalism demonstrates that southerners learned about intellectual culture in the North through periodicals and books.[53] Ultimately, southerners were as dismissive of Transcendentalism as most northerners, describing the movement as mystical nonsense. Southern writers did not reject Transcendentalism out of hand, however, and some reviewers credited the movement and Emerson with a high level of creativity and originality of thought.[54] Far from intellectually isolated or obtuse, southern writers were active participants in, and contributors to, national debates about important new ideas.

One of the earliest southern discussions of Emerson came from Caroline Gilman's husband Samuel in the Charleston weekly *Southern Rose*.[55] In an 1838 issue of the magazine, Samuel Gilman wrote a lengthy analysis of Emerson, who had only a few months before delivered his "Divinity School Address" and had only begun to win fame. "A new comet, or rather meteor," the essay announced with enthusiasm, "is shooting athwart the literary sky of old Massachusetts, in the person of Ralph Waldo Emerson."[56] Samuel Gilman's essay offered a lengthy analysis of Emerson's addresses before Dartmouth College and the Harvard Divinity School. The essay finds much to praise in Emerson's addresses, although Gilman qualified his positive assessments with some criticism. "The character of his mind," Gilman explained, "is poetical and imaginative, and he is strongly inclined to certain mystical and visionary habits of thought and discussion. His talents are unquestionably

[53] Jay B. Hubbell, "Ralph Waldo Emerson and the South," in *South and Southwest: Literary Essays and Reminiscences* (Durham, 1965), 123–53. See also Linda T. Prior, "Ralph Waldo Emerson and South Carolina," *South Carolina Historical Magazine* 79 (October 1978), 253–63.

[54] Ralph E. Luker has identified at least one southerner who might loosely be grouped with the Transcendentalists. Luker discusses the religious philosophy of Charleston's James Warley Miles, brother of prominent writer William Porcher Miles, and its similarities with European Transcendentalism. See "God, Man and the World of James Warley Miles, Charleston's Transcendentalist," *Historical Magazine of the Protestant Episcopal Church* 39 (June 1970), 101–36.

[55] For a biographical treatment of Samuel Gilman, see Daniel Walker Howe, "A Massachusetts Yankee in Senator Calhoun's Court: Samuel Gilman in South Carolina," *New England Quarterly* 44 (June 1971), 197–220. Howe credits Gilman with removing "the stigma" of Unitarianism in Charleston but argues that the New Englander never fully adopted his new home (201). Howe depicts Gilman as "a talented and conscientious man enervated by a stifling environment" (202).

[56] Samuel Gilman, "Ralph Waldo Emerson," *Southern Rose* 7 (November 24, 1838), 100.

of a respectable order, though, as it appears to us, much inferior to the scale assigned them by his fervent admirers."[57] Gilman correctly placed Emerson and his philosophy with Thomas Carlyle and the German romantics, and he found much in Emerson's addresses that were original and even inspiring. But Gilman, himself a Unitarian minister, was offended by Emerson's attacks on the clergy, calling them "offensive, wild, and unintelligible."[58] He, like many readers North and South, found Emerson difficult to understand, too often derivative, and unnecessarily provocative. "On the whole," Gilman summarized, "we cannot help concluding, that a writer, who seems to entertain no clear and definite principles ... is destined to make no very deep or permanent impression on the minds of his generation."[59] Despite his rather incorrect assessment of Emerson, Gilman's account almost certainly ranks as the first mention of the New England philosopher in any southern magazine. The Gilmans were more familiar with Emerson than perhaps any one else in Charleston because of their close ties to Boston. Because of this essay, Charlestonians and other southerners who subscribed to the *Southern Rose* may well have been acquainted with Emerson even before many northerners learned about him.

Despite her New England ties, Gilman vigorously defended her adopted region, and like many writers in the region she thought literature could help achieve southern intellectual independence from the North. Sarah Lawrence Griffin, like Gilman a woman who came to the Old South from New England, employed her literary and editorial talents to the *Family Companion and Ladies' Mirror*, which she started in 1841. More in line with the traditional women's periodical fare of the kind published in Gilman's magazines than with the outspoken views expressed by Barney and Royall, Griffin's monthly journal nonetheless contributed in important ways to Georgia's rich history of periodicals. She published the usual poetry and helpful hints for women, but she also included works by respected authors and thinkers. As she stated in the *Family Companion*, "While by our tales and essays we would enliven the fancy, cultivate the taste, and establish correct moral principles, we would cultivate the higher intellectual powers by essays of a more labored character.... Science, stripped of its mystery, tales, education, the house and garden will each receive its share of attention in our pages."[60] Griffin, new to journalism, sought advice from fellow author William Alexander Caruthers, who wrote to her in 1841, "You have madam, undertaken an arduous task, for one of your sex – yet I don't know but you endure & persevere under difficulties better than ours."[61]

[57] *Ibid.*

[58] *Ibid.*, 104.

[59] *Ibid.*, 105.

[60] *Family Companion and Ladies' Mirror*, 1 (October 15, 1841), 64.

[61] William Alexander Caruthers to Sarah Lawrence Griffin, May 30, 1841, published in Curtis Carroll David, "Dr. Caruthers Aids a Lady," *Georgia Historical Quarterly* 56 (Winter, 1972), 585.

One key feature of Griffin's journal was that it provided southern authors, including dozens of women both famous and unknown, with a forum for publishing their poetry, essays, and short stories. As Griffin stated in her introduction, "We ... hope that our COMPANION, may be the means of giving impetus to the talent of the ladies of Georgia, and become the organ of conveying some spark of the fire from Heaven ... which shall obliterate narrow prejudice."[62] She followed through on this promise.[63] She welcomed contributions from northern female authors such as Sigourney, Caroline Orne, Frances Sargent Osgood, and Emma Embry as well as southern writers and thinkers.[64] Griffin, like many transplanted northerners, did not question slavery and even complained about northern schoolbooks with an abolitionist bias being used in southern classrooms. Perhaps due to her pro-southern viewpoints, Griffin earned respect in and around Macon for her editorial and literary efforts. The *Macon Weekly Telegraph* praised Griffin as "a lady whose talents, attainments, experience and attractive amenity of deportment so amply qualify her" to edit a periodical. The paper, reflecting the frustration felt by many southerners when it came to supporting a regional magazine, remarked wryly, "We trust the generous patronage extended to the publication throughout the State, may be proved, that the productions of a fine mind and a pure heart, will be, not less cared for in Georgia, than those of Corn and Cotton."[65] Griffin's magazine reflected the eclectic nature of women's periodicals, and she offered literary fare that could be found in other publications like *Godey's*.

Other southern women editors, however, sought to generate a different readership altogether, presenting readers with articles on science, history, philosophy, or mathematics. Almira Spencer's *Young Ladies' Journal of Literature and Science*, published in Baltimore at the same time as Barney's *National Magazine*, offered diverse essays on topics from education to magnetism. Like Barney, Spencer made it clear in her opening essay "To the Public," a title that reflected the self-consciously public role that women editors played in the South, that she wanted to steer women away from reading "the silly love stories in which the genius of the times is so abundantly fruitful."[66] Her magazine consisted largely of light reading, with poetry and essays on female friendship, travel, and moral tales. Famous authors like Sigourney published numerous poems and short stories in the magazine, as did dozens of lesser-known women. Despite her desire to see young women read more substantive literature, Spencer was willing to print what Barney would not. Spencer's magazine

[62] Griffin, *Family Companion* 1 (December 15, 1841), 3.

[63] See Robert A. Rees and Marjorie Griffin, "Index and Author Guide to the *Family Companion*," *Studies in Bibliography* 25 (1972), 205–12.

[64] For a discussion of Simms' contributions to the magazine, see Rees and Griffin, "William Gilmore Simms and *The Family Companion*," 109–29.

[65] Anonymous, *Macon Weekly Telegraph* 15 (June 8, 1841), 3.

[66] Almira Spencer, "To the Public," *Young Ladies' Journal of Literature and Science* 1 (October 1830), 4.

was directed at a younger audience than Barney's *National Magazine*, and Spencer welcomed pieces such as "A Love Story" into her pages.[67]

Editors as far away as Vermont reprinted Spencer's magazine prospectus, testimony of the willingness of other editors to see the magazine succeed. Editors often printed such advertisements *gratis*, expecting that the favor would be returned in kind. Thus, without having to pay for her lengthy prospectus to be printed, Spencer was able to secure publication of her notice in the *Vermont Gazette*, the *Connecticut Mirror*, and the *Baltimore Patriot*.[68] Spencer believed she knew what parents and young women were looking for in a magazine because she had been involved in female education previous to establishing her journal. She spent nine years as a teacher in Philadelphia and two in Boston prior to moving to Baltimore, and she had served as the principal of a seminary for girls and young women.[69] The content of her magazine, despite its ambitious title, often harkened back to earlier notions of how best to prepare southern women for genteel society. Indeed, Spencer made clear that she intended her periodical "to foster the growth of learning, morals and piety in the hearts of those who, if properly trained, are to make sensible, enlightened, and accomplished women." She added that the need for such a journal "is highly approved by Ladies and Gentlemen of taste and judgment."[70]

"Taste" and "judgment" were, of course, highly subjective, and women editors like Spencer found it difficult to keep their magazines afloat. Journals rarely lasted more than a year or so, reflecting the demands on time and money that running a periodical required. One magazine that endured longer than most was Catherine Webb Barber's *Madison Visitor*. Like Gilman and Griffin, a native of Massachusetts, Barber came to the South to attend Alabama's Lafayette Female Seminary after the death of her father in 1843. After a brief stint as a teacher there, she moved to Georgia where she became one of the state's most prominent literary women as editor of the *Madison Visitor* newspaper from 1850 to 1853. The *Madison Visitor* included poetry and reviews of literature as well as local and national news. In addition to her editorial duties with the *Visitor*, Barber served as editor of the "Women's Department" of numerous magazines and newspapers.

Whereas she wrote for many southern periodicals, Barber achieved her greatest recognition as editor of the *Southern Literary Companion*, a weekly newspaper published in Newnan, Georgia, during the Civil War. The paper consisted mostly of occasional pieces of war news mixed with the poetry and prose by dozens of southern women, most of whom never

[67] Anonymous, "A Love Story," *Young Ladies' Journal of Literature and Science* 1 (December 1830), 106–11.

[68] See ads in *Vermont Gazette* 49 (August 9, 1831), 3; *Connecticut Mirror* 22 (September 11, 1830), 3; *Baltimore Patriot* 36 (August 31, 1830), no page number.

[69] Information taken from the prospectus printed in the Baltimore Patriot 36 (August 31, 1830), no page number.

[70] Prospectus for the *Young Ladies' Journal of Literature and Science*, *Baltimore Patriot* 36 (August 31, 1830), no page number.

achieved fame.[71] Below the masthead of her paper, Barber printed a motto that could have served as the cry of southern intellectuals, male and female alike: "A People's Education is a Nation's Best Defense." Barber represents well a much larger group of northern men and women who ventured South to carve out for themselves a small but important role in the intellectual life of the South, particularly in smaller towns.

Gilman, Barney, Spencer, Griffith, and Barber were fairly wealthy women, at least before financial hardship struck Barney when her husband was fired. The class implications are clear. Women editors hailed from upper- or middle-class backgrounds. Few, however, were as prominent socially as Lucy Virginia Smith French, who edited the *Southern Ladies' Book* in New Orleans in 1852 and 1853. French came from a well-educated Virginia family. Her father, Mease W. Smith, was professor of Greek and Latin and later president of Washington College. After schooling in Pennsylvania, Lucy Virginia Smith moved to Memphis to teach elementary school; and when she found the time, she sent poems to the *Louisville Journal* under the pseudonym "L'Inconnue." Her literary talents caught the eye of William T. Leonard, a New Orleans doctor who published the *Southern Ladies' Book* but who was searching for an editor to assume daily responsibilities for the journal. Leonard invited Smith to become associate editor of the magazine, soon leaving the endeavor entirely in her hands. Shortly after assuming her position as editor in early 1852, Smith married a wealthy Tennessean, Johns Hopkins French. She continued to edit the magazine until July 1853. French enjoyed editing, writing, and managing her periodical and was reluctant to end it even after marriage. Besides the requisite bow to the importance of female education, her *Southern Ladies' Book* proved more in tune to the literary currents of the period than many other women's magazines and attracted the notice of other periodicals throughout the region.[72] For example, the January 1853 issue contained reviews of both Harriet Beecher Stowe's *Uncle Tom's Cabin* and Sarah Josepha Hale's *Northwood*.[73] The journal contained discussions of periodical literature, examples of intelligent women from history, and a poem on Henry Clay.[74] After moving to McMinnville, Tennessee, with her husband late in 1853, French edited Nashville's *Southern Homestead*, and after the war she edited many

[71] See, for example, news about the war in *Southern Literary Companion* 6 (April 19, 1865) and Lincoln's assassination in 6 (May 17, 1865).

[72] For example, see the notice in the Marshall, Texas, *Star State Patriot* 5 (June 26, 1852), 2.

[73] "Uncle Tom's Cabin," "Northwood," *Southern Ladies' Book* 1 (January 1853), 175–81, 182–4. Smith published another, lengthy discussion of *Uncle Tom's Cabin* in the following (February 1853) issue, 226–38. The first discussion of *Uncle Tom's Cabin* was reprinted from the *Southern Standard*. Predictably, the essay criticized the novel: "This book, then, in our opinion, is one calculated to do serious harm; not at the South, but among that class of readers in the Northern States, who are prejudiced against the institution of slavery." See page 175.

[74] B. Birdeye, "Periodical Literature," *Southern Ladies' Book* 1 (November 1852),39–41; "Women of Genius," 1 (December 1852), 120–2; George D. Prentice, "Henry Clay," 2 (May 1853), 5.

other magazines and newspapers, including the *Sunny South* and the *Ladies' Home*. Like many southern women journalists and writers, French delivered public lectures throughout the region. "Mrs. L. Virginia French," a Georgia newspaper reported soon after the outbreak of the Civil War, "a lady of decidedly literary talent and reputation, has written a series of lectures, appropriate and relating to the times, which it is her intention to deliver through the principal cities in the South – the proceeds to be appropriated to the purchase of winter clothing for the Confederate soldiers in Missouri."[75]

Though French supported the Confederacy, she was not completely blinded by sectional animosity. Like fellow male and female southern authors and editors, French viewed careers in journalism and writing as legitimate professions of their own. After the war, she felt compelled to defend her southern colleague, editor John R. Thompson, who moved from Virginia to New York to continue his career. Thompson was chastised by some southerners for his supposed betrayal of his native region. But French came to his aid, proclaiming that the professional author and journalist had an obligation to uphold standards and rates of pay even if the pursuit of those rewards was detrimental to the cause of southern literature. "When we have a commodity to sell," French reminded southerners, "we *will* sell to the highest bidder. We may deprecate the *necessity* of selling the best brains of the South to *Harper*, which for years past has undergone torments to prove that the South *has no brains at all* – but is it not a splendid contradiction to this theory that 'Harper' now buys Southern brains at higher rates than the South itself is willing to accord them?"[76] By the time of her death in 1881, French had acquired enough of a national reputation to warrant an obituary in the *New York Times*.[77]

French also contributed to other southern periodicals for women, such as Mrs. E. M. Eaton's *Aurora*, a "Monthly for the Mothers and Daughters of the South and West," published in Murfreesboro, Tennessee, in the late 1850s. Like other magazines for women, the *Aurora* consisted largely of light poetry and essays, with occasional articles on female education and examples from history and biography of "Genius in Women."[78] In common with many other periodicals North and South, Eaton fretted over unpaid subscriptions. The financial state of the enterprise was at one point so bleak that Eaton wrote in the *Aurora* of a $3,000 debt. She even threatened to name in print "a list of subscribers who are in arrears," but the journal survived only a few issues.[79] Most women's periodicals lasted little longer than the myriad other northern and southern magazines that appeared briefly, only to perish with the ubiquitous plea: "Subscribers: pay up!" on their final, dying pages. Historians have enough testimony from southern editors to

[75] *Macon Daily Telegraph* (September 9, 1861), 4.

[76] French, "Pen-Feather," *Land We Love* 6 (December 1868), 148, quoted in Jay B. Hubbell, *The South in American Literature* (Durham, 1954), 711.

[77] April 1, 1881, page 5, column 4.

[78] "Genius in Women," *Aurora* 2 (August 1859), 410–1.

[79] See the end of the *Aurora* issue 2 (May 1859).

know that southerners' sense of honor was mysteriously absent when it came to paying for subscriptions. Still, the southern press faithfully carried out its duty to provide the journal with free publicity; the Texas *State Gazette*, published in Austin, told its readers that Eaton's journal was "neatly gotten up" and deserved their patronage.[80]

During the 1850s, women continued to edit periodicals, though there appears to have been fewer published in the South in the years immediately preceding the Civil War than there were in the 1830s and 1840s. In addition to Virginia Smith French and Eaton, Frances Webb Bumpass edited Greensboro's *Weekly Message* in the 1850s.[81] Keeping a literary enterprise afloat was a difficult task, made all the more so when the duties of editorship were thrust on women. Sidney D. Bumpass's *Weekly Message*, a Greensboro, North Carolina, newspaper that began in October 1851 as a religious and literary paper interspersed with news on local and national affairs, exhibited an interest in women's issues from its first number. After Bumpass's death only one month later, his widow Frances assumed the editorship and conducted the paper for many years. Paying particular attention to female education in North Carolina, the *Weekly Message* contained news about the teachers, students, examinations, and other affairs of the Greensboro Female College, the Somerville Female Institute, and the Carolina Female College.

Mrs. E. P. Elam of Richmond started a magazine for women and children titled the *Family Christian Album* in January 1855. The first issue contained "Remarks of the Editress," which recounted her purpose in beginning a family periodical. "To mothers," Elam remarked on her paper, "who are solicitous for the moral and religious training of their children, I especially dedicate it." Even given the traditional content, however, Elam admitted to "feelings of timidity and much anxiety" in the first sentence of the magazine.[82] In her thirty-page monthly paper, Elam included articles such as "Maternal Thoughts," "Filial Affection," and "The Value of a Good Countenance." There were few flourishes and no pictures or woodcuts that might have appealed to readers, but Elam did include sections such as "Juvenile Department" and "Gleanings," the latter included brief observations and musings on subjects as various as "Egyptian Discoveries" and war in China.[83] The *Family Christian Album* must have acquired enough subscribers to keep it afloat at least until September 1856, when it appeared in an advertisement in the *American Publishing Circular*.[84] Indeed, as the fellow Richmond journal *Southern Literary Messenger* remarked in language common to magazines that wished to provide positive comments for other editors, "We trust it will be universally welcomed into the family circle, and that the gifted lady who has undertaken

[80] Texas *State Gazette* 9 (May 15, 1858), 2.

[81] On Bumpass, see Wells, *Origins of the Southern Middle Class*, 125–7.

[82] Mrs. E. P. Elam, "Remarks of the Editress," *Family Christian Album* 1 (January 1855), 1.

[83] *Family Christian Album* 1 (January 1855).

[84] *American Publishing Circular and Literary Gazette* 2 (September 6, 1856).

its management will be rewarded with the most abundant patronage of the lovers of Christian literature."[85]

Elam's social class appears not to have equaled the high standing and wealth of women literati like French. But women of middling status also found ways to edit periodicals. Rachel Jones Holton found herself head of a small business with the death of her husband Thomas in 1860. Although she eventually settled in North Carolina, Holton was born in Richmond in 1813. She became a teacher and moved to Cabarrus County in southwestern North Carolina where she met Thomas Jefferson Holton, then editor of the *Catawba Journal*. After marrying in 1834, they moved to Charlotte where Thomas Holton edited a newspaper titled the *Miners' and Farmers' Journal*, which lasted five years and consisted of local news, articles selected from northern periodicals, and essays on farming. Although Thomas Holton claimed in the opening issue of the *Journal* that "it is to be no party paper," the Whiggish political leanings of the Holtons found their way into the paper in essays favorable to railroads, canals, and other internal improvements.[86] The *Miners' and Farmers' Journal* became the *Charlotte Journal* in 1835; in 1851, the Holtons dropped all pretenses of nonpartisanship and changed the paper's name to the *North Carolina Whig*. Although Thomas was mainly responsible for the daily operation of all of the papers, Rachael remained an important part of the enterprise. This experience proved valuable when Thomas died just two days after Christmas in 1860, leaving Rachel alone to raise their eleven children. Yet, unlike Frances Bumpass, who struggled with self-doubt and waited months before taking over the *Weekly Message*, Rachel immediately seized the operation of the *North Carolina Whig*. The paper lasted well into the Civil War, long after the Whig party itself managed to survive.

One of the most remarkable magazines edited by a female editor was Petersburg, Virginia's *The Kaleidoscope*, published in the mid-1850s. The newspaper-size periodical was one of the only weekly journal edited by a southern woman before the Civil War, but what really made the eight-page paper unusual was its outspokenness on gender, politics, and literature. Rebecca Brodnax, born in Brunswick County, Virginia, in 1823, was educated at a school in Richmond. At the age of twenty-one, she married Dr. Benjamin Isaac Hicks, and the couple eventually had four daughters. Like other southern literary women, Hicks did not let her domestic duties impede her desire to write. She published poems in *The Southern Literary Messenger* in the early 1850s and a serialized tale in New York's *Putnam's Magazine*. By the time she had set her sights on becoming a magazine editor, she had published two novels: *The Lady Killer* (1851) and *The Milliner and the Millionaire* (1853).[87]

[85] John R. Thompson, "Editor's Table," *Southern Literary Messenger* 21 (March 1855), 190.

[86] See, for example, "Canals in the United States," *Miners' and Farmers' Journal* 1 (October 18, 1830). Quotation comes from 1 (September 27, 1830).

[87] Barbara Browder, *A Virginia Woman of the 1850s Speaks Out* (unpublished ms., 1988); copy available at the Virginia Historical Society.

Hicks knew that to run a periodical she needed to have access to writers, printers, and the post office, all of which were in short supply in the small town of Lawrenceville. However, given her husband's medical practice the family could hardly afford to move, so each week Hicks left Lawrenceville and her family and ventured into Petersburg to conduct the business of running a magazine. Of course, this was highly unusual, and her commute did not escape the notice of friends and neighbors. Leaving home to edit and conduct the business of a journal, however, was merely the beginning of her willingness to counter tradition.

Although *The Kaleidoscope* was subtitled "A Family Journal, Devoted to Literature, Temperance, and Education," Hicks wasted little time in delving into a wide range of political topics. Literature did indeed occupy much of the weekly; Hicks herself published two serialized novels in the paper in 1855 and 1856, "The Miser's Daughter" and "Coy Fannie Vane." She published poetry by both women and men and printed short fiction, biographies, commentaries on authors and other periodicals, and essays on topics such as education. Each issue was an eclectic mix of prose, fiction, and poetry, with four large columns filled with material Hicks hoped would attract a long list of subscribers to her magazine, priced at the moderate sum of two dollars per year. As rich as the literary columns are, however, Hicks made her mark as a woman editor by publishing an editorial nearly each week, addressing topics from women's rights to temperance to slavery and the South.

In one of her first editorials, published in January 1855, Hicks made clear her forthrightness and exhibited an engaging style, and even some tongue-in-cheek boasting of the importance of her magazine. "The intellect of Petersburg pines for us before we came," she asserted, "and we aspire to be the nucleus around which nascent ideas may revolve.... Who dares say that the Kaleidoscope is an interloper?"[88] In the same issue, she defended the northern writer Fanny Fern against critics, solicited advertisements for her paper, reviewed new books, published a new chapter of her serialized novel "The Miser's Daughter," printed stories for children, reported news on farming, and corresponded with letter writers to the journal. She carried on this hectic pace, writing and editing while also conducting the journal's business, not to mention raising a family. Nearly each week she returned to offer subscribers a collection of mostly original works, including her often bold editorials.

Hicks, like most southern women journalists, did not wish to be seen in the same light as British or northeastern advocates of women's rights, but her editorials nonetheless were sometimes as audacious as anything written in the North. In just the fourth number of *The Kaleidoscope*, Hicks published a lengthy editorial, "Woman's Rights," in which she expressed her views on gender roles. "That the sole object of a woman's life is *not* fashion, dress, establishments, and matrimony," she declared, "I sincerely hope the nineteenth

[88] Rebecca Hicks, "To Our Readers," *The Kaleidoscope* 1 (January 24, 1855), 13.

century will triumphantly prove."[89] She devoted most of the editorial "to prove that we have good cause for complaint" because of how "unfair" the "injustice" to women has been. In six lengthy columns of newsprint, she argued "that men are often unjust and ungenerous in their requirements of us." "In the first place," she contends, "they set themselves up as judges and lawgivers over us – viewing everything from *their* standpoint, and nothing from *ours*." Even worse, perhaps, men used that power to suppress women: "Then they are eternally meddling with our little preferences, our weaknesses, our imperfections, and even our personal defects." "I should like to hold the mirror up to men, and let them see themselves as we women see them ... to ridicule them, to sneer at them, to annihilate their provoking conceit."

Hicks was insightful enough to realize that differences in the accomplishments of the sexes were due to differences in upbringing, not innate abilities. She prefigured later feminists in arguing that perceptions of appropriate pursuits for women were based merely on tradition and discrimination and not on biological distinctions. She angrily protested that women were shunned if they expressed interest in traditionally masculine subjects: "They deny us all interest in matters of importance, and then sneer at us for being interested in matters of no importance! They swear we shall not vote or take any part in the affairs of the nation, and then cry out because of the importance we attach to our bonnets and dresses! ... Woman shall be nothing, and she shall be everything, cries ungenerous man." Hicks felt, as did many women journalists and writers, that her abilities warranted a broader sphere of influence. For her, editing a magazine and freely offering her opinions on discrimination was the most effective path to persuading readers of the need for greater gender equality.

In the same editorial, Hicks stressed the double standards of nineteenth-century society, particularly in regard to marriage. Though she herself seems to have had a better marriage than most, Hicks could see clearly the price women paid for being loyal wives:

> "She shall be useful, and she shall be ornamental. She shall be universally admired, and yet scorn all men but her lord and master.... She shall bring all her treasures and the fortune her father gave her, and lay it, with her love and fealty at my feet; and I may take all this thanklessly, and squander it in any way I like, and abuse her, and maltreat her, and leave her children destitute, and she shall not dare to open her lips! ... She shall be faithful, cries ungenerous man, though I am unfaithful; tender though I am harsh.... She shall yield to my wishes, though I scorn to consult hers. She shall be wise, and yet foolish enough to think *I* am her superior!"

In the repetition of the phrase "she shall," Hicks echoed the list of complaints of the Seneca Falls Declaration just a few years before. And like her northern

[89] Rebecca Hicks, "Woman's Rights," *The Kaleidoscope* 1 (February 7, 1855), 28. The italics are in the original. The next several quotations come from this editorial, which covered much of pages 28 and 29.

sisters, she argued that women should be allowed into all professions. "I, who have seen man-milliners, and man-dress-makers, can see nothing ridiculous in a female physician for females.... And I *do* say, at the risk of everything, that when [men] come *en masse*, and seize all our employments, and leave nothing in the world whereby we can make a decent living, that it is nothing more than fair play, that we should don the pantaloons, and try to drive them back to their places." Hicks understood that her unusual occupation as an editor provided a public forum for expressing opinions unavailable any other way, and she referred to her status as a journalist often. In Hicks, the political power and intellectual freedom of editorship was the vital platform for denouncing gender discrimination.

Because her role as editor was central to her identity, Hicks reacted angrily when she was treated differently from her male counterparts. Her outspokenness apparently generated opposition, for rumors circulated that her husband strongly disapproved of her periodical. In response, Benjamin Hicks wrote a short explanation that was printed on cards and published in a few issues of *The Kaleidoscope* in the summer of 1855. Dr. Hicks wanted to make clear that he supported his wife, and that "those who *profess* to be *his* friends would remember that *nobody can be a friend to him who is not a friend to his wife*."[90] Hicks continued to feel keenly that she was unwelcome among the male editorship. When a convention of editors met in Richmond, she devoted a lengthy editorial to the unjustness of her exclusion. "Among the journalists of Virginia," she wrote, "whether we are regarded as an interloper, or a *rara avis*, or both we cannot say." When she failed to receive even a notice of the convention, let alone an invitation to attend, she reacted hurtfully, lamenting that "no intimation was given to us that we were recognized as one of the profession." She criticized the "awful conclave" for its secrecy and for leaving her out, claiming that perhaps the editors should be classed with the same fraternity of "Free Masonry, Odd-Fellowship, and Know-Nothingism."[91] With hurt feelings, but perhaps feeling even more acutely the disrespect of what she considered her journalist colleagues, Hicks lashed out with her pen, scorning "the cowardly wretch who had first proposed the meeting." Hicks would go on to write for many years until her death after the war, and her legacy was an important one. With unusual boldness on questions of gender, she laid bare society's discrimination against women.

Despite the substantial number of southern women editors, historians know little about them, and thus female intellectual culture, much like the intellectual culture of the Old South in general, remains hidden. The literary women of the Old South are worthy of further study, beginning with basic biographical research, because they can tell us much about the South in the antebellum

[90] Benjamin Hicks, "Special Notice," *The Kaleidoscope* 1 (June 20, 1855), 180.

[91] Rebecca Hicks, "That Editorial Convention," *The Kaleidoscope* 1 (November 14, 1855), 348.

period. The magazines and newspapers are in part a reflection of these women's own values, what literature they thought worthy of publishing, which news articles they deemed of interest to their readers, and which authors they thought would bring respect to their enterprise; but the magazines also reflect more flexible notions of southern womanhood than we expect. Indeed, some periodicals, like Mary Chase Barney's *National Magazine*, served as important platforms for the expression of personal and political views while also printing literature simply for the quiet enjoyment of leisure. Whether or not they used the pages of their magazines explicitly to attack traditional notions of gender roles, women editors by their very occupation challenged the idea that woman's sole province was the domestic sphere. At the same time, only a modicum of protest ever emerged from those opposed to women as editors, suggesting that southerners accepted women in positions as business and literature that were traditionally defined as masculine. Women editors, regardless of their ideological position, demonstrate that the notion of separate spheres was contested and complicated in the Old South, as it was in the antebellum North.

After 1820, however, increasing educational opportunities and higher literacy among southern women laid the foundation for greater numbers of women to assume the duties of editorship.[92] Southern women like Barney and Royall provide evidence that female editors sometimes stepped significantly beyond the accepted boundaries of woman's domestic sphere. Unlike early literary women who studiously avoided delving into political debates, Barney and Royall foreshadow later nineteenth- and early twentieth-century southern women like Georgia's Rebecca Latimer Felton who used their work in literature as platforms from which to launch political careers promoting women's rights. Moreover, unlike the women editors of the early 1800s, who relied on public sympathy with their widowhood to assume editorships, Barney and Royall were not widows at the time at which they began their literary and political careers. The southern women who edited periodicals in the first decades of the nineteenth century were indeed pioneers, and their efforts were carried on in the later antebellum decades in a continuing effort to push gender boundaries. It would be the work of later nineteenth-century female journalists who would expand on these efforts as well as suffragettes in the postwar period who would carry the work of women editors to its logical fruition. Women who could effectively engage politics and literature in the precarious business of periodical editing could also lay claim to broader participation in the political process.

[92] For a discussion of literary and educational advances made by women in the early years of the nineteenth century, see Mary Kelley's essays, "'Vindicating the Equality of Female Intellect,'" and "Reading Women/Women Reading," 401–24.

PART THREE

WOMEN JOURNALISTS AND WRITERS IN THE NEW SOUTH

At the end of the nineteenth century, a new invention sparked a revolution in home publishing. Early in the century, young women like Sarah Cooper, Nannie Grant, and Paulina Warinner dreamed of editing their own newspapers, and the power of those aspirations is reflected in the details they incorporated into their hand-drawn magazines. Although meant only for private reading among friends, the hand-drawn periodicals were tangible expressions of southern women's dreams of a life beyond domesticity. Soon after the Civil War, inventors began experimenting with smaller printing presses designed for the home. Benjamin Woods of Boston offered one of the first of these early presses for sale, and his Novelty Press attracted buyers across the country. In 1872, Connecticut's William A. Kelsey developed a new small printing press, offering the invention for sale in periodicals like the *Youth's Companion*. By 1875, Kelsey's press was self-inking, rendering the publishing and distribution of magazines even more accessible to children and adults.[1]

Twelve-year-old Eva H. Britton began printing her amateur paper, *The Hurricane*, from her Charleston home in 1879. The subtitle of the paper, "Devoted to Fun, Frolic and Fancy," mirrored the earlier hand-drawn papers. But *The Hurricane* was more professional-looking than aspiring female editors could have hoped for in the early 1800s. With a masthead, three columns of text, and four pages, each amateur newspaper had the look and feel of nationally distributed journals. And unlike the handcrafted papers sketched by earlier women, Britton's magazine was offered to the public for subscriptions.

In *The Hurricane*, Britton offered readers poetry, short bits of local news, and serialized stories. Even though many of the articles were no doubt gathered from other sources, Britton's personality shines through the pages. She is listed on page two as "Editress and Proprietress," and each issue contained a section entitled "Our Say." In the September 1879 issue, Britton commented on local politics, noting that the Charleston mayoral race approached. "The

[1] Truman J. Spencer, *Amateur Journalism* (New York, 1957), 15.

political sky is rapidly clouding," Britton remarked, "and the politicians have begun their accustomed 'mud-throwing.' Every claimant for the Mayorality claims to be the regular Democratic candidate, and things will be pretty mixed on election day if there are three *regular* Democratic tickets in the field." Despite her grown-up assessment of one-party rule in the Solid South, Britton was still obviously a child. She remarked in the same section how much she looked forward to the end of summer vacation and to sitting next to her friends again at school. On the last page, she claimed a circulation of 500, printed advertisements for an array of goods and services, and announced that paying subscribers "would not miss 30 cents a year."

The Hurricane was not the only amateur newspaper edited by a southern woman. Addie Humble edited *The Southernwood and Myrtle* in Washington, Louisiana, and Mary M. Darr published *The Sumter Mirror* in South Carolina, among dozens of others. In fact, Kelsey's press helped inaugurate an amateur publishing craze that swept the country. Hundreds, perhaps thousands, of amateur newspapers sprung up throughout the nation, and southern men and women actively joined in the trend. Clubs like the Southern Amateur Press Association and the South Eastern Amateur Press Association flourished, and southern men and women eagerly joined national amateur press associations.

However, southern racism kept out African Americans who wanted to join in the small press enthusiasm. In 1879, the same year that Britton started *The Hurricane*, the National Amateur Press Association elected an African American, Ohio's Herbert A. Clarke, to its leadership as third vice president. White southerners like North Carolina's Edward Oldham and George M. Carr reacted angrily to Clarke's election, and southern whites stormed out of the proceedings to form their own whites-only press association. The Amateur Anti-Negro Admission Association reflected the extent to which virulent racism had penetrated into every corner of southern life. The group's constitution stated the chief aim: "To prevent the admission of negro members into the white amateur journalists' associations of the United States."[2] Members had to pledge an oath to follow the policy of supporting only white candidates for offices in national and local associations. The group's plan to publish a new paper called *The Anti-Negroite* apparently never came to pass, but the prejudice of the whites-only group was clear enough.

The struggle over race demonstrates the possibilities and certainly the limitations of justice in the South. The amateur press allowed larger numbers of southern women new opportunities to publish their own papers, opening spaces in the public sphere for self-expression, individuality, and creativity. However, while gender equality found expression in southern periodicals in the late nineteenth century, so too did prejudice. In the late 1800s, southern white and black journalists – both men and women – continued to talk

[2] John Travis Nixon, *History of the National Amateur Press Association* (Crowley, LA, 1900), 59–60.

past each other. White racism kept amateur associations segregated, a pattern paralleled in the professional groups of the era. Because of segregation, African-American men and women would form their own press associations, and periodicals led by black female editors would flourish despite continued white racism.

6

New South Periodicals and a New Literary Culture

In 1876, *The People's Advocate*, an African American newspaper published in Alexandria, Virginia, printed an article titled "How a Woman Reads a Newspaper."[1] Mocking female readers, the newspaper chided them for cherishing "a vague belief that newspapers are the enemies of her sex, and editors its chief oppressors." "She never reads the headlines ... she is greedy for local news, and ... marriages and deaths are always interesting reading to her, and advertisements are exciting and stimulating.... Views are of no importance in her estimation, but facts are everything ... she reads stories, and sketches, and paragraphs indiscriminately, and believes every word of them." After such reading, the article claimed, the disappointed woman puts down the paper, convinced that if she only "had a chance she could make the only perfect newspaper the world has ever seen." Such ridicule heaped on women readers was, of course, grossly unfair, because by 1876 women were clearly not only reading national news, editorials, and highly opinionated columns but writing them as well.

Still, the denigrating tone of the article in *The People's Advocate* did stumble upon one truth: that many women did indeed believe that they could produce more interesting periodicals than their male journalistic colleagues. As editors, authors, and readers of periodicals during the Civil War and in the New South, southern black and white women established important precedents for female journalism in which virtually no subject was beyond their purview. From the harshest days of the war to the turn of the twentieth century, these women played central roles in the expanding publishing industry.

We know that white southern women nursed soldiers behind the battle lines, often tending to wounded or dying men. Women comforted soldiers by bringing water, mopping damp foreheads, changing dressings, or by simply holding the hand of the dying. As soldiers' letters and diaries attest, reading aloud was one of the most important ways in which women comforted patients.

[1] "How a Woman Reads a Newspaper," *The People's Advocate* 1 (May 13, 1876).

Long recognized for the important part they played as Confederate nurses, southern women also calmed soldiers by reading them novels, poetry, and periodicals.

In the earliest months of the war, southern women were already gathering books and other reading material to ease the suffering of men hurt in battle. In August 1861, Eliza Howland helped to soothe the injured in her hometown. The local college had been converted to a hospital, and while other women served as nurses she elected to use whatever literary talents she possessed to aid the war effort: "We spent the morning there helping them, reading to the men, writing letters for them, etc."[2] She continued these contributions throughout the early years of the war, remarking in a letter in October 1861 that she was "just going up the Columbian College to cover and arrange a nice box of books ... to form the nucleus of a hospital library – an excellent selection of books, histories, biographies, etc; half-worn, but the covering and labeling we mean to put them through will make them" much appreciated by the soldiers.[3]

Soldiers often found special meaning in the readings. As Judith McGuire recorded in her diary in 1862, "I returned to my post by the bedside of the soldiers. Some of them are very fond of hearing the Bible read; and am yet to see the first soldier who has not received with apparent interest any proposition of being read to from the Bible." McGuire was careful to select stories that would have relevance to the soldiers. As McGuire continued, "To-day, while reading an elderly man of strong, intelligent face sat on the side of the bed, listening with interest. I read of the wars of the Israelites and the Philistines. He presently said, 'I know why you read that chapter; it is to encourage us, because the Yankee armies are so much bigger.'"[4] McGuire referred to her "post" as a reader, indicating that she believed she was making an important contribution to the cause. Like McGuire, Kate Cumming also worked hard to find reading of interest to the wounded. As she wrote in her diary in 1862, "I have spent the day talking and reading to the men; they like to hear us read to them, but they do not seem to care much for reading themselves." Picking up copies of the *Illustrated London News*, Cumming read to the men about the Crimean War, for "I thought if anything would interest them these would."[5]

Women also read to stay informed during the war, especially by perusing newspapers. "I see all the Washington papers," Blanche Butler Ames remarked

[2] Eliza Newton Woolsey Howland to Joseph Howland, August, 1861, in Georgeanna Woolsey Bacon and Eliza Woolsey Howland, eds., *Letters of a Family During the War for the Union* (New Haven, 1899), 142.

[3] Eliza Newton Woolsey Howland to Joseph Howland, October 1, 1861, in Bacon and Woolsey, eds., *Letters of a Family*, 194.

[4] Entry dated March 1862, Diary of Judith White Brockenbrough McGuire, in *Diary of a Southern Refugee During the War* (New York, 1867), 97.

[5] Entry dated May 1862, Diary of Kate Cumming, in Richard Barksdale Harwell, ed., *Kate: the Journal of a Confederate Nurse* (Baton Rouge, 1998), 31.

in 1864, "and some of the New York."[6] Like Ames, Ella Gertrude Thomas noted in her diary in the summer of 1864, "Tonight since tea have been reading the papers. The subject of an armistice is attracting general attention. I do not feel sanguine with regard to it and indeed think that it would be a suicidal move on the part of our government to agree to an armistice."[7] Of course, reading the newspapers could worsen fears. As Catherine Edmondston boiled, "Have just been reading the accounts of the outrages of the Yankees about Elizabeth City [North Carolina] and am at fever heat."[8]

Despite the potential for frustration, women also used reading as a diversion from the troubles surrounding them. As Ella Gertrude Thomas revealed toward the end of the war in March 1865, "I strive to get away, to forget in reading or in writing or in talking the ever present, the one absorbing theme of war and thus it is thrust upon me."[9] But whether southern women read to serve at their post beside the casualties of war, to stay informed of the happenings on the battlefield, or to try to escape the horrors of the time, reading was a vitally important activity, even a necessity, for women during the Civil War. Periodicals, as much as novels, provided a diverse reading experience, particularly when it came to discussions of the meaning of gender differences.

Periodicals were one of the few wartime forums in which discussions of gender equality could receive a public hearing. In a fall 1861 essay in *De Bow's Review*, for example, the fight for southern independence became a fight for greater opportunities for women. Any deficiencies in the elevation or treatment of women were due to "Yankee influence." "We can but believe that there was in the minds of Southern women," the essayist continued, "an instinctive perception of the great advantages which would result to their sex from Southern independence, which helped to make them such bold advocates of secession." Exactly what women's reward might be, the author did not say. However, this author argued, "In demanding a more extended mental culture and a more enlarged sphere of action, woman demands no more than is just and reasonable." In arguing for a more enlarged range of opportunities, this author employed the term "woman's rights." "We are in favor of woman's rights in the highest, noblest sense, and therefore we plead her claim for a higher intellectual culture." The contributor to *De Bow's* rejected the "Yankee version" of woman's rights that would allow women to venture into careers occupied by men, but admitted that "the woman's rights movement had some basis of truth."[10] So just as they had before the Civil War, southerners interested in debating the meaning of gender difference found magazines to be essential, even during the exigencies of war.

6 Blanche Butler Ames to Sarah Hildreth Butler, June 1, 1864, in *Chronicles from the Nineteenth Century*, 106.

7 Entry for August 1864, Diary of Ella Gertrude Thomas, in Burr, ed., *Secret Eye*, 233.

8 Entry for April 1862, Diary of Catherine Ann Devereux Edmondston, in Crabtree, ed., *Journal of a Secesh Lady*, 160.

9 Entry for March 1865, Diary of Ella Gertrude Thomas, in Burr, ed., *Secret Eye*, 257.

10 "Education of Southern Women," *De Bow's Review* n.s. 6 (October/November 1861), 383, 387, 388, 390.

Southerners started new periodicals even in the midst of the Civil War and Reconstruction. Throughout the 1860s and 1870s, dozens of magazines launched. Between 1860 and 1869, 182 quarterly, monthly, and weekly journals began, some of which were fleeting, comprising only a few issues, others of which endured for years. In the wartime South, paper became increasingly hard to come by, and one scholar found that at least thirteen periodicals were printed on wallpaper.[11] Acquiring quality contributions and engaging printers proved equally challenging. A Virginia publisher complained during the war as he closed down his paper, "The proprietor has been reluctantly compelled to this decision in consequence of the lack of paper, ink, editors and printers.... He furthermore begs to state that in consequence of the editor, the compositors and the printers having gone off to war, the devil only is left in the office."[12]

Battling scarcity of paper and machinery during the war, not to mention the diverted attention of writers, illustrators, poets, and other potential contributors, wartime periodicals were surprisingly resilient. Many journals reported on the events of the war, defended slavery and states' rights in support of the Confederate cause, or published poems (particularly by women authors) to celebrate fallen soldiers and the glory of the fight against Yankee tyranny. The *Southern Monthly*, published in Memphis in 1861 and 1862, lasted only a few issues but provided a forum for wartime literature. As they had before the war, magazines like the *Southern Monthly* advocated the creation of a distinctly southern literature that was free from the taint of northern sentiments. Though not directed specifically at a female audience, journals like the *Southern Monthly* eagerly published works by southern women, such as the poetry of Lena Lyle of Germantown, Tennessee.[13] Similarly, *Southern Punch*, a Richmond weekly published between 1863 and 1865, reminded readers of the need for humor in the midst of war. The *Southern Illustrated News*, the *Magnolia*, and the *Illustrated Mercury* were other magazines that filled an important need for readers and authors on the home front.[14]

The *Southern Illustrated News*, published in Richmond from 1862 to 1865, was a particularly important periodical for southerners. That women and girls read the magazine is evidenced by the many poems by female contributors, as well as letters to the editor written by female readers. For example, in late 1862, a young woman from Virginia wrote to complain of being ostracized by her peers for wearing a homespun dress. "Don't you think it would be more patriotic in our girls to wear home spun dresses," a letter writer named Louise asked the editors, "instead of wearing such doleful faces about the blockade, just because they can't get such lots of fine dresses and other finery

[11] Ray Morris Atchison, "Southern Literary Magazines, 1865–1887," (Ph.D. dissertation, Duke University, 1956), 16.

[12] Quoted in Frank Luther Mott, *American Journalism: A History, 1690–1960* (New York, 1963), 363, and in Atchison, "Southern Literary Magazines," 15.

[13] Sam G. Riley, *Magazines of the American South* (Westport, CT, 1986), 247–9.

[14] *Ibid.*, 247.

as they used to in times back?"[15] The editors agreed with "Louise" and chastised those who scorned such a prudent southern girl. When Louise asked if she should wear such a dress again, the editors responded forcefully. "Advise you to wear it again? Why, most assuredly; and when it is worn out, send us a piece, that we may put it away with other highly prized mementoes of this war, to remind us in after years that there was one brave little heart somewhere in the Old Dominion, that pulsated with *genuine patriotism*, and with whom '*duty*' was a higher word than '*fashion*.'"[16]

Whereas the *Southern Illustrated News* often published news from the battlefields, *The Southern Field and Fireside* was an important periodical published during the war years that leaned more toward literature and domestic articles. Published in Augusta, Georgia, *The Southern Field and Fireside* was a treasure trove of short fiction, poetry, and serialized novels by leading women writers like Sue Petigru Bowen, Mary Edwards Bryan, Annie R. Blount, Eliza Cook, Mary Bayard Clarke, Laura Lincoln, Julia Pleasants Creswell, and others. Important male writers, including Paul Hamilton Hayne and John R. Thompson contributed to the weekly paper as well. Although the magazine was generally focused on literature, child rearing, agriculture, and domesticity, it occasionally offered views on the military and political course of the war.[17]

Unlike the *Southern Illustrated News* and *The Southern Field and Fireside*, both of which appealed to male and female readers alike, the *Magnolia: A Southern Home Journal*, published in the Confederate capital from 1862 to 1865, targeted a female readership; the title page of the weekly journal featured a picture of a female writer busy at her desk.[18] Although avoiding politics, the paper published reports of the latest battles as well as news of Confederate government activities. Mixed in with such reports were short stories, serialized novels, poems, and letters to the editor, Charles Bailie. By 1863, the paper's title page featured a picture of "a more warlike woman with a helmet surrounded by globe, easel, writings, and books."[19] A new feature was added, titled "Notes on the War," bringing women subscribers updated information on the progress of Confederate forces. The magazine ceased publication in April 1865, shortly before Lee surrendered to Grant, enduring until the lack of supplies rendered continuation of the paper impossible.

Lack of resources and supplies, the diverted attention of contributors and readers, and the collapsing transportation infrastructure worked together to make wartime journalism in the South an immensely difficult task. Almost as

[15] "The Home Spun Dress," *Southern Illustrated News* 1 (November 8, 1862), 3.

[16] *Ibid.*

[17] "The Housewife's Manual," *Southern Field and Fireside* 1 (March 14, 1863), 87.

[18] Kathleen L. Endres, "The Magnolia: A Southern Home Journal," in Endres and Therese L. Lueck, eds., *Women's Periodicals in the United States: Consumer Magazines* (Westport, CT, 1995), 205.

[19] *Ibid.*, 206.

soon as the fighting ended, however, southern editors optimistically embarked on new journalistic endeavors. The immediate postwar period witnessed a number of important periodicals begun by enterprising editors, some of which catered to female readers. *Scott's Monthly Magazine*, published in Atlanta beginning in December 1865 by William J. Scott, was significant as the home of many postwar southern authors, such as Hayne, Sidney Lanier, and Henry Timrod. Alongside these important southern male writers, dozens of poems and short stories by women authors also appeared.[20] Catherine Webb Barber, an editor herself, published her novelette *Briarbrook* over several numbers in 1866 alongside work by prominent southern male authors, including Timrod and Hayne.[21]

Indeed, though edited by a man, *Scott's Monthly* actively encouraged women's literary endeavors. The journal published news of a National Woman's Rights Convention held in New York, reported on L. Virginia French's visit to Atlanta, and helped to promote a new family monthly paper edited by Barber.[22] Regarding Barber, who had already edited at least two other Georgia magazines before and during the Civil War, Scott remarked that "those who are acquainted with the literary qualifications of Miss Barber need no assurance that [she] is entitled to a liberal patronage from a generous and appreciative public."[23] Given the destruction wrought by the war, Atlanta was a difficult city in which to start a new periodical. In fact, several newspapers there folded between 1868 and 1872.[24]

Many of the same problems that plagued prewar editors, male and female alike, continued into the post–Civil War era. Nonpayment of subscriptions was a constant source of editorial frustration. *Scott's Monthly Magazine*, which cost five dollars per year, complained in July 1866 that "we still have a number of subscribers who have neglected to remit us the amount of their subscriptions." Editor Scott did not question his readers' honesty, remarking that "in a majority of instances this is the result of forgetfulness." But he still wished the nonpayers would "lighten our present burden" by sending in their five dollars, and he hoped that "there will be no occasion to allude to this subject again."[25] Nonpaying readers continued to irritate editors, and many a departing journalist complained bitterly about the absence of honor when it came to receiving promised money from subscribers.

Until the postwar period, the gender of editors remained the same during the periodical's entire run. Periodicals rarely alternated between male and female editors over their publishing lives. One of the first postwar magazines to break this trend was Atlanta's *Ladies' Home* (1866–1867), which alternated

[20] Riley, *Magazines of the American South*, 200.

[21] For Chapters 6, 7, and 8 see Catherine Webb Barber, "Briarbrook," *Scott's Monthly Magazine* (May 1866), 380–8.

[22] *Ibid.*, 433, 437.

[23] *Ibid.*, 437.

[24] Ted Curtis Smythe, *The Gilded Age Press, 1865–1900* (Westport, CT, 2003), 41.

[25] William J. Scott, "Reviews, Notices, etc.," *Scott's Monthly Magazine* 2 (July 1866), 580.

between male and female editors. The magazine's founder, Thomas S. Powell, a Georgia physician who later also established the *Southern Medical Journal*, wanted the *Ladies' Home* to be "an elegant Home for the suffering and afflicted females of our country."[26] L. Virginia French edited the first few issues of the literary periodical and tried to give southern women an outlet for creative expression by publishing poems and short fiction by female writers, including Annie R. Blount and Catherine Ann Warfield. Reflecting the notion that reading could be a vital solace in the midst of postbellum melancholy, the motto of the *Ladies' Home* was "Life without Literature is Death."[27] However, unlike some other women's magazines, the *Ladies' Home* was very conservative in its approach to women's political equality. In an 1867 article on "Women at the Ballot-box," the periodical came out strongly against women's suffrage: "What demon ever suggested the notion of giving woman the right of suffrage has not yet transpired.... The idea of having her participate in ugly political brawls is too utterly abhorrent to be thought of. Woman has her sphere, and she can in no wise transcend it without sacrificing her dignity and self-respect."[28] Thus, simply because a magazine opened its pages to female contributors did not mean that it assumed a progressive view of women's equality. In fact, the *Ladies' Home* emphasized traditional views of gender roles.

On the other hand, periodicals led by male editors did not always offer merely boilerplate defenses of separate spheres. For example, the Nashville *Home Monthly*, edited by A. B. Stark, advocated women's suffrage in an 1868 editorial. In Stark's mind, women had earned the right to vote through intellectual improvement and the accumulation of property. He also believed that women's kindness and sensitivity would help to balance the aggressive and often brutal world of male-dominated politics.[29] Similarly, although edited by men, *The Monthly Visitor* began publication in 1871 in Norfolk and included prose and poetry by female writers like Fanny Downing.

Prominent among southern editors and authors after the war, Downing was born in Portsmouth, Virginia, in 1835, the daughter of a leading attorney. Before the war, she had married a Florida politician and lived in the frontier state, an experience that later served her well in a series she wrote for the *Southern Home Journal*.[30] Downing, like many southern women who specialized in writing for periodicals, exhibited versatility, publishing a biography, several serialized novels, numerous poems, and short fiction in postwar magazines like *The Monthly Visitor*.[31] In addition to Downing, the journal

[26] Powell quoted in Atchison, "Southern Literary Magazines," 103.

[27] *Ibid.*, 105.

[28] "Women at the Ballot-box," *Ladies' Home* 2 (March 16, 1867), quoted in Atchison, "Southern Literary Magazines," 111–2.

[29] Atchison, "Southern Literary Magazines," 146.

[30] "Fanny Murdaugh Downing," *The South in the Building of the Nation* (vol. XI, Richmond, 1909–1913), 291–2.

[31] See, for example, Downing, "The Virtues of Nothing," *The Monthly Visitor* 1 (September 1871), 44–5.

printed works by Mary Bayard Clarke, Nora Cannon, and other southern women. Equally significant, *The Monthly Visitor* demonstrates the extent to which literary ties between the North and South had been reconstructed as early as 1872; for in February alone, the magazine received thirty-six periodicals in free exchange, including the *Chicago Schoolmaster*, *Kansas Magazine*, *Philadelphia Business Advocate*, and *New York Courier*.[32]

The vast majority of magazines published in the South before 1870 were edited, written by, and read by a white readership. Still, promising signs for an African American periodical culture existed before the Civil War, particularly among the literary societies established by free blacks in Baltimore prior to 1835. At least two such organizations were founded, the Young Men's Mental Improvement Society and the Phoenix Society, with other debating and literary clubs formed by African Americans in Washington, D.C.[33] By the late nineteenth and early twentieth centuries, a thriving black literary culture produced many magazines aimed at black subscribers. The content of these magazines, particularly those published by activist editors, provided essential forums for appeals to both racial and gender equality.

Despite seemingly insurmountable obstacles, a few black periodicals were launched in the antebellum North. As Charles A. Simmons points out in *The African American Press* (1998), the earliest such periodical was *Freedom's Journal*, published in New York City in 1827.[34] Edited by John Russwurm and Samuel Cornish, two prominent African Americans, this newspaper lent a black voice to the abolitionist cause.[35] Although it is hard to gauge the extent of free black southern readership, we do know that in July 1827 free blacks in Virginia welcomed the new magazine as a worthy contribution to the abolitionist cause.[36] Although the paper lasted only two years, other editors would take up the cause, such as *The Rights of All*, edited by Cornish after the termination of his first endeavor.[37] In addition, *The Anglo-African Magazine*, edited in New York by Thomas Hamilton beginning in 1859, eagerly published work by black women. Frances Harper and Mary A. S. Cary published poems and occasionally brief essays in the pages of the monthly magazine, in much the same way that poetry by white women were welcomed into the pages of *Harper's* and *Scribner's*.[38]

32 "Exchanges Received," *The Monthly Visitor* 2 (March 1872), 103.

33 Dorothy B. Porter, "The Organized Educational Activities of Negro Literary Societies, 1828–1846," *The Journal of Negro Education* 5 (October 1936), 558, 573–4.

34 Charles A. Simmons, *The African American Press* (Jefferson, NC, 1998), 9.

35 Dickson D. Bruce, Jr., *The Origins of African American Literature, 1680–1865* (Charlottesville, 2001), 163.

36 *Ibid.*, 165.

37 *Ibid.*, 175.

38 In 1859, Harper published at least four poems and short essays in *The Anglo-African Magazine*: "Gone to God," 1 (April 1859), 123; "Our Greatest Want," (May 1859), 160; "The Dying Fugitive," (August 1859), 253–4; and "The Two Offers," (September 1859), 31–3. Cary published and essay titled "Trifles." See (February 1859), 55–6.

Scholars have argued that periodicals such as *Freedom's Journal* and *The Rights of All* used literature and print culture as vehicles for abolitionism. With African American editors and contributors, such papers used the "credibility and authoritative character of the African American voice" to discredit the notion that slavery was a benevolent institution.[39] Thus, periodicals for black Americans began primarily to serve the abolitionist cause, with papers like the *Mirror of Liberty* and the *National Reformer* attracting subscribers in the North. New York and Philadelphia, with larger numbers of literate free blacks, became centers of antebellum black print culture. African American women, notes Frankie Hutton in *The Early Black Press in America* (1993), were actively involved in these papers, primarily as contributors. Periodicals "were diligent in helping to counter negative images of black women," according to Hutton, and offered material directed at female readers, including personal advice columns that boldly advocated a greater role for women in society.[40]

Southern African Americans would begin to form their own print culture not long after the first Union troops entered the South.[41] There appears to have been no periodicals published by or for African Americans in the South before the Civil War. Some white southern magazines, particularly before the regional trauma caused by Nat Turner's Rebellion in 1831, gave limited voice to African American aspirations. For example, the *Virginia Religious Magazine*, published in Lexington, printed an antislavery poem by William Cowper titled "The Negro's Complaint."[42] Even the vaunted *Southern Literary Messenger* published two poems by the North Carolina slave poet George Moses Horton in the early 1840s. "Ode to Liberty" and "Lines to My –" appeared with a short introduction indicating that Horton was "a negro boy, belonging to a respectable farmer, residing a few miles from Chapel Hill."[43] Thus, rarely, even white establishment periodicals might shed a little light on black literary interests. But such insight was fleeting at best before the Civil War.

During and after the war, African American periodicals sprang up quickly. By most accounts, the first journal published by southern African Americans was *L'Union*, published in French and English in New Orleans beginning in 1862.[44] In *The Afro-American Periodical Press, 1838–1909* (1981), Penelope L. Bullock notes that *L'Union* was published primarily for the free black community in and around the port city. She also notes that black churches often led efforts to create and sustain periodicals. The A. M. E. church, for example, moved the *Repository* to Baltimore in January 1862 and turned it into a monthly magazine of general interest, offering religious and literary news.

[39] Bruce, *Origins of African American Literature*, 273.
[40] Frankie Hutton, *The Early Black Press in America, 1827–1860* (Westport, 1993), 57–67.
[41] Penelope L. Bullock, *The Afro-American Periodical Press, 1838–1909* (Baton Rouge, 1981), 1–3.
[42] *Ibid.*, 97.
[43] See *Southern Literary Messenger* 9 (April 1843), 237–8.
[44] Simmons, *African American Press*, 13–4.

Supported by contributions from male writers like the Charleston native Daniel A. Payne, the *Repository* was also sensitive to the interests of women readers. As Bullock points out, the journal published a "Mothers' Department" and a "Young Ladies' Lecture Room" to broaden its appeal to female subscribers.[45] The earliest southern black periodicals, therefore, indicated that women were actively engaged in shaping the region's nascent African American print culture.

African American newspapers and magazines after the Civil War actively and boldly attacked discrimination, publicized violations of civil rights, promoted literacy and literature among the freed people, and provided a strong voice in favor of the Republican Party. It is testimony to the potential of a black southern literary culture that as soon as emancipation and the end of the Civil War rippled through southern communities, periodicals directed toward black readers began to emerge. Rising rates of literacy certainly helped. Just five years after the Civil War ended, nearly 80 percent of African Americans were illiterate, a number that dropped to about 45 percent in 1900 and 30 percent by 1910.[46] Augusta's *Colored American*, Richmond's *True Southerner*, Mobile's *Nationalist*, and the *South Carolina Leader* all appeared in 1865, and the *Charleston Journal* was published the following year.[47] According to one scholar's estimate, some 500 African American newspapers were published between 1865 and 1889, including dozens in the South.[48]

Most magazines were headed by enterprising black men, such as Alabama's Jesse Chisholm Duke, who founded the *Montgomery Herald* in 1886.[49] Yet, black periodicals owned and operated by men opened their pages to women. *McGirt's Magazine*, a Greensboro journal edited by James E. McGirt, published works by Anna Julia Cooper, Mary Church Terrell, Frances Harper, and other leading black women writers.[50] As editors like Duke understood, the diversity of contributors enhanced a periodical's appeal. The 1880s in particular witnessed a dramatic rise in the number of black periodicals, and not all originated in large cities. Alabama had nearly thirty newspapers and magazines by 1890, published in ten different towns.[51] Many such editors, including Duke, were born into slavery and yet within a generation had advanced the African American press. Middle-class status characterized many black journalists who often simultaneously held other occupations as teachers or

[45] Bullock, *Afro-American Periodical Press*, 44–7.

[46] *Ibid.*, 9.

[47] Henry Lewis Suggs, ed., *The Black Press in the South, 1865–1979* (Westport, CT, 1983), 3–4.

[48] Noliwe M. Rooks, *Ladies' Pages: African American Women's Magazines and the Culture That Made Them* (New Brunswick, 2004).

[49] Allen W. Jones, "The Black Press in the 'New South:' Jesse C. Duke's Struggle for Justice and Equality," *Journal of Negro History* 64 (Summer 1979), 216.

[50] Bullock, *The Afro-American Periodical Press*, 79. See also Heather Andrea Williams, *Self-Taught: African American Education in Slavery and Freedom* (Chapel Hill, 2005).

[51] Jones, "The Black Press," 216.

merchants. Duke represented this trait well; he was a businessman, teacher, and politician in addition to an editor.[52]

The rapid journalistic progress made by African Americans was not lost on contemporary observers. As a writer in the African American newspaper *The Petersburg Herald* noted in 1892, "Journalism among the Afro-Americans is of quite a recent date but they have achieved a most wonderful success. As the race grows more interested, subscribes and pays for some good papers, and then reads them, the success will be more marked, and more good along this line will be accomplished."[53] Circulation of these papers, according to one scholar, usually ranged between 100 and 1,000 subscribers, but more prominent newspapers, such as the *Dallas Express*, claimed a circulation of 5,000 in 1889.[54]

The emergence of the black press after 1865 reflected a remarkable hunger for newspapers and magazines devoted to the concerns of African Americans. Indeed, many freedmen and freedwomen believed that consistent periodical reading would be of significant educational and intellectual benefit to the race. In an editorial published during Reconstruction, Virginia's *People's Advocate* relied on testimony from schoolteachers to demonstrate the importance of reading newspapers. Teachers claimed that black students who had access to periodicals at home were better readers, spellers, and writers and were often "taking the lead in debating societies."[55]

Beyond educating the young, however, periodicals could prove a powerful force in combating discrimination. According to Hayward Farrar, Baltimore's *Afro-American* newspaper "constantly exposed racism in education, jobs, housing, and public accommodations, encouraged its readers to right racism, and publicized their activities when they did."[56] As a black paper argued in 1889, the press was "the most powerful agency for the accomplishment of great achievements that the world has seen.... If the colored people have made any progress ... it is through the medium and by the agency of the colored newspapers." In addition, claimed the writer, "when white men want to know the attitude of the colored people they look into the colored papers."[57] Still, journalists complained that African Americans failed to take newspapers as seriously as editors believed that they should. According to one estimate, of nearly fifty black papers started in Texas before 1900, "only eight existed for at least 10 years."[58] Editors cried that black folks did not "understand that a well supported paper can do more good for the race by far, than all of the conventions ever held in any country." "A good newspaper," the *People's*

[52] *Ibid.*, 225.

[53] "Race News," *The Petersburg Herald* 5 (December 31, 1892).

[54] Charles William Grose, "Black Newspapers in Texas, 1868–1970," (Ph.D. diss., University of Texas, 1972), 45.

[55] "Influence of Newspapers," *The People's Advocate* 1 (July 1, 1876).

[56] Hayward Farrar, *The Baltimore Afro-American* (Westport, 1998), xv.

[57] "The National Colored Press Convention," *The National Leader* 2 (March 9, 1889).

[58] Grose, "Black Newspapers in Texas," 55.

Advocate agreed, "is a thing of first importance to every family, and not a colored child in our schools should be without a paper."[59]

Just as white southern women considered the press vital to expanding women's rights, so too did African Americans place a great deal of emphasis on journalism for advancing the cause of racial justice.[60] For example, the *Freeman's Press*, printed in Texas in 1868, called for an end to racist Jim Crow laws in public accommodations and denounced the Democratic Party. Many of these papers were also concerned with encouraging black self-help as well as economic and intellectual development. As the Arkansas *Freeman* put it in 1869, "A plow made by a black man tells us more than a hundred first class speeches."[61] Thus, after emancipation a wave of southern black journalists sought to fill the need for news and entertainment among a black readership. Considering the often violent opposition to black voices, the story of the success of these newspapers is all the more inspiring. Indeed, as white on black violence escalated after Reconstruction, black newspapers became a source of defiance and strength. What is remarkable is that even with relatively low literacy rates, a life of oppression, and little economic power, black newspapers and their editors prospered as much as they did.

Such newspapers were not without problems, however. African American periodicals often teetered on the edge of insolvency for many months before folding. As was true of papers aimed at white readers, black periodicals often had difficulties securing subscribers and experienced similar frustration in getting subscribers to pay. Businesses were often reticent to pay for advertisements. The *Arkansas Weekly Mansion* complained in 1883, "In canvassing among the merchants, we find it as a rule, very difficult to secure advertisements." The problem was that businessmen believed illiterate blacks would not be reached by such ads. "The merchants' plea," according to the *Mansion*, "is that the colored people are too ignorant to be guided by advertisements, that they get just as much colored trade without as with advertisements in colored papers." But what really angered the black press was that "those same merchants have large advertisements in all the white papers of the city."[62] White and black members of the press competed for scarce advertising dollars to keep their papers afloat, and in that competition businessmen often placed their ads in more established white periodicals.

Whereas most newspapers for black readers were perpetually in danger of folding, energetic and determined editors managed to keep publishing for many years. Some states harbored a more successful and resilient black press than others. Virginia was the home of many important black periodicals after the Civil War. Joseph T. Wilson's *True Southerner* was perhaps the state's first paper for black readers, starting in Norfolk in 1866.[63] Despite the fact that

[59] "Colored Journalism," *The People's Advocate* 6 (October 8, 1881).

[60] Henry Lewis Suggs, *The Black Press in the South, 1865–1979* (Westport, CT, 1983), 13.

[61] October 5, 1869; quoted in *ibid.*

[62] "To the Colored People of Little Rock," *Arkansas Weekly Mansion* 4 (October 20, 1883).

[63] Ronald E. Cutler, "A History and Analysis of Negro Newspapers in Virginia," (MA Thesis, University of Richmond, 1965), 5.

Wilson was threatened by white mobs who destroyed his presses, other freedmen in Virginia bravely undertook editorships, including Magnus Robinson of the *Virginia Post*, Jonathan Cromwell of the *People's Advocate*, David C. Carter of the *Virginia Critic*, and George F. Bragg of the *Lancet-Recorder*.[64] All of these newspapers, published in the last three decades of the nineteenth century, were important voices for the black community. Two other newspapers, the *Richmond Planet* and the *Virginia Star*, became prominent periodicals that were read by African Americans outside Virginia.

Despite such success in establishing black newspapers after the war, and despite sometimes opening their pages to female contributors, postwar African American newspapers published surprisingly little that might appeal directly to women. Whereas southern white periodicals even in the early decades of the 1800s devoted sections of the paper to a "Woman's Column" or some other direct plea for female readers, and whereas white newspapers often included poems and short fiction by women, postwar black newspapers remained almost entirely male bastions until after the turn of the twentieth century. Women could occasionally be found as subjects or authors, but on a scale much less than could be found in white periodicals much earlier. Undoubtedly, women read a range of articles, not just those specifically aimed at them. We know that in both the black and white communities periodicals were not only read by the subscriber but also circulated among any number of friends and relatives. Because most subscribers to magazines and newspapers were men, it is difficult to determine the extent to which female spouses and relatives also read the periodicals. Even in African American papers that contained little direct reading targeting women, the kind of women's columns intentionally designed to attract women to issues like fashion, literature, homemaking, and child rearing, there is evidence that women were at least perusing periodicals generally aimed at men. Alabama's *Huntsville Gazette*, for example, did not publish traditional women's newspaper fare but did contain advertisements for women's products, such as cosmetics and clothing.[65]

One of the papers that did give women more of a voice in the black press was the *Washington Bee*, which became one of the nation's leading examples of African American journalism. Edited at first by William V. Turner, *The Bee*, as it became known, published a section titled "For the Fair Sex" that provided news of women's activities. Throughout the 1880s, the paper published articles with headings like "Ladies' Department" or "For Feminine Readers," which often consisted of news on fashion. However, to an extent unusual among postbellum African American newspapers, *The Bee* also printed news of women who moved beyond traditional gender boundaries. In an 1883 issue, the paper noticed that a school of pharmacy had opened for women in Kentucky and that women were earning respect as

[64] *Ibid.*, 6.

[65] See the ad for Mrs. A. Herstein's dress and fancy goods store, *Huntsville Gazette* 2 (June 18, 1881).

physicians.[66] Similar issues published news of women who held political and professional jobs, including in dentistry.[67] Other African American papers, although not consistently featuring columns by or for women, nonetheless highlighted the lives and careers of individuals. *The Weekly Pelican*, published in New Orleans and edited by John L. Minor beginning in 1887, presented a picture and biography of Sojourner Truth on its front page.[68] The paper also included news of a co-ed literary club that included many single and married women.[69]

Just as with the white press, there was no guarantee that periodicals friendly to female readers would also offer progressive views on equality. Not all references to women in black newspapers promoted a progressive agenda regarding gender; in fact, these periodicals were often conservative in their approach to women in society. Alice King wrote an article for the *Georgetown (S.C.) Planet* about "Woman's Power" in which she explicitly denied the wisdom of giving women the right to vote. King maintained that in gaining direct influence on politics through voting, women would be surrendering the myriad influences they already possessed in family and society.[70]

Although newspapers directed toward a black audience expanded, magazines were slower in developing. The first step was for African American writers to contribute to established white magazines, a process that started before the Civil War ended. Sometimes black writers had to conceal their racial identity to get published; Charles W. Chesnutt learned this lesson early and hid his race from publishers for a time.[71] However, other white journals embraced the new perspectives that a black voice might bring to their pages, particularly northern magazines. Charlotte Forten, for example, a black school teacher in South Carolina during the Civil War, published pieces in *The Liberator* and the *Atlantic Monthly*. The latter contributions, essays on her experience in areas of the South controlled by Union forces, were sympathetic accounts of her attempts to relate to the people of the coastal islands.[72]

Similarly, the *Southern Workman*, published in Hampton, Virginia, in association with the Hampton Institute, was an important early journal for African Americans. Lasting from 1872 until 1939, the *Southern Workman* enjoyed one of the longest runs of any southern magazine, white or black. For much of its history the magazine was edited by Samuel Armstrong, a former Union General who advocated industrial education as the best means of black

[66] "News and Notes for Women," *The Bee* 1 (May 12, 1883).

[67] "Women as Dentists," *The Bee* 1(February 17, 1883); "Women Who Hold Office," 3 (September 6, 1884).

[68] "Sojourner Truth," *The Weekly Pelican* 1 (July 23, 1887).

[69] "Calanthe Literary Circle," *The Weekly Pelican* 1 (September 3, 1887).

[70] Alice King, "Woman's Power," *Georgetown Planet* 1 (May 31, 1873).

[71] M. Marie Booth Foster, comp., *Southern Black Creative Writers, 1829–1953* (New York, 1988), xiii.

[72] Bruce, *Origins of African American Literature*, 308–9.

advancement.[73] Until 1899 or so, the magazine steered clear of controversial issues and avoided wading into heated debate. However, beginning with issues in 1899 and lasting until the periodical folded during the New Deal, the *Southern Workman* became an important voice for black authors like Paul Laurence Dunbar and his wife Alice Dunbar-Nelson. Along with leading forums for black intellectual life like the *Crisis*, the *Southern Workman* was a conduit for the discussion of racial issues and a prominent place for talented black authors to publish.[74]

Among the earliest and most important periodicals edited by African Americans for a black audience was the weekly *Colored American*, published in Augusta soon after the war ended. The prospectus for the paper promised political, religious, and general news, but its earnestness in asking for white respect is particularly affecting. The prospectus declared that the *Colored American* would "be devoted to the promotion of harmony and good-will between the whites and colored people of the South, and untiring in its advocacy of Industry and Education among all classes." Bearing no ill will toward their former masters, but perhaps aware that outright support from whites would not be forthcoming, the freedmen instead asked for "the cordial support of our white friends at the South."[75] Still, the managers of the paper, Reverend James Lynch of Baltimore and J. T. Shuften of Augusta, did not place racial harmony above racial justice. Shuften in particular considered newspapers and magazines to be vital to "the work of elevating his people." The plan for the paper also stated clearly that "it will fearlessly remonstrate against legal and constitutional proscription by appeal to the public sense of justice."[76] Although a strong advocate for racial justice, the paper rarely attacked gender discrimination or embraced women as writers or subjects, aside from the occasional poem penned by a female author.[77] The paper, though important for its earnestness and initial commitment, did not endure long and was abandoned in February 1866 due in part to "the bad faith of the stockholders."[78] But other African American periodicals soon appeared, including *The Colored Tennessean*, Baltimore's *True Communicator*, Mississippi's *The Colored Citizen*, and *The New Orleans Louisianan*. Of the thirty or so periodicals published by black editors in 1880, sixteen were published in the southern states.[79] Nearly all of the postwar periodicals for African Americans were edited by men, though as we shall see, important women like Ida. B. Wells could be found at the helm of a few key publications in the later nineteenth century.

[73] Brian Joseph Benson, "The Southern Workman," in Walter C. Daniel, ed., *Black Journals of the United States* (Westport, 1982), 350–1.

[74] *Ibid.*, 354–7.

[75] Prospectus printed in *The Anglo-African* 5 (June 1865); quoted in I. Garland Penn, *The Afro-American Press and its Editors* (Springfield, MA, 1891), 101.

[76] *Ibid.*

[77] Sarah E. Shuften, "Ethiopia's Dead," *The Colored American* 1 (December 30, 1865).

[78] *Ibid.*, 104.

[79] *Ibid.*, 105–113.

As was the case with periodicals for white readers, the choices for African American subscribers increased in the 1880s. This decade was particularly important for the growth in numbers of white female editors; during this period, some of the first press associations for women were being formed, indicating an increasing self-awareness and a desire for greater respect through the professionalization of their field. The same is true of African American editors and periodicals. One census found 31 periodicals published throughout the United States in 1880, a number that had risen to 154 just ten years later in 1890. The South witnessed important gains, even in the midst of hardening segregation and the entrenchment of Jim Crow. Although in 1880 just sixteen black periodicals were published in the former Confederate states, by 1890 those states could count ninety-six.[80] Magazines with titles like *The Southland*, emanating from Salisbury, North Carolina, indicated a defiant co-opting of southern white identity.

During the 1890s, African American newspapers and magazines were more likely to make appeals to a female readership. During this decade, *The Petersburg Herald* routinely published a "Woman's Column," whereas the paper had rarely included such a section in the 1880s. By the 1890s, however, spurred by both the Chicago Exposition as well as by the growing numbers of black female authors and a new gender consciousness evinced in the black women's club movement, periodicals like the *Herald* thought it wise to open its pages to female readers. Much of the writing on women was traditional, such as references to women as "the precious porcelain of human clay, to be handled gently and admired from a distance."[81] Still, the paper routinely printed news of progress in female education and actively promoted the activities of local schools for girls.[82]

Many prominent African American magazines were associated with religious denominations, such as Baltimore's *A.M.E. Church Review*. B. T. Tanner, who had been active in church-related publishing for more than fifteen years, was tapped to edit the *Church Review* beginning in 1884.[83] According to a contemporary observer, by the early 1890s the journal could boast of a circulation of more than 1,500 subscribers from the United States, Europe, the Caribbean, and Africa.[84] Although the *Review* certainly supported church doctrine, it was more open than many other black periodicals to denunciations of lynching, job discrimination, and Jim Crow. Indeed, according to one scholar, the *Review* became "a weapon for civil rights, education, and religious zeal."[85] Late nineteenth-century journals like the *Southern Workman* and the *A.M.E. Church Review* proved that black periodicals could endure for decades and remain viable and important venues for discussions of race

[80] *Ibid.*, 114.
[81] "Woman's Column," *The Petersburg Herald* 5 (December 31, 1892).
[82] *Ibid.*
[83] Daniel, *Black Journals*, 27.
[84] Penn, *Afro-American Press*, 126–7, also quoted in Daniel, *Black Journals*, 27.
[85] Daniel, *Black Journals*, 28–9.

and politics, helping to lay the groundwork for early twentieth-century journals like Atlanta's *Voice of the Negro*.

In addition to money from subscriptions, as unreliable as payments might be, black and white editors earned revenue from advertisements, which increased notably in southern periodicals after the war. In antebellum southern magazines, ads were few or nonexistent; newspapers were more open to accepting advertisements, as papers from the eighteenth and early nineteenth centuries attest. However, many editors of literary magazines in the prewar period wished to keep their journals as elevated and dignified as possible, and that meant rejecting ads from the latest fashions or for the most recent self-proclaimed cure for a variety of ailments. After the war, magazines like *Scott's* eagerly printed ads for a range of services and products, perhaps more deliberately copying the practices of northern journals. *Scott's* published advertisements in the year following the war for commission merchants, hardware, repair shops, china and glass dealers, wholesale grocers, hotels, physicians, druggists, saddle makers, insurance, lawyers, and boots. The remarkable range of goods and services advertised represented businesses and professionals primarily from Atlanta where the magazine was published, but other ads came from Augusta, Savannah, Chattanooga, Tennessee, and Auburn, Alabama. The Travelers Insurance Company of Hartford, Connecticut, evidently hoped to attract Georgia buyers, promising insurance against "accidents of all kinds."[86]

A willingness to publish ads expanded opportunities for revenue and contributed to the growth in the number of magazines published after the war. Table 6.1 shows the breakdown of publications started by year, indicating that there was indeed a drop in the numbers of periodicals started during the war, but that new enterprises were not squelched altogether. After the slowdown during the war, the four years after Appomattox averaged about twenty new journals per year.

The fact that these new magazines were distributed throughout the South suggests that the dramatic increase in the numbers of periodicals after 1820 did not end with the war or with the economic hardships suffered during Reconstruction. Table 6.2 reflects this distribution across the southern states. Moreover, whereas magazines became ubiquitous throughout the postwar South, so too did they become increasingly important to the women of the region. Almost as soon as the war was over, southerners began to plan for the publication of new periodicals that were put on hold during the fighting. In 1866, for example, Susan Bradford Eppes noted in her diary that "Colonel Wyatt Aiken was here a few days ago and … he is preparing to bring out a new farming magazine, 'The Rural Carolinian,' and is gathering all available material."[87]

[86] For representative advertisements, see *Scott's Monthly Magazine* 2 (July and August 1866).

[87] *Diary of Susan Bradford Eppes*, April 1866, in *Through Some Eventful Years*, 324, reprinted in North American Women's Letters and Diaries.

TABLE 6.1. *Number of New Southern Magazines Undertaken by Year, 1860–1869*

Year	Number of Magazines Started
1860	36
1861	10
1862	13
1863	14
1864	14
1865	13
1866	23
1867	18
1868	22
1869	19

Source: Sam G. Riley, *Index to Southern Periodicals* (Wesport, CT, 1986), Appendix B.

TABLE 6.2. *Numbers of Magazines Published in Southern States, 1862–1880*

State	Number of Magazines
Alabama	22
Arkansas	7
Florida	4
Georgia	41
Kentucky	46
Louisiana	33
Maryland	8
Mississippi	8
North Carolina	18
South Carolina	15
Tennessee	35
Texas	17
Virginia	49

Source: Riley, *Index to Southern Periodicals*, Appendix B.

Thus, a pent-up demand for southern literature stymied during the war led to the development of many periodicals in the immediate postwar period.

The notion that southerners refused to support adequately native publications persisted into the decades after 1865. To the dismay of native southern authors, readers in the region still seemed to prefer Boston, New York, and Philadelphia productions. Magazines published in the North like *Harper's* and *Atlantic Monthly* continued to receive the eager patronage of southern men and women, and antebellum complaints about prejudice against southern publications were heard in the postwar era as well. As one southern female author wrote in an 1869 letter to Hayne, "Within the last month I have had various letters from the Editor of *The New Eclectic* about their magazine. The proprietors are somewhat disheartened in the attempt to maintain a distinctively Southern journal.... An extended subscription list is all they require to give permanency to the magazine, and to afford them the means of enlarging its attractions. If *it* fails, through the inertia and apathy of the Southern people, then farewell to any attempt to sustain a magazine south of Philadelphia."[88] The fact that the editor of *The New Eclectic* had "sunk $5000" in the magazine in the attempt to keep it afloat reflects the optimism – and perhaps the naïveté – of some literary entrepreneurs.[89]

One postbellum periodical that earned significant patronage among white southerners was *The Land We Love*, published in Charlotte, North Carolina, by Daniel H. Hill, a graduate of West Point who had seen action in the Mexican War. He participated in numerous Civil War battles in Tennessee, Virginia, and North Carolina and led troops at the Battle of Antietam. After the war, Hill settled in North Carolina and became a mathematics professor at Davidson College. In *The Land We Love*, which he began as a monthly in May 1866, Hill offered a forum for women authors. Although no friend of progressive reforms and certainly no advocate of women's rights, Hill's journal published dozens of poems and short pieces by women like Margaret Junkin Preston, Fanny Murdaugh, Mary Bayard Clarke, and Fanny Downing. It was not uncommon for a single issue to publish four or five works by southern women authors, almost always with their names printed in the table of contents or next to the work itself. Books by women, such as Emily V. Mason's *Southern Poems of the War*, were also reviewed, providing further public recognition for female writers.[90] The back of the magazine frequently printed advertisements for women's schools, such as the Charlotte Female Institute.[91] Occasionally, views favorable to greater gender equality made their way into the pages of *The Land We Love*, such as the 1868 review of a book by Virginia Penny on *The Employments of Women*. Burwell Carter, a resident of Williamstown, Kentucky, praised the book. "Such a volume has never before been accessible to our wives and daughters," Carter approvingly stated. "It is, in some sense, a vindication of woman's natural right to occupy places and positions suitable to her talent, tact, and taste; from which man, in too many instances, has pushed her aside to make room for himself."[92] For white

[88] Margaret Junkin Preston to Paul Hamilton Hayne, September 13, 1869, in *Life and Letters of Margaret Junkin Preston*, 249–50.

[89] *Ibid.*

[90] For the review of Mason's book, see *The Land We Love* 3 (May 1867), 91.

[91] See, for example, *The Land We Love* 3 (September 1867), 442.

[92] Burwell N. Carter, "Book Notices" *The Land We Love* 3 (August 1867), 364.

women in the postwar period, there was no shortage of southern magazines like *The Land We Love* eager to publish their work.

The New South was a place of significant journalistic activity among both African Americans and whites. After a difficult recovery period immediately after the war, the region's periodical culture once again became vibrant, diverse, and filled with new energy by the 1880s to an extent not seen since before secession. Perhaps most notably, even in the Jim Crow South, when racial violence constantly threatened the very lives of black southerners, bold and courageous African American journalists put fear behind them and started new newspapers and magazines. Along with schooling, another important cause of the freedmen and freedwomen, journalism was seen as the key to bettering the condition of African Americans. It would be editors, papers, and correspondents, black journalists argued, who would be among the leaders in revealing injustice, advocating racial equality, and improving the general knowledge of black readers. With similar boldness and bravery, black and white women authors and journalists would seek to change the region by providing prominent examples of female literary professionals.

7

Writing a New South for Women

The devastation wrought by the Civil War left many southern women feeling that careers and occupations were no longer a luxury but an utter necessity. In an 1868 North Carolina magazine article titled "The Women of the South," one commenter noted that "Fortunes have been swept away; we are nearly all poor. Many who were born and reared in affluence, now find it difficult to get bread, while those who were always poor are poorer still.... We can no longer live the life of ease to which we have been accustomed. We must work or perish."[1] Yet, beyond small-scale needlework or farming, opportunities for women remained circumscribed by traditional notions of gender roles. Women were becoming teachers in greater numbers, but the most alluring paths for many educated women were careers in writing and editing. As they had before the war, postbellum women entered the fields of literature and journalism with optimism. According to contemporary observers, such careers carried with them a new sense of urgency in the postwar miasma. "The pursuit of letters," claimed the editor of a southern magazine in 1867, "is not now a recreation, but an earnest effort for a livelihood."[2] Women could be found as fiction writers, essayists, editors, translators, poets, and periodical contributors. By 1870, one Nashville editor could claim, "This is the era of woman's reign in the republic of letters."[3]

Despite such effusions, major obstacles stood in the way of aspiring women journalists. Printers and publishing houses across the region suffered heavy damage as a result of the war, and although a few printers could be found in important cities like New Orleans, Charleston, and Richmond, what little publishing industry the region had begun to build up before the war was now largely decimated. Union troops destroyed both personal and public libraries. Those libraries that were not destroyed were sometimes sold off to northerners to help raise badly needed money. Postwar southern authors, such as Paul Hamilton Hayne,

[1] "The Women of the South," *The Carrier Dove* 1 (July 1868), 129.

[2] Quoted in Hubbell, *The South in American Literature*, 711.

[3] Anonymous editor quoted in Atchison, "Southern Literary Magazines," 281.

Augusta Jane Evans, Mary Edwards Bryan, and John Esten Cooke, turned to northern houses to publish their latest works. Evans ventured to New York after the war to reconnect with northern publishers like J. C. Derby, who was stunned by her haggard appearance. Her father, Evans told Derby, had "lost everything, the slaves had been freed and all property confiscated."[4] Financial necessity required beating the pavement, even if that meant going outside the South to do so.

Postwar copyright laws proved only slightly more protective of authors' rights than they were in the antebellum era. As Meredith L. McGill found in *American Literature and the Culture of Reprinting* (2003), republishing literary works before the Civil War was "not a violation of law or custom, but a cultural norm."[5] The Confederate copyright law, which female writers like Evans had been instrumental in enacting, could protect authors who knew their rights. As one scholar has observed, Evans was an especially "canny player in the literary field" in the 1860s "who understood and exploited the possibilities of shifting national narratives shaped by copyright law."[6]

In the postwar South, many observers were willing to grant women the right to earn income outside the home, especially if they elected not to marry or if they could not find a husband. An editorial by A. B. Stark in Nashville's *The Home Monthly* in 1868 remarked that "there are a few women who do not want husbands, and thousands who cannot get them. What are these to do?" Given the devastation to the male population as a result of the war, many southern women went without a husband. "Is it just to exclude them," asked Stark, "from a fair competition in the active pursuits by which money is made? To us it seems most unjust and tyrannical."[7]

Other southern postwar women writers were motivated not just by financial desperation but also by an equally powerful desire for intellectual stimulation. In the latter years of the nineteenth century, white women in Richmond formed the Saturday Afternoon Club for sophisticated discussion of complicated topics. At their first series of meetings in 1896, they discussed "Goethe and His Contemporaries," and in later meetings they tackled the modern short story, social science, Dante, and child labor.[8] Although these topics were more advanced than the themes and questions discussed in antebellum women's literary and debating clubs, it is important to realize that associations like the Saturday Afternoon Club had hundreds of antecedents in the region.

As Lucretia Mott and Elizabeth Cady Stanton called for more diverse responsibilities for women, southerners continued to expand women's sphere. Indeed, one of the active participants of the Saturday Afternoon Club was

[4] Derby quoted in William Perry Fidler, *Augusta Evans Wilson*, (University, AL, 1951), 122, and in Atchison, "Southern Literary Magazines," 30.

[5] Meredith L. McGill. *American Literature and the Culture of Reprinting, 1834–1853* (Philadelphia, 2003), 3.

[6] Homestead, *American Women Authors and Literary Property*, 194, 196.

[7] A. B. Stark, "Book Notices," *The Home Monthly* 4 (March 1868), 147.

[8] Saturday Afternoon Club Records, Virginia Historical Society.

Emily Earl Chenault Runyon, one of the first female doctors to practice in Virginia. Sophia Bledsoe Herrick began her career as a writer and editor through the efforts of her father, Albert Taylor Bledsoe, who edited the *Southern Review* during Reconstruction. Herrick contributed biographies, literary criticism, and book reviews for her father's periodical, which later led to her appointment with *Scribner's Monthly*, where she worked as an editor from 1879 to 1906.[9]

Whereas racial violence characterized white culture's reaction to the end of slavery, many white southerners remained open to discussions of gender equality. In spite of the fact that racial equality was largely an anathema in the post-Civil War South, a notion hardly worth even entertaining in the public sphere except in rare cases, the drive for the expansion of women's rights was often discussed in public forums. In revealing the lost lives and careers of black and white southern women journalists and writers, we can fully grasp the diversity of ideas circulating in what is often justly regarded as a closed, highly conservative society. Southern women show that even in the midst of such a society, room could be found for the discussion of new gender roles.

One of the most significant southern women authors of the second half of the nineteenth century was Mary Edwards Bryan, a prolific author and journalist who hailed from Florida and Georgia. Although much historical and literary work has helped us to understand better the lives and careers of southern women authors such as Mary Bayard Clarke, Sarah Morgan Dawson, and Evans, Bryan herself remains largely forgotten.[10] Among late nineteenth-century southern women, Bryan stands virtually alone in her literary, journalistic, and editorial contributions. Like her much better known contemporary, Augusta Jane Evans, Bryan was a productive author who sold thousands of copies of her novels. Evans, the author of *Beulah* and *Macaria*, has received much attention from historians and literary scholars for her illustrious career as a best-selling author. However, Bryan's literary career was more varied than that of Evans, because Bryan edited numerous newspapers and magazines in addition to her work in fiction and poetry. As a journalist and novelist, Bryan was well known in the North and South throughout a literary life that spanned nearly six decades.

[9] Atchison, "Southern Literary Magazines," 287–8.

[10] The reprinting of two of Evans' novels, *Beulah* (Baton Rouge, 1992) and *Macaria; Or, Altars of Sacrifice* (Baton Rouge, 1992), edited by Elizabeth Fox-Genovese and Drew Faust, respectively, demonstrates the scholarly attention that Evans and her works have received recently. See also Terrell Armistead Crow and Mary Moulton Barden, eds., *Live Your Own Life: The Family Papers of Mary Bayard Clarke, 1854–1886* (Columbia, SC, 2003); Rebecca Grant Sexton, ed., *A Southern Woman of Letters: The Correspondence of Augusta Jane Evans Wilson* (Columbia, SC, 2002); Giselle Roberts, ed., *The Correspondence of Sarah Morgan and Francis Warrington Dawson, with Selected Editorials Written by Sarah Morgan for the Charleston News and Courier* (Athens, GA, 2004).

Born on the untamed Florida frontier in the early 1840s, Bryan and her family lived on an isolated plantation in Gadsden County. Her parents, Florida native John D. Edwards and Louise Houghton of Athens, Georgia, could offer her little in the way of friends given their isolation, but they nonetheless ensured that her education at the Fletcher Institute in Thomasville, Georgia, would facilitate her growth as a writer. According to one observer, Bryan was "reading Shelley and Byron at seven, and reciting Shakespeare at nine."[11] She was prone to wandering her parents' plantation, reading all manner of books, and when her family removed to the Gulf Coast during the summers she found further areas to explore.[12] While still in school, she married a wealthy Louisiana planter named Jerdell Bryan, although after moving to that state she soon returned home. At the young age of fifteen, she felt ill prepared for marriage. As she later recalled, "I, like a thoughtless, disobedient girl as I was, married, and left books, music, and teachers behind, while I entered a somewhat sterner school, away out in the wilds of the West. During the one year I was a wife, with housekeeping duties and nobody to take an interest in my improvement, I made no progress whatever, and did not even read anything worth remembering."[13] This view of marriage, as an obstacle to women's intellectual development, was to color her views on the institution for the rest of her life. She must have made some accommodation with her husband because in 1862 she returned to live with him in Louisiana, and together they had five children.[14]

At sixteen years old, Bryan began contributing essays and poems to a local newspaper, the *Temperance Banner*, published in the small Georgia towns of Penfield and Newnan. In the late 1840s and early 1850s, the paper had become important to local girls and young women. Like many newspapers, the *Banner* had a "Ladies' Department" that printed poems and short stories of interest to women, and news about female education was reported often. Advertisements for institutions such as the Woodland Female Seminary and the Forsyth Female Collegiate Institute appeared in the newspaper's pages, as well as reviews of the latest issues of women's magazines like *Peterson's*.[15] Contributions from prominent southern women authors, such as L. Virginia French, Catherine Webb Barber, and Octavia Le Vert, appeared often in the paper, and Bryan herself began publishing poems and short essays in its pages.[16] Her involvement in the paper resulted in her appointment as editor of

[11] Mildred Lewis Rutherford, *The South in History and Literature* (Athens, GA, 1906), 242.

[12] Simms, *War Poetry of the South* (New York, 1866), 317.

[13] Bryan to W. W. Mann, February 18, 1860, reprinted in James S. Patty, "A Georgia Authoress Writes Her Editor," *Georgia Historical Quarterly* 41 (December 1957), 427.

[14] Glenn R. Conrad, ed., *A Dictionary of Louisiana Biography* (New Orleans, 1988), 123–4.

[15] For advertisements and reviews of interest to women, see *Temperance Banner* 15 (May 29, 1852) and 20 (February 18, 1854).

[16] See Smith, "The Two Angels of Fever and Frost," *Temperance Banner* nsv1 (August 2, 1856), Barber, "The Nice Match" *Temperance Banner* nsv2 (February 26, 1857), and Le Vert, "Souvenirs of Travel," *Temperance Banner* nsv3 (January 28, 1858).

the Ladies' Department in early 1858. "Only when Mrs. Bryan took charge of the magazine," one observer has written, "did it get beyond being solely the organ of the Temperance movement in Georgia."[17] Although Bryan was far from the first southern woman to edit a periodical, her appointment earned praise from neighboring publications. As the *Bainbridge Argus* reported shortly after her appointment, "As a resident of her section of the state, we feel proud of Mrs. Bryan; and in welcoming her to the fraternity editorial, heartily wish that her career as a writer may be a bright one.... The proprietor of this excellent Literary Journal has been fortunate in procuring the services of one so well qualified for the position she has assumed, and will doubtless find that she will not only contribute to the literary worth of his paper, but add largely to his subscription list."[18] Other Georgia newspapers, including the *Macon Weekly Telegraph*, offered encouragement as well.[19]

As editor, Bryan contributed essays to the *Banner*, including some that were unusual in their boldness, on topics ranging from temperance to novels. One of her first essays, a short piece titled "Why Ladies Should Read Newspapers," argued that women should not be limited to "fashionable literature" but instead that they should be exposed to "this actual world and its transpiring events." "Let the gilded annuals and poems on the center table," she suggested, "be kept apart of the time covered with the weekly and daily journal."[20] Bryan also made clear that she expected women to be serious readers as well as writers: "But not for you shall I write pretty butterflies of fashion, who listlessly take the paper in your jeweled fingers to while away a moment's time while waiting for a carriage, or for the adjustment of patterns at your dressmaker."[21] She continued this theme in another editorial titled "A Plea for the Ladies:" "I have heard gentlemen of reputed sense and refinement speak as though the only qualifications necessary in a lady, were to be a good cook and housekeeper. As though digestion were the grand business of life, and gastronomy the most important of sciences!" She warned young men and women that once the honeymoon was over, they had to talk with one another, and intellectual compatibility was the key to a lasting marriage. Young women who were "not removed above biscuit-making and darning socks" would make poor companions.[22] Bryan signed her contributions, thus welcoming the public recognition that would come with her publications.

In her opening address to her readers as associate editor of the *Temperance Banner* early in 1858, Bryan set forth the tone and character of her future columns and offered views on the state of southern literature in general and

[17] Bertram Holland Flanders, *Early Georgia Magazines: Literary Periodicals to 1865* (Athens, GA, 1944), 162.

[18] Quoted in *Temperance Banner* nsv3 (January 28, 1858).

[19] "Notice," *Macon Weekly Telegraph* 32 (January 26, 1858), 2.

[20] Mary Edwards Bryan, "Why Ladies Should Read Newspapers," *Temperance Banner* nsv3 (January 7, 1858).

[21] Bryan "Salutatory," *Temperance Banner* nsv3 (January 28, 1858).

[22] Bryan, "A Plea for the Ladies," *Temperance Banner* nsv3 (February 11, 1858).

southern women authors in particular. Despite her unusually bold admonishments to lazy readers, Bryan was popular with subscribers and the paper prospered. As head of the literary department of the weekly paper, Bryan had ample opportunity to offer her views on women and literature. In addition to contributing dozens of poems and short stories to the *Temperance Banner* (her writings occupied almost the entire front page of the paper on March 4, 1858), Bryan offered marriage advice.

Before the Civil War Bryan was well known in the South for publishing prose and verse in various magazines, including the *Southern Field and Fireside*. She often proved a perceptive critic of southern literature, but she still struggled against stereotypes of female writers. "I am *not* one of those female scribblers," she wrote to Mann in 1860, "who imagine themselves perfect because they have recieved [sic] indiscriminate and wholesale puffs and praise from the press and the public – our southern press not yet understanding that judicious criticism will do more to help the literature they are anxious to build up than injudicious and universal praise."[23]

On the eve of the Civil War, Bryan accepted a generous salary from James Gardner, editor of the *Southern Field and Fireside*, to become coeditor and contributor. In this position, she continued to express herself boldly on questions regarding gender roles. In "How Should Women Write?" published in 1860, Bryan called for greater acceptance of women writers. "Men," she complained, "after much demur and hesitation, have given women liberty to write; but they cannot yet consent to allow them full freedom." As long as women write "of birds, of flowers, sunshine, [or of] love, religion, and domestic obligations," female authors are permitted to continue their literary endeavors. However, she wrote, "those who seek to go beyond the boundary-line are put down with the stigma of '*strong-minded*.'" Bryan protested that authors such as Fanny Fern, who wrote "to strike a blow at the root of social sin and inconsistency," were "annihilated by the epithets of 'bold' and 'indelicate.'" To the question, "How should women write?" Bryan answered, "As men, as all should write to whom the power of expression has been given – *honestly and without fear*."[24]

On her return to her husband in Louisiana in the early 1860s, Bryan edited the *Semi-Weekly Times* in Natchitoches, writing essays, poems, and short stories for the paper. Yet she complained about the distractions that women authors faced as they struggled to fulfill their duties as wives and mothers. She lamented that male writers did not have to contend with "the infliction of 'calls' – morning and evening. Positively, my hours for reading, writing, etc., are so broken in upon by company, that I am almost ready to give up in despair."[25] As she wrote to the southern poet Paul Hamilton Hayne in 1881, "I wish I could have a season of rest with no family cares to distract me. These

[23] Patty, "A Georgia Authoress Writes Her Editor," 423.

[24] Bryan, "How Should Women Write?" reprinted in Simms, *War Poetry of the South*, 336–7.

[25] Bryan to W. W. Mann, February 18, 1860, reprinted in James S. Patty, "A Georgia Authoress Writes Her Editor," 424.

domestic ties tugging always at the heart – they do pull down the imagination, but then life would not be worth living without them."[26] Evidently Bryan found a way to balance these demands because she remained a productive author while raising a family.

After she left Louisiana in the late 1870s, Bryan edited an Atlanta weekly magazine called the *Sunny South* (which later merged with the important monthly *Uncle Remus' Magazine*). Her duties at the *Sunny South* ranged from writing poems and stories to fill pages to maintaining correspondence with contributors to writing captions for engravings. "Sometimes," she admitted, she wrote "under another name, if I do not care to acknowledge the necessarily hurried work."[27] Despite these extensive responsibilities, Bryan found time to pen her first novel, *Manche* (1879). The latter work sold thousands of copies and became a popular traveling play that was performed all over the country, but her publishers failed to copyright it, and the novel was pirated across the country.[28] Thus, even before her successful novel *Wild Work* (1881), Bryan was an accomplished and widely recognized author and editor.

Wild Work drew extensively from the real people, events, and landscape of Red River Parish. Louisiana after the Civil War harbored a volatile combination of native whites who fervently wished to regain political control of their state from the federal government, Republican carpetbaggers, and freedmen seeking justice and equality.[29] Such a combination was bound to explode violently. Scholars such as Bertram Wyatt-Brown, Kenneth Greenberg, and Gilles Vandal have devoted much attention to the ubiquity of violence that was bound up in southern honor culture.[30] The often brutal nature of life in the nineteenth-century South so well described by Wyatt-Brown is evident in *Wild Work*. Red River Parish, created by the Louisiana legislature in 1871, was particularly susceptible to the kind of passions that might result in conflict because it was the powerbase of Vermont carpetbagger Marshall Twitchell.[31] Although much has been written about other violent periods in

[26] Mary E. Bryan to Paul Hamilton Hayne, November 14, 1881, in Hayne Papers, Perkins Library, Duke University.

[27] Mary E. Bryan to Mrs. Paul Hamilton Hayne, May 5, 1880, in Hayne Papers, Perkins Library, Duke University.

[28] "Mary Edwards Bryan," in *National Cyclopedia of American Biography* vol. 8 (New York, 1925), 374–5.

[29] Useful works on Reconstruction Louisiana include James G. Hollandsworth, Jr., *An Absolute Massacre: The New Orleans Riot of July 30, 1866* (Baton Rouge, 2001); Ted Tunnell, *Crucible of Reconstruction: War, Radicalism and Race in Louisiana, 1862–1877* (Baton Rouge, 1984); Joseph G. Dawson, *Army Generals and Reconstruction: Louisiana, 1862–1877* (Baton Rouge, 1982); Jo Gray Taylor, *Louisiana Reconstructed, 1863–1877* (Baton Rouge, 1974).

[30] Bertram Wyatt-Brown, *Southern Honor: Ethics and Behavior in the Old South* (New York, 1982); Kenneth Greenberg, *Honor & Slavery* (Princeton, NJ, 1996); Gilles Vandal, *Rethinking Southern Violence: Homicides in Post-Civil War Louisiana, 1866–1884*, (Columbus, OH, 2000).

[31] On the history of the Red River region, see Carl N. Tyson, *The River in Southwestern History* (Norman, OK, 1981); Carol Wells, ed., *War, Reconstruction and Redemption on Red River: The Memoirs of Dosia Williams Moore* (Ruston, LA, 1991).

Reconstruction Louisiana, including the New Orleans riot of 1876, comparatively little has been written about the murders in Red River Parish. As the only novel to deal with this tragedy, *Wild Work* records in lively detail a crucial incident in the postwar South. In fact, *Wild Work* is quite similar to Albion Tourgee's popular *A Fool's Errand*, a similarity that was not lost on contemporaries. The *Atlanta Phonograph* remarked angrily that the novel by Tourgee, a carpetbagger greatly resented by many in the South, was "a wholesale plagiarism upon a serial story called *Wild Work*, written by Mrs. Mary E. Bryan for the *Sunny South* three years before Judge Tourgee's book appeared." Although unsubstantiated, the Atlanta paper delighted in claiming that "the cormorants of the Radical party want to prey on Southern brains as well as everything else."[32]

After *Wild Work*, Bryan went on to pen ten more novels and to edit the *Sunny South* magazine for nearly a decade. So successful was Bryan that in 1885 she moved to New York to edit *The Fashion Bazaar* and *The Fireside Companion*. In fact, she was renowned not only in her native South, but (uncommon for a southern woman) she was also recognized as a member of New York literati.

Success was marred by personal tragedy. Shortly after Christmas Day in 1887, Bryan's thirteen-year-old son Fritz nearly accidently killed himself. As a Georgia newspaper reported, "Young Bryan ... made a fireball out of barrel hoops, covering the hoops with cotton balls dipped in oil. He then threw the ball up into the air, and when it came down it fell on the boy's head.... It is said that both eyes are so terribly burned that his sight is completely destroyed, while his face is fearfully charred."[33] Bryan was in New York at the time, and she rushed back home to Clarkston, Georgia, to care for her son. The boy apparently survived, and the tragedy did not dissuade Bryan from her literary and journalistic career. The *Kansas City Star* reported the following year that Bryan was earning "about $6000 per year with her pen."[34]

Despite such gains, just a year after her teenage son Fritz nearly died from his burns, Bryan's family suffered another drama when another of her sons was indicted for murder in Monticello, Florida. In this case, her son, who was involved in Florida politics, became embroiled in a fight in which he was stabbed by a freedman named Judson Cason. The wound to the young Bryan was not mortal, but he felt justified in hunting down the alleged perpetrator and, along with three friends, stabbed Cason more than a dozen times and dumped his body in a nearby body of water where it was soon discovered. Bryan, never in favor of emancipation and strongly opposed to the political and social equality of the races, supported her son. "My son thought this negro was the one who stabbed him, and I assure you he thought he was doing

[32] Comments from *Atlanta Phonograph* reprinted in *Macon Weekly Telegraph* (February 19, 1881), 2.

[33] "A Helmet of Fire," *Macon Weekly Telegraph* (December 28, 1887).

[34] "Starbeams," *Kansas City Star* 14 (July 13, 1888), 2.

perfectly right when he helped to kill the negro."[35] The claim was reprinted in newspapers as far away as Philadelphia.

Undeterred by these familial traumas, Bryan remained in New York in the early 1890s, expanding opportunities for women in journalism and politics. Her home became a gathering place for literary women and, importantly, as a forum for budding female journalists. For example, in December 1890, Bryan held a reception at her home on 61st Street to protest the treatment of women in Russia. The case of one woman, Sophie Gunsberg, condemned in Russia on "very slight cause or none at all," attracted the support of Bryan and her female colleagues. The reception for Gunsberg, according to one newspaper, "called together most of the women writers of New York City. It was remarked at this reception that the general impression of the 'unkemptness' of the 'blues' was finally refuted for good and all."[36] Soon, Bryan was being paid $10,000 yearly to write serialized stories for publisher George Munro, and she served as chairwoman of literature in the Sorosis Club and Vice President of the Woman's Press Club of New York. Despite this fame, Bryan remained politically unreconstructed. As one newspaper observed in 1891, "In one corner of her drawing room, on an easel, stand pictures of Jefferson Davis ... and Henry Grady, who was one of her dearest friends."[37] Clearly she had left the South for a time but never abandoned her prosouthern political views.

Bryan returned to the South and to her post as editor of *The Sunny South* in 1891 and around the same time purchased a magazine titled *The Old Homestead* for $10,000, which she conducted with her son-in-law.[38] She was now editor and owner of two different periodicals at the same time, a highly unusual feat for any early female journalist. Yet, before her death near Atlanta in 1913, Bryan was to face one more personal series of crises involving her family. In a widely publicized affair, Bryan's daughter divorced her husband, Charles P. Byrd, one of the most important publishers in Atlanta. Whatever caused the divorce was so egregious that Bryan's daughter came to live with her in New York and refused to return home to Georgia despite the personal appeals of her husband. Remarkably similar to Bryan's own leaving of her husband nearly thirty years earlier, her daughter's divorce undoubtedly affected the couple's children.[39] For, three years later, Bryan's fourteen-year-old granddaughter Ada eloped with the teenage son of Georgia's governor.[40]

Bryan's personal life read too much like one of her tragic novels, but her career is significant for a number of reasons. First, the ease with which she

35 "Authoress's Son in Trouble," *Philadelphia Inquirer* 119 (November 27, 1888), 1.

36 "From the Great Metropolis," *Columbus (Georgia) Daily Enquirer* 32 (December 7, 1890), 3.

37 "Bright Women These," *Idaho Daily Statesman* 27 (January 24, 1891), 5.

38 "People Worth Talking About," *Morning Olympian* 1 (November 5, 1891), 4; "Mrs. Mary E. Bryan," *Columbus Daily Enquirer* 32 (December 13, 1891), 4; "Mrs. Mary E. Bryan's New Venture," *Idaho Daily Statesman* 28 (March 29, 1892), 3.

39 "A Sensational Divorce," *Columbus Daily Enquirer* 35 (August 23, 1894), 1.

40 "Son of Georgia's Governor," *The State* (Columbia, SC) (April 3, 1897), 1.

moved between northern and southern cultures reflected a common characteristic of male and female authors and journalists both before and after the war. Intellectuals throughout the nineteenth century traveled freely and often felt equally comfortable in New York City or small-town Georgia. Such flexibility served women like Bryan well because it allowed them to earn substantial regional reputations while also taking advantage of big-city opportunities. There is ample evidence in the nineteenth century that southerners and northerners often struggled mightily when confronted with local customs. Antebellum northern intellectuals decried slavery and recorded in their travel journals the horrors of seeing slaves in chains. But equally striking is the sense of familiarity that nineteenth-century Americans experienced when traveling to a different part of the country, or at least a sense of undeterred adventure. The friends Bryan made in both the North and South are testament to the existence of a national literary culture before and after the Civil War.

In addition, Bryan's successful career suggests a southern society more open to bold and accomplished women than we might have otherwise believed. The intellectual culture of the New South was flexible enough to accommodate white women even as it stiffened in opposition to any advances made by African Americans. Rarely did late nineteenth-century southerners openly deny that men and women were intellectually equal or that girls and young women should be educated. The region was not a bastion of reform sentiment, nor was suffrage for women a popular political position. However, the extent to which Bryan and other white women like her were treated fairly in an open literary market is remarkable.

If Bryan were the only example of such a successful southern woman, she might be treated as an extreme aberration. However, the literary career of Margaret Junkin Preston paralleled in many ways those of writers like Bryan. Preston was born in the North and spent her early years in Pennsylvania. Her father, George Junkin, brought the family to Virginia when he became president of Washington College in 1848. Although her father never seemed to warm to the new location, Margaret apparently felt quite at ease in Lexington, Virginia. In fact, she would later become a strong supporter of the Confederacy, and her sister, Eleanor Junkin, was the first wife of Stonewall Jackson.[41] In the early 1850s, Margaret began publishing poetry in leading periodicals, such as the *Southern Literary Messenger*, *Sartain's Magazine*, and the *Southern Presbyterian*. She wrote at least eighteen short stories and poems for the *Messenger* alone between 1849 and 1853.[42] One scholar has claimed that "her new society did not tolerate her publishing career," but there is little evidence to suggest that she faced any rebukes from southerners

[41] Hubbell, *The South in American Literature*, 617.

[42] Stacey Jean Klein, "Wielding the Pen: Margaret Preston, Confederate Nationalistic Literature and the Expansion of a Woman's Place in the South," *Civil War History* 49 (September 2003), 222.

for her desire to write and publish.[43] Indeed, in Virginia and elsewhere in the region, women not only became prominent authors but editors as well. According to Preston's biographer, because Preston usually signed her full name to the poems and stories she published, these quickly "won her considerable respect" among her fellow Virginians.[44] She penned a novel, *Silverwood* (1856), which attracted the notice of the *Messenger* and other prominent periodicals.[45] With her literary reputation secure, Preston also entered the public intellectual sphere by attending lyceums and the proceedings of local debating societies.

A year after she published *Silverwood*, Margaret married John Preston, a professor of Latin at the Virginia Military Institute, who became an important champion of her literary ambitions. Preston, a widower who brought seven children to his marriage with Margaret, was often ambivalent about his new wife's literary endeavors. He admired her talents, once proclaiming that "she is a genius and she is my darling."[46] But he was also wedded to the notion that although women might legitimately pursue literature and intellectual interests in private, women should not appear in print with their names attached. As Margaret later remarked, John "did not in his heart of hearts approve of his wife's giving any part of herself to the public, even in verse."[47] Although Preston was reluctant to have his wife's name printed in public forums, he supported her writing and eventually warmed to her desire to become a well-known author.

When Virginia seceded, Margaret's family, like many, divided over whether to join the Confederacy or remain in the Union. Her father refused to support secession and moved back to the North, but Margaret and her husband became strong advocates of the new Confederate government. Her husband had deep roots in the South (Senator William C. Preston was his cousin), and Stonewall Jackson was her brother-in-law. There appears to have been little anguish over secession or hesitation at remaining in Virginia. John Preston became Chief of Staff in Jackson's army, and Margaret assisted the southern war effort with her pen. Both would pay dearly for their support of the Confederacy. Like Mary Bayard Clarke, Preston became more political in her writing during the war. Undoubtedly, both women saw the war as an opportunity to employ their literary talents to aid Confederate nationalism. They saw a way to build on their previous literary successes to earn even greater respect in the region. Preston wrote poetry that buttressed the Confederates politically and militarily, in much the same manner that a southern politician might use a Fourth of July speech to rally support for the southern cause.

[43] Klein, "Wielding the Pen," 223.

[44] Mary P. Coulling, *Margaret Junkin Preston: A Biography*, (Winston-Salem, NC, 1993), 62, 80.

[45] Baym, *Women's Fiction*, 240–1.

[46] Coulling, *Margaret Junkin Preston*, 119.

[47] Preston quoted in Hubbell, *The South in American Literature*, 618.

As her biographer Stacey Jean Klein has shown, Preston published widely during the war, writing poems tinged with political statements about the just battle the South was waging for its independence.[48] As one scholar has noted, her poem "Dirge for Ashby" (though initially printed in her local newspaper) became one of the most celebrated poems of the war. Leading Stonewall Jackson's cavalry in Virginia, Brigadier General Turner Ashby was killed in the summer of 1862.[49] In her poem championing Ashby and his troops, Preston engaged in a political act as powerful as many others performed by southern men who gave speeches or organized parades. By proclaiming that Ashby, and by extension his fellow officers and soldiers, were "Bold as the lion's heart/Dauntlessly brave/Knightly as knightliest," Preston promoted the political argument that fallen Confederates were martyrs who earned the eternal respect of the southern people. When she added that "Jackson, the victor, still/Leads at your head!" Preston was reminding the soldiers that heroic leaders still remained.

Jackson's death at Chancellorsville hit the family and especially Margaret very hard. The Confederate leader seemed to Margaret larger than life, almost invincible in the face of mere human challenges, and thus his death was a shock. As she wrote in her war journal in an entry dated May 12, 1863, "Jackson is indeed dead! My heart overflows with sorrow. The grief in this community is intense; everybody is in tears.... Never have I known a holier man. Never have I seen a human being as thoroughly governed by duty."[50] Jackson's death, as painful as it was for Margaret and her family, provided another opportunity for her to engage in the political act of supporting the Confederate struggle. Based on Jackson's last words ("let us cross over the river, and rest under the shade of the trees"), Preston composed a poem that eulogized Jackson titled "Under the Shade of the Trees."

Margaret's public and political support for fallen Confederates stood in sharp contrast to her private grief and misgivings about the war. She began keeping a detailed war journal in April 1862, and just one year into the battles, she lamented the misfortune that had befallen the region: "Darkness seems gathering over the Southern land; disaster follows disaster; where is it all to end? My very soul is sick of carnage. I loath the word – *War.* It is destroying and paralyzing all before it."[51] She complained bitterly about the difficulty in purchasing food and other items: "Goods not to be bought, or so exorbitant that we are obliged to do without."[52] However, Preston realized that the problems she faced in securing daily items needed to run a household and to feed her seven stepchildren were trifling compared to the deaths experienced

[48] Stacey Jean Klein, *Margaret Junkin Preston: Poet of the Confederacy* (Columbia, 2007).

[49] Klein, "Wielding the Pen," 224.

[50] Entry for May 12, 1863 in Elizabeth Preston Allan, *Life and Letters of Margaret Junkin Preston* (Boston, 1903), 165.

[51] Entry for April 3, 1862 in *ibid.*, 134.

[52] *Ibid.*

by families in both North and South. After one of her stepsons suffered an amputated arm, another was slain on the battlefield at Manassas. "The worst has happened," she lamented in her journal in September 1862, " – our fearful suspense is over: Willy, the gentle, tender-hearted, brave boy, lies in a soldier's grave on the Plains of Manassas! This has been a day of weeping and of woe to this household."[53]

By 1863, Preston was desperate for the return of her husband from the battlefields and frantic for the war to end. After Jackson's death, she wrote in her journal, "Oh the havoc that death is making! ... Who thinks or speaks of victory? The word is scarcely ever heard. Alas! Alas! When is the end to be?"[54] But the war was to have one more trial for Preston. In June 1864, as Union soldiers stormed through her town of Lexington, Virginia, Preston faced the threats of starved men on her doorstep. Alone she had to confront soldiers demanding the keys to her cellar and smokehouse, soldiers who bullied and terrorized her while threatening to burn down her home. "I protested their pillage," she recorded in her journal, "... with a score of them surrounding me, with guns in their hands." She begged them, "by the respect they had for their wives, mothers, and sisters, to leave me a little meat. They heeded me no more than wild beasts would have done; swore at me; and left me not one piece." The next morning the soldiers returned and stole her stepchildren's breakfast, and then set fire to the Virginia Military Institute and many homes.[55]

Through these trials, Preston remained interested in writing and in literature. She continued to search for ways to contribute to the war effort with her pen even as those closest to her were falling in battle. Realizing the power of Margaret's abilities to support the Confederacy, John Preston became a more consistent advocate of his wife's literary career. Near the end of the war, John sent his wife a poem titled "Wee Davie." "It is a rather pretty thing," John wrote to Margaret, "but you could do something much better in the same line."[56] Margaret accepted the offer, and in short period she had composed *Beechenbrook: A Rhyme of the War*, an epic poem nearly sixty-five pages long. Based in part on her own war-time experiences, *Beechenbrook* tells the story of Alice Dunbar, a woman whose dedication to the war effort only deepened as she faced hardships. In fact, Alice laments that she must pass the time idly, consumed with trivial tasks, while the men are fighting and dying on the battlefield.[57] Alice's bravery in the face of danger and suffering stems from her unwavering support for the Confederate war effort.[58]

Preston's propagandistic rendering of southern motives in the war was buttressed by her portrayal of the strength of southern women. Indeed, when the

[53] Entry for September 4, 1862 in *ibid.*, 147.
[54] Entry for May 12, 1863 in *ibid.*, 165.
[55] Entries for June 11 and 12, 1864, in *ibid.*, 189–90.
[56] Hubbell, *The South in American Literature*, 618. Also quoted in Klein, "Wielding the Pen," 232.
[57] Margaret Junkin Preston, *Beechenbrook: A Rhyme of the War* (Baltimore, 1866), 11.
[58] *Ibid.*, 12.

poem was reissued after the war, it was dedicated "To every southern woman who was widowed by the war." Preston ensured that southern women would be depicted with strength and fortitude, and Alice Dunbar exhibited these qualities well. Southern women in Preston's poem did not shrink from their responsibilities with weakness:

> Brave-hearted, – yet quaking, – high-souled, – yet so pale, –
> Is it thus that the wife of a soldier should quail,
> And shudder and shrink, at the boom of a gun,
> As only a timorous girl should have done?
> Ah! wait until custom has blunted the keen,
> Crushing edge of that sound, and no woman, I ween,
> Will hear it with pulses, more equal, more free
> From feminine terrors and weakness, than she.[59]

After the death of Alice's husband, she stubbornly and bravely still proclaims her belief in the virtue of the Confederate cause. The poem concludes with a stirring tribute to the notion that the war was driven by a desire for southern independence, and Preston gives not an inch to those who would deny the righteousness of southerners' motives.

In presenting a brave woman who was emboldened during the war by the difficulties she faced, Preston was not being honest with herself or her audience. For we know from her war journal that Preston repeatedly questioned the wisdom of continuing to fight as losses mounted, and she was less concerned with Confederate victory than she was in ending the war before she and her family experienced further suffering. Thus, *Beechenbrook* should be seen not as a kind of personal story so much as another attempt by Preston to assert herself as a public figure playing a political role in the Confederate cause. John Preston read *Beechenbrook*, which received the warm approval of fellow officers, and then invested $2,600 for two thousand copies to be printed in Richmond. All but fifty copies were destroyed by fire as Lee's army left the city, but it was reprinted in 1866 and sold more than 7,000 copies.[60]

The publication of *Beechenbrook* and the end of the war marked a significant new phase in Preston's career as an author. After the war she contributed innumerable books reviews, poems, and short stories to periodicals. The *Land We Love*, a new literary magazine published in Charlotte and edited by Civil War veteran Daniel Hill, was the forum for many of Preston's contributions in the years after the war. As her biographer notes, many of her works continued to reflect pro-South sentiments so evident in *Beechenbrook*.[61] In 1867, Preston also developed what would become a twenty-year correspondence with the

[59] *Ibid.*, 16.

[60] Hubbell, *The South in American Literature*, 618–9. See also Klein, "Wielding the Pen," 234 and Louis D. Rubin, et al., *The History of Southern Literature*, (Baton Rouge, 1985), 190–1.

[61] Coulling, *Margaret Junkin Preston*, 153.

important Charleston author and editor Paul Hamilton Hayne. Before the war, Hayne had edited a key literary periodical titled *Russell's Magazine*, and by the time he and Preston began writing to one another he was regarded as one of the South's leading authors. Although Hayne and Preston never met, they valued their correspondence. They offered critical advice, mutual support, and opinions on authors and literary trends.

Although discussions of authors and their works consumed many of their letters, often Hayne and Preston entered a more personal realm. In an 1872, letter Preston let Hayne know that her husband was still a bit uneasy with her public role as a writer. Hayne responded with friendly support for her career as a female author. "No man could by *any* possibility desire to see all the delicacies which surround your sex, more carefully preserved, than I do," Hayne wrote, "*but there is no sex in genius*, and, I would, with my dying breath uphold a woman's *right* ... to appear before the world as *Teacher & Consoler*, thro the force, or beauty of her *thoughts*, as presented in *poem, novel, essay*, or drama!!"[62] They also often commiserated after a harsh or critical review. After one particularly nasty review in 1878, Hayne lashed out at critics in general: "But *Critics*, now-a-days, seem to me for the most part, a precious set of Donkeys, with boundless powers of *self-assurance*, and unlimited capacity for ... *braying*!!"[63] With Hayne's support, Preston published four more poetry collections, all of which bore her full name upon publication: *Old Song and New* (1870), *Cartoons* (1875), *For Love's Sake* (1886), and *Colonial Ballads, Sonnets and Other Verse* (1887). After a lifetime of trying to reconcile her desire for a public career as an author with John's intermittent apprehension over these desires, Preston and her husband had finally become comfortable with her role as a highly visible female writer. When one scholar published a history of southern literature in the early twentieth century, Preston was deemed "the best woman poet of the South."[64]

As the literary legacy of Bryan and Preston suggests, the postwar period was a fertile one for women journalists and authors. Whereas Bryan and Preston advanced southern women's literary standing by publishing poetry and reviews in periodicals such as *The Land We Love*, other women ventured into writing essays. Sarah Morgan, an important Civil War-era diarist, played an important role in the postbellum years as a leading woman editorialist. Morgan's editorials are a crucial link between the literary endeavors of southern women and the broader fight for gender equality. Appearing originally in the Charleston *News and Courier*, a newspaper edited by her future husband Francis Warrington Dawson, Morgan's editorials demonstrate clearly that southern periodicals were most often the vehicles through which women challenged traditional notions of gender boundaries.

[62] Hayne to Preston, April 9, 1872, in Rayburn S. Moore, *A Man of Letters in the Nineteenth-Century South: Selected Letters of Paul Hamilton Hayne* (Baton Rouge, 1982), 100.

[63] Hayne to Preston, July 26, 1878, in *ibid.*, 153.

[64] Rutherford, *The South in American Literature*, 431.

The Civil War years and their aftermath were unkind to Morgan. Born in New Orleans in 1842, the daughter of a prominent Louisiana judge, Morgan grew up in a wealthy family that owned eight slaves as house servants.[65] However, she lost two brothers during the war: one during the fighting and another to a duel. And her family's financial losses, like those of many previously wealthy families, mounted during the Union occupation of New Orleans. Additionally, Sarah remained unmarried in the 1860s and early 1870s and so had to depend on the kindness of relatives. In 1873, she and her mother moved to South Carolina to live with Sarah's brother, James. The comfort and familiarity of James's home changed, however, when he married. James' new wife apparently resented the presence of his sister and mother, creating an awkward situation. Thus, when a suitor named Francis Warrington Dawson began to seek Sarah's affections, the possibility of leaving her brother's household and moving out on her own might have appeared as an attractive alternative to remaining an unwelcome guest.

Sarah repeatedly rebuffed Francis's advances, however, and a man less persistent would likely have given up. Perhaps Sarah had cause to question the authenticity of Francis's affections. A British immigrant who came to the South in 1862, Dawson worked as a reporter for the *Richmond Daily Examiner* and then for the *Charleston Mercury*. By 1873, he had purchased his own paper and appointed himself editor of the new Charleston *News and Courier*.[66] His seemingly good fortunes ended, however, with the death of his wife, Virginia, in December 1872. Almost immediately Dawson set his sights on Sarah, and her friends and family repeatedly noted the impropriety of pursuing another woman's hand so soon after the death of his first wife. In January, just a few weeks after her passing, Francis was hinting of his feelings for Sarah; by early February he addressed his letters to "my darling"; and by July he called her "my beloved saint." Such tributes to southern womanhood were ubiquitous in the nineteenth-century South, but Francis' love for Sarah and his commitment to winning her hand strike the modern reader as legitimate. Sarah, however, gave Francis little hope of winning her love, and she remained unwavering as late as mid-September that he was to regard her only as a friend. So Francis changed strategy and withheld his affection in their correspondence. The plan worked. Sarah moved to Charleston in the fall, and they were married in January 1874.[67]

Francis's position as newspaper editor provided Sarah with an unusual opportunity to employ her talents as a writer. However, despite her abilities as a keen observer of and commentator on southern society, talents that modern

[65] Roberts, *The Correspondence of Sarah Morgan and Francis Warrington Dawson*, xvii–xviii. See also Clara Junker, "Behind Confederate Lines: Sarah Morgan Dawson," *Southern Quarterly* 30 (Fall 1991), 7–18.

[66] Roberts, *The Correspondence of Sarah Morgan and Francis Warrington Dawson*, xxvii–xxviii.

[67] *Ibid.*, xxxi, xlv.

readers can appreciate through her published diaries, Sarah was reluctant to throw herself into the realm of writing editorials. She harbored doubts about the legitimacy of women as public figures, particular in expressing views on politics and culture. But eventually Sarah, moved by Francis's encouragement, realized that the opportunity to publish editorials on a range of subjects that would be widely read, as well as the opportunity to earn considerable income to facilitate her financial independence from her brother, proved to be too important to pass up.

Morgan's editorials, particularly those on women, created a stir among Charleston readers. Often Morgan questioned the institution of marriage. In one editorial, titled "Old Maids," Morgan criticized women who married only because southern society expected them to:

> An infinite number of foolish virgins prefer marrying men unworthy of a good woman's respect to facing the jibes and sneers of their mating and mated associates. O women who seek this so-called "respectability," can you, do you, believe it decent to marry not only without love but actually without aversion? Is it more reputable to marry a man for *his* money, than to catch *your* fish with a golden hook? Is it "proper" to marry John because Thomas is not available?

It is clear from Morgan's editorials that she herself faced scorn and ridicule as a thirty-one-year-old unmarried southern woman. "Put it to a vote," she declared, "a year, a month, a week after marriage and how many women would secretly black-ball their choice! Yet these same wives, smiling in ghastly faintness to conceal some hidden stroke, will scoff at Old Maids who have no one to marry." For Morgan, the independence she coveted as a single woman was an integral part of being an advocate of women's equality. The unmarried woman, she claimed, "has no terror of the marital lion roaring for a retarded meal, or growling over an over-done roast. She has no fear for the future: for, at the worst, her destiny is in her own hands, and she is not chained to a dead hope and a living despair."[68] Such a jaded view of marriage helps to explain Morgan's initial rejection of Dawson's advances.

In her 1873 editorials on women, Morgan approved of the nation's "steady liberalization of opinion on the Woman question," particularly in regard to the expansion of careers opening to women.[69] She praised northern efforts "to open a wider field of labor for women," and she urged the South to follow the North's lead.[70] Who was to blame for the limited career options for women? Clearly the blame lay with men who offered tributes to traditional roles for women. "Men of blessed memory have agreed that women were made to

[68] Morgan, "Old Maids!" reprinted in *ibid.*, 57–8.

[69] Morgan, "The Property of Married Women," reprinted in Roberts, *The Correspondence of Sarah Morgan and Francis Warrington Dawson*, 60.

[70] Morgan, "Work for Women," reprinted in Roberts, *The Correspondence of Sarah Morgan and Francis Warrington Dawson*, 61.

become mothers; nothing more," she lamented.[71] "Some men still cling," she complained, "to the ancient prejudice of woman's sanctity, and maintain that she is desecrated by labor."[72] Morgan proved quite forward thinking in her views, offering a proto-feminist perspective on equal pay and equal opportunity in occupations. As she stated in an April 1873 editorial for the *News and Courier*, "The most modest and retiring may hail the promise of a day when the equality of the sexes will be established on the true basis of equal remuneration for equal services." In her mind, women were being denied opportunities to expand their interests and their occupations merely because of tradition: "And public prejudice ... shuts her out from work she could do, perhaps better than the man to whom the preference is given."[73]

Morgan was equally outspoken on the movement for women's rights. For her, "Woman's Rights" meant "the right of doing as she will with her own."[74] "Marriage," she declared, "is *not* the end of woman!"[75] However, Morgan was not willing to accept, at least by 1873, that women should serve in political office. Of course, she engaged in political acts by writing on society and culture, but she was not prepared to throw herself with the northern women's movement for suffrage, which she called "sheer nonsense."[76] On matters of race, she seems to have differed little from the majority white opinion that blacks were by nature inferior, and she had doubts about the ability of the freedmen to survive in the South on their own.

Morgan dismissed Dawson's affections until she moved to Charleston in the fall of 1873. As scholar Giselle Roberts points out, "The move marked a turning point in Sarah's relationship with Frank."[77] She and Frank married in late January 1874 and apparently shared a loving relationship that bore three children. She published few editorials after her marriage but continued to contribute book reviews to southern periodicals and offered advice to Frank on the *News and Courier*. Unfortunately, her husband was killed in 1889 in a fight with Thomas McDow, who Dawson suspected of having an affair with Dawson's governess. Although McDow was brought to trial he was acquitted on the basis of self-defense, and for Sarah the lack of justice in punishing her husband's killer was a bitter pill. No longer comfortable living among those

[71] Morgan, "The Natural History of Woman," reprinted in Roberts, *The Correspondence of Sarah Morgan and Francis Warrington Dawson*, 67.

[72] Morgan, "Work for Women," reprinted in Roberts, *The Correspondence of Sarah Morgan and Francis Warrington Dawson*, 62.

[73] *Ibid.*, 63, 64. See also E. Culpepper Clark, "Sarah Morgan and Francis Dawson: Raising the Woman Question in Reconstruction South Carolina," *South Carolina Historical Magazine* 81 (January 1980), 8–23.

[74] Morgan, "Work for Women," reprinted in Roberts, *The Correspondence of Sarah Morgan and Francis Warrington Dawson*, 61.

[75] Morgan, "Young Couples," reprinted in Roberts, *The Correspondence of Sarah Morgan and Francis Warrington Dawson*, 75.

[76] Morgan, "Suffrage-Shrieking," reprinted in Roberts, *The Correspondence of Sarah Morgan and Francis Warrington Dawson*, 205.

[77] Roberts, *The Correspondence of Sarah Morgan and Francis Warrington Dawson*, 249.

who denied her husband justice, she moved to Paris in 1898, a city that years before she and Francis had dreamed of seeing.[78] She died in Paris in 1909. Morgan's willingness to explore in public discourse ideas that openly questioned traditional opinions on gender and woman's place in society stand out boldly. Using the region's periodicals as a forum for debate over gender equality, she expressed views that called for greater equality.

That literature and particularly periodical writing could be vitally important vehicles for furthering women's independence is further illustrated by the life and career of Katherine McDowell, who wrote under the penname Sherwood Bonner. Born in Holly Springs, Mississippi, in 1849 to a planter family and then married to what she thought was a promising and ambitious southern gentleman, Bonner would seem hardly the kind to become one of the South's boldest literary women. After attending the well-regarded Holly Springs Female Seminary and another school in Montgomery, Alabama, during the Civil War, McDowell began writing short poems and fiction for literary periodicals. Her first story was published in Boston's *Ploughman* in 1869.

McDowell married a fellow native of Holly Springs, with whom she had a daughter in 1872. The marriage did not last, however, and McDowell left her husband and moved to Massachusetts, leaving her daughter behind as well, in 1873. Once in New England, McDowell wasted little time in writing to Henry W. Longfellow, who became a mentor to the ambitious young woman.[79] Despite her move to the North, she maintained literary ties to her native region, publishing a series of letters in 1875 in the Memphis *Avalanche*, and shortly afterward published her only novel, *Like unto Like*. Like many southern women authors, McDowell contributed to magazines, including popular northern literary magazines such as *Harper's*, *St. Nicholas Magazine*, and *Lippincott's*, even as she wrote longer fiction.[80]

McDowell was unusual, however, in that she divorced her husband in 1881, and her independence was reflected in her writings. An important early contributor to the local color genre, she used African American dialect long before better-known male authors did so. She seems to have veered little from traditional southern notions of black racial inferiority, but in other matters she was intellectually divorced from her upbringing. She openly questioned the Christian faith in which she was raised, and at only twenty years old, Bonner scorned the "bullying denunciations from the pulpit" and rejected organized religion. She called herself a "happy heathen" and chose not to have her infant daughter baptized.[81]

Her vigorous independence was reflected as well in her views on suffrage and gender. Angry that she could not vote in the late 1860s, she remarked,

[78] *Ibid.*, 251–2.

[79] William L. Frank, *Sherwood Bonner* (Boston, 1976), 49–50. See also the fine biography of Bonner by Hubert Horton McAlexander, *The Prodigal Daughter: A Biography of Sherwood Bonner* (Baton Rouge, 1981).

[80] Frank, *Sherwood Bonner*, 72–3.

[81] McAlexander, *The Prodigal Daughter*, 147.

"What a grand privilege it is to be a man!"[82] While living in the North, she criticized her native region for imagining "that a woman who wants to vote, or stands on a platform to make a speech, of necessity unsexes herself, and must be bold, unwomanly, and false to her higher duties."[83] In the 1870s, Bonner befriended prominent suffragist Elizabeth Avery Meriwether, a Tennessee native who published a pro-suffrage newspaper and who was elected vice president of the National Woman's Suffrage Convention in 1876.[84] Bonner and Meriwether must have found much in common, two southern women radicals who hailed from wealthy families and who used print culture to further the cause of independent womanhood.

In her novel *Like unto Like*, Bonner created an unusual southern character, Roger Ellis, a radical whom McDowell depicts in a favorable light, perhaps aware that southern male critics would find the character troubling. Paul Hamilton Hayne reviewed the novel for a Louisville newspaper and claimed that although the book was "very clever, sometimes brilliant," the character Roger Ellis should not have been drawn by "a Southern woman, one Southern in principle." Hayne chastised McDowell for having "lingered with such apparent pride, satisfaction and delight over many traits of his ultra Radical nature, and many expressions of his ultra Radical belief."[85] Yet even as Hayne found reason to fault McDowell, others embraced her openly and praised her talents. At her untimely death, she was remembered for having made important contributions to the South's intellectual life in spite of untraditional views on religion and gender roles.

White women could be subject to harsh criticism from prominent reviewers like Hayne, but at the same time they had greatly expanded their roles in southern intellectual culture by the 1890s. Bold, even radical, women could be found in the Old South, as the careers of Anne Royall, Mary Chase Barney, and Rebecca Hicks prove. During the latter half of the century, the number of white women who edited newspapers and magazines or who attained celebrity status as authors expanded greatly. White society in the New South proved more open and flexible when it came to successful and powerful women active in the public sphere.

The same could not be said for white society's reaction to southern black women journalists and intellectuals. At best, white southern intellectual culture almost completely ignored black literary and journalistic progress, as if whites and blacks lived in wholly different universes. However, if white women like Bryan and Morgan had taken the time to notice, they would have found much that was familiar in the pages of African American periodicals and novels. Former slaves earned notoriety in the postwar period by publishing memoirs of their lives in bondage. Annie Louise Burton, Louisa Picquet,

[82] *Ibid.*, 34.
[83] *Ibid.*, 68.
[84] *Ibid.*, 106.
[85] Hayne, "Like unto Like," Louisville *Argus*, (November 17, 1878), quoted in *ibid.*, 137.

Ellen Craft, and many other freedwomen published their stories, sometimes via coauthors, attracting notice for their abilities to convey in rich narratives bravery under cruel conditions. Such narratives by former slaves were important steps in creating a space in the literary culture for black women.

For African American women, the end of the war meant the end of slavery and finally the freeing up of latent literary and intellectual talents. As literacy rates rose for black women, so too did their interest in writing and editing. By the close of the nineteenth century more than a dozen African American women could be called journalists or editors, and dozens more were regular contributors to periodicals published for a black readership.

The new era in African American women's intellectual culture began with the entrance of such women into new occupations. While white women like McDowell forged literary careers in late nineteenth-century periodicals, black women made inroads into a wider range of traditionally white positions. Effie Cox, for example, was appointed postmaster by Benjamin Harrison and reappointed by William McKinley.[86] Elizabeth Keckley earned fame as a seamstress in the Lincoln White House.[87] Historians Sonya Ramsey and Adam Fairclough have recently argued convincingly that African American teachers became important members of the black middle class, whereas Leslie Brown has similarly illuminated the significance of black women workers in Durham.[88] By the end of the nineteenth century, there were even a few African American publishers in the South, including the A.M.E. Zion Publishing House, which was moved from Pittsburgh to Charlotte in 1895, and the Christian Methodist Publishing House found a home in Memphis beginning in 1870.[89] With such advances, freedmen and freedwomen carved out lengthy careers as publishers and authors, frequently under threat of violence. In fact, Effie Cox was forced to abandon her post office position in 1902 due to intimidation from whites.

Careers for black women in the postwar South often originated in work with reform movements, particularly temperance, or with the church, and such active involvement in the community facilitated the growth of black women's clubs at the end of the nineteenth century. Often periodicals helped to publicize clubs and their activities. The *National Association Notes*, for example, published in Tuskegee, Alabama, by Margaret Murray Washington, was vital in encouraging literacy among African Americans as well as in reporting on the news of the Tuskegee Woman's Club. According to scholar Elizabeth

[86] Thomas D. Clark, *The Southern Country Editor* (reprinted edition, Columbia, 1991), 314.

[87] Johnnie M. Stover, *Rhetoric and Resistance in Black Women's Autobiography* (Gainesville, 2003), 11–12.

[88] Sonya Ramsey, *Reading, Writing, and Segregation A Century of Black Women Teachers in Nashville* (Urbana, 2008); Adam Fairclough, *A Class of Their Own: Black Teachers in the Segregated South* (Cambridge, 2007); Leslie Brown, *Upbuilding Black Durham: Gender, Class, and Black Community Development in the Jim Crow South* (Chapel Hill, 2008).

[89] Donald Franklin Joyce, *Black Book Publishers in the United States: A Historical Dictionary of the Presses, 1817–1990* (Westport, 1991), 7–9, 71–5.

McHenry, "Cultivating the habit of reading was an integral component of black clubwomen's conception of literary work as a strategy of resistance."[90] In 1899, the club distributed more than fifteen hundred books, magazines, and other printed matter to needy African Americans.[91]

Individual black women contributed significantly to the literary culture emerging in the New South. Many of them are forgotten, like the careers of their white southern sisters. However, the recent rise of studies of African American life and culture has brought to life many of these powerful black women, from Anna Julia Cooper to Mary Church Terrell. Cooper was born a slave in Raleigh in 1858, but after the war she studied at St. Augustine's Normal School and quickly earned a reputation as an agitator. She protested that the girls' curriculum was not as rigorous as the boys', and she angrily denounced the sexism that pervaded both the school and society, lamenting that "the only mission open before a girl ... was to marry" a minister.[92] Her persistence paid off with an invitation to attend Oberlin, where she enrolled in a more arduous curriculum than female students typically took. She earned a master's degree and embarked on a career as a prominent teacher. Remarkably she never ceased striving, for in 1925, at the age of sixty-seven, she earned a doctorate from the University of Paris, just the fourth African American woman to be awarded the degree.[93]

Her education and teaching careers are remarkable by themselves, but Cooper was also an author and a well-respected lecturer. In *A Voice from the South* (1892), Cooper's only book-length work, she incorporated many of the same themes that won her acclaim as a public speaker, and she spoke out powerfully against racism and sexism. Writing on female education, Cooper praised the advances made in the nineteenth century that had sent "out yearly into the arteries of this nation a warm, rich flood of strong, brave, active, energetic, well-equipped, thoughtful women ... women who can think as well as feel, and who feel none the less because they think."[94] Cooper scorned the "barbarian brawn and brutality" that Western society seemed to value over the feminine, and she attacked the sexism of society in language similar to that employed by antebellum white women. She complained that "women must be pretty, dress prettily, flirt prettily, and not be too well informed."[95] Her writings emphasized the ability of women to be both compassionate and intelligent, feeling and rational. In both her speeches and her writings, Cooper contributed significantly to women's activism in the late nineteenth and early

[90] *Ibid.*, 225.

[91] Elizabeth McHenry, *Forgotten Readers: Recovering the Lost History of African American Literary Societies* (Durham, 2002), 222–3.

[92] Drema R. Lipscomb, "Anna Julia Cooper," in Richard W. Leeman, *African-American Orators: A Bio-Critical Sourcebook* (Westport, 1996), 41.

[93] *Ibid.*, 43.

[94] Cooper quoted in Bert James Loewenberg and Ruth Bogin, *Black Women in Nineteenth-Century American Life* (University Park, PA, 1976), 319.

[95] *Ibid.*, 323.

twentieth centuries. In "The Higher Education of Women," Cooper complained that though women were allowed into colleges, higher education was still available "only to a select few."[96]

Whereas Cooper seems to have spoken out particularly against gender discrimination, she was conscious of her unusual success as a black woman. At the 1893 Columbian Expo, black women had to struggle mightily to earn a place, and ultimately only six African American women attended as representatives, including Cooper, who spoke before the mostly white audience in Chicago. She unflinchingly declared that she spoke "for the colored women of the South" in offering hope for a biracial movement for women's rights. "The colored woman," Cooper asserted, "feels that woman's cause is one and universal." In fact, she made a case for broader justice as well. "Woman's wrongs are this indissolubly linked with undefended woe, and the acquirement of her 'rights' will mean the triumph of right over might, the supremacy of the moral forces of reason, and justice, and love in the government of the nations of earth."[97] She did not waste her opportunity to call white women's attention to the plight of blacks by pointing out that "the white woman ... could at least plea for her own emancipation," while "the black women of the South [had] to suffer and struggle and be silent."[98] Johnnie M. Stover has argued that Cooper presented a voice for black women that emphasized a collective awareness. "While Cooper celebrates a woman's role as moral stabilizer of the home," Stover argues, "she also speaks in favor of a woman's entry into the public arena."[99] Thus, even women like Cooper who might be viewed as advocates of women's traditional domestic roles in society could also be powerful supporters of expanding those roles to include writing, lecturing, and editing.

Whereas Cooper was known largely within the black community, Mary Eliza Church Terrell won considerable fame in both the black and white communities as a writer, teacher, and public speaker. Terrell, however, was not born a slave. A native of Memphis born in 1863, she grew up in an elite home after her ex-slave parents became businesspeople. In her autobiography, *A Colored Woman in a White World*, Terrell highlighted her determination to succeed academically, and her success in school prepared her well for teaching. Like other black women educators, Terrell branched out into lecturing, a field that for decades won her added income and reputation. "As a lecturer," scholars have written, "she was known for her elegance, candor, and ability to articulate her concerns, not only in her native tongue, but in three foreign languages."[100] Her intellectual abilities and speaking skills led to her election as the president of the National Association of Colored Women in 1896,

[96] Cooper, "The Higher Education of Women," quoted in *ibid.*

[97] Philip S. Foner and Robert James Branham, *Lift Every Voice: African American Oratory, 1787–1900* (Tuscaloosa, 1998), 775.

[98] Lipscomb, "Anna Julia Cooper," 44.

[99] Stover, *Rhetoric and Resistance*, 175.

[100] Ruthleon W. Butler and A. Cheree Carlson, "Mary Eliza Church Terrell," in Leeman, *African American Orators*, 320.

an important organization for black women activists that included Ida B. Wells and Frances Ellen Watkins Harper. The NACW was "the first cohesive network of communication among black women throughout the United States."[101]

In her capacity as head of the National Association of Colored Women, Terrell delivered powerful speeches that called attention to racism and sexism. Like Cooper, she recognized fully the need to fight against both at the same time. In an important 1897 speech, Terrell argued, "We proclaim to the world that the women of our race have become partners in the great firm of progress and reform." Indeed, black women were vital participants and leaders in temperance and religious movements. Yet, racism in white women's organizations had necessitated the formation of black women's clubs. Thus, in explaining the need for the National Association of Colored Women, Terrell claimed that "we denominate ourselves colored, not because we are narrow ... but because our peculiar status in this country at the present time seems to demand that we stand by ourselves in the work for which we have organized ... colored women feel their responsibility as a unit, and together have clasped hands to assume it."[102]

Terrell was one of the few black women to cross the boundaries set by whites, and she was invited in 1898 to give a speech before the National American Woman Suffrage Association. In her lecture, "The Progress and Problems of Colored Women," Terrell pointed out to her largely white audience the remarkable strides that black women had made in the short time since the end of slavery. They had attended college, embarked on careers as teachers and domestic workers, and some had even entered the professions.[103] She carried similar themes with her to the meeting of the National American Woman Suffrage Association in 1900 and to other prominent events. At such speeches, Terrell vigorously struggled against racism and sexism, providing further evidence that women intellectuals were vital to the southern women's rights movement.

Not all southerners, of course, appreciated her activism. In a speech before the National Association of Colored Women in 1907, Terrell and other speakers denounced the abuse and murder of African Americans, especially women. In fact, Terrell proclaimed that "no servant girl is safe in the homes of the white people," a claim that led to the headline "Furious Address against the South" in a South Carolina newspaper. Terrell, the paper complained, had charged that white southerners "had plotted to shut out the children of the blacks from an education, and that the courts had refused to protect colored women."[104]

[101] Beverly W. Jones, "Mary Church Terrell and the National Association of Colored Women, 1896 to 1901," *Journal of Negro History* 67 (Spring 1982), 24.

[102] Butler and Carlson, "Mary Eliza Church Terrell," 322.

[103] *Ibid.*, 323.

[104] "Furious Address against the South," Columbia *State* (November 2, 1907), 6.

Remarkably little has been written of women like Terrell, but even more obscure black women writers like Clarissa M. Thompson of South Carolina await their biographers. Thompson, a novelist, poet, teacher, and temperance reformer from Columbia, attended lectures at South Carolina University and earned her teaching credentials before moving to Fort Worth, Texas, in 1886. Like other prominent African American authors, she began by contributing short works to widely read periodicals like the *Christian Recorder*.[105] Thompson parlayed her shorter inroads into periodical publishing into serialized novels in the *Boston Advocate*. As the careers of Cooper, Terrell, and Thompson suggest, black women spoke out boldly against gender inequality, while at the same time remaining cognizant that especially in the so-called New South, racism, violence, and murder were ever-present dangers for African American women and men.

The rich legacy of postbellum black and white women authors, both famous and obscure, offers insight into how literary women used their talents as a path to gender equality. White southern female writers rarely missed opportunities to call for the expansion of women's rights and responsibilities. As Martha S. Jones has recently argued in *All Bound Together* (2007), black women saw themselves at the forefront of movements for both racial and gender equality.[106] However, to take advantage of their literary talents fully, they needed to move beyond writing for periodicals to careers as professional journalists.

[105] M. A. Majors, *Noted Negro Women*, (Chicago, 1893), 69.

[106] Martha S. Jones, *All Bound Up Together: The Woman Question in African American Public Culture, 1830–1900* (Chapel Hill, 2007).

8

Postwar Women and Professional Journalism

In 1889, two rival newspapers sponsored around-the-world trips by female journalists. The impetus for the race was the widespread popularity of Jules Verne's 1873 novel *Around the World in 80 Days*, but the use of two women, one southern and one northern, to test the feasibility of such a trip indicated the growing prominence of female members of the press in late nineteenth-century America. By the 1880s, enough female journalists had made their careers and reputations that the prospect of two women traveling alone around the world sparked little moral indignation.

One of the travelers was Elizabeth Bisland, venturing west under the auspices of the *Cosmopolitan*. Born on a plantation in Louisiana in 1863, Bisland had forged a regional reputation through her contributions to local newspapers, including the New Orleans *Times-Democrat*, for which she later became literary editor. Like many southern women journalists in the postwar period, Bisland left her native region for a time to seek greater renown in New York, and soon she was hired as the literary editor of the *Cosmopolitan*. The notion of a race around the world against Nellie Bly, who ventured eastward for the *New York World*, proved a success as both women relayed their experiences to their home papers. Although Bly bested Bisland by a few days, both completed their trips in less than the eighty days it took Phileas Fogg, and Bisland published an account of her adventure in *A Flying Trip Around the World*.[1]

Such a trip by a southern or even a northern woman would have been highly unlikely before the Civil War. By the 1870s, however, there were hundreds of female journalists throughout the former slave states. Many of these women, following precedents laid down in the 1840s and the 1850s, wrote columns specifically aimed at female readers. Whereas a newspaper or periodical might hire a male editor for the overall production, women often directed a "women's department" or "woman's column," covering a range of topics. For example, the Macon, Georgia, *Weekly Telegraph* contained a section, "Of

[1] Frances E. Willard and Mary E. Livermore, eds., *American Women: Fifteen Hundred Biographies* (v2, New York, 1897), 86.

Interest to Women," that printed society news, information on the Daughters of the Confederacy meetings, local history, receptions, out-of-town visitors, and various clubs and organizations.[2] Articles on household remedies and chores were common, as were essays and advice columns on child rearing. Pages were often devoted to political and community news, information on charity events, and social functions. Periodicals not edited by women often had female correspondents who added perspectives that male journalists did not offer.

As we have seen, women operated newspapers and magazines on their own in the antebellum era, a trend that grew significantly after the war. As they had before the war, southern women in the postbellum period were responsible for finding suitable contributions, paying authors, handling subscriptions, and sending the finished draft to the printer. Together with female columnists, women editors held highly visible roles in the postwar intellectual and political culture of the region, which scholars are only now beginning to appreciate. Southern women were active participants and leaders in the growth of journalism as a profession.

As they worked to define a new career path for women in journalism, female members of the press also helped to encourage the emergence of the suffrage movement in the South. Key to this development was the formation of press associations in the region beginning in the 1870s, groups that gave women professional respect, a training ground for coordinated activism, and a foundation for advocating greater political and intellectual equality.

Newspapers and magazines of the postwar South are dotted with biographies of contemporary female journalists, and periodicals reported widely on the new press associations being formed by these professional women. Some continued careers begun in the antebellum period. Mary Edwards Bryan, for example, continued to edit southern columns for women and dramatically expanded her reputation by taking editorial positions in New York City. Other women were new to the profession in the 1870s, and although they could rely on a tradition of southern female journalists that dated back to the eighteenth century, in many ways they had to reassert their right to be journalists and editors after the war.

In the latter decades of the nineteenth century, there still existed reluctance on the part of many to accept women in public roles previously reserved for men. In the Biloxi, Mississippi, *Herald Weekly*, for example, a postwar writer poked fun at the new wave of female editors. A fictional young female editor was depicted as sobbing to her father over the trials of her job. "My editorials were praised," she proclaims, "by the entire Texas press, and I got flattering

[2] See, for example, "Of Interest to Women," *Macon Weekly Telegraph* (February 16, 1896), 2. A comparable section of the Columbus, Georgia, *Daily Enquirer* was entitled "Woman's World" and published news about journalists, women stevedores, housekeeping, and the "modern woman." "Woman's World," *Columbus Daily Enquirer* 36 (November 10, 1895), 7.

words of encouragement from even the large dailies. I was, oh, so proud of the fact that, although a woman, I had been admitted as an equal member of the great brotherhood that exercises such an influence upon the mind and morals of the people." Here this fictional editor alluded to the common practice of periodicals giving notices of new magazines. However, this young editor suffered when she wrote a mildly critical article about a neighboring weekly paper. In return for this criticism, the paper responded by calling her a "loathsome, nock-kneed, piebald jabberwack" who published "disgusting, idiotic drivel." The competing editor continued the rain of insults, calling her a "clapper-jawed, squirrel-headed, slab-sided puddle duck that spoils paper" as well as a "hump-backed, putty-faced vermin," all of which sent the distraught young journalist into the arms of her father. The implication, of course, was that women were not suitable for the rough-and-tumble world of journalism any more than they were prepared for the coarse political arena. The story ended with the woman asking her father "to buy me a cook book and some long aprons" so that she could "stay at home and help mother about the house."[3] This hypothetical scene, reprinted in Houston and Biloxi newspapers, was read no doubt with much delight by male journalists who resented the infringement of women into the arena of periodical publishing.

In addition to derision from male editors, female journalists had to contend with the widespread perception that they were stepping beyond the normal spheres of their gender and that they were unfeminine. "No Woman," claimed the *Dallas Morning News*, "can safely work a day long in an office and give evening after evening to society, the theater, or to delightful, but overstimulating clubs, where she must read and discuss papers and chat with bright women."[4] Despite the substantial record of successful antebellum women journalists, old battles had to be fought again. Arguments heard in the earlier decades of the century were heard once again, especially the claim that women were not biologically or temperamentally suited to the confinement of an office.

Female journalists also had to confront stereotypes of bold women, particularly in terms of dress. One New York editorial that was reprinted prominently in the Dallas *Weekly Times Herald* charged that at a recent meeting of literary women there were "frocks and bonnets [that] set your teeth on edge," that one poet wore "execrable raiment," and that "the tastefully dressed writer is an anomaly." At the reception, the observer complained, the number of "well dressed women" could be counted "on the fingers of one hand."[5]

The charge was not just that literary women had poor taste in clothes but that they did not know how to dress and act properly in polite society. To fight such stereotypes, female journalists often began their comments on politics or

3 "Woman Editor's Trials," *Biloxi Herald Weekly* 12 (June 20, 1896), 5.

4 "The Woman Who is an Editor," *Dallas Morning News* (February 2, 1896), 11.

5 "'Woman's World' A Charge that Literary Women are Dowdy Dressers," *Dallas Weekly Times Herald* 6 (May 17, 1890).

current events with the caveat that they were not "blue stockings," a code word for bold female advocates of political equality. To counter these stereotypes, women members of the press continued to dress conservatively even as they worked in unconventional roles. Many bristled against the limitations placed on their ability to work because of societal expectations regarding clothing and appearance. As one northern woman editor put it, "Fancy a man trying to write an editorial article on the tariff or the sugar trust with his neck clasped almost to the point of congestion by a high, stiff collar, every movement of his arms restricted by a tight-fitting sleeve, and his chest and body held firm and unyielding in a panoply of bone and drilling!"[6]

Despite the fear of being stereotyped as an activist, many southern journalists did believe that they lived in a more enlightened era when it came to gender, particularly in regard to women's acceptance in literary and journalistic circles. "The old maid of the past," editor Mary Edwards Bryan claimed in a Georgia newspaper, " – sour, scandal-loving, sharp of temper and of features – is now almost an unknown quantity.... The unmarried woman of today, who has past her twenties, is cheery, active, busy and useful. Generally, she is [in] business, or has some special art, profession or accomplishment to which she devotes herself.... She has little time for gossip and less inclination."[7] Bryan, in common with her journalist sisters, wished to stress that female members of the press were serious in a focused pursuit of a career. In an editorial reprinted in a Columbia, South Carolina, newspaper in 1894, Jennie de la Lozier, the president of the literary club Sorosis, argued that there were "great surprises in store for the men of today in the remarkable development of our modest, retiring and as yet imperfectly known sex." She suggested that the region was witnessing the emergence of the "woman architect, woman doctor, or woman journalist" who would demand "equal pay with the men for equal work." She advised that a female editor and writer "should not sacrifice her individuality to a newspaper, and, above all, should be endowed with a sense of personal responsibility and loyalty to her own sex." The author concluded that "women are successful in journalism and make charming Bohemians. They are brave, plucky, tactful creatures, and deserve well of the reading public."[8] The connection between the success of women journalists and gains in gender equality was clear. Southerners recognized that the success of female editors and correspondents marked a new and significant moment in gender roles and equality. As the *Charlotte Observer* noted when two young women took over a Lincolnton newspaper, "The *Observer* is glad to see the women of the South branching out into new lines of business. The individual and not the sex determines one's success."[9]

[6] Margaret H. Welch, "Is Newspaper Work Healthful for Women?" *Journal of Social Science* 32 (November 1894), 114.

[7] Mary E. Bryan, "Mrs. Mary E. Bryan," *Macon Weekly Telegraph* (May 31, 1900), 4.

[8] Jennie de la Lozier, "Women as Journalists," *Colombia State* (January 12, 1894), 3.

[9] "Women Editors," *Charlotte Observer* 8 (August 6, 1895).

If women could pursue careers dominated by men, some southerners reasoned, the path should be opened to political participation as well. A. B. Stark argued in Nashville's *The Home Monthly* in 1868 that "the whole question of Woman's Rights must be lifted from its present disreputable position and earnestly, calmly discussed by the thoughtful men and women of the age." Stark was hopeful that a new era dawned, even in the South. "Just now," he observed, "we apprehend, the advocates of woman suffrage are not numerous in the South. We are inclined to think the number of advocates will be largely increased within the next decade."[10] Stark was unusually bold among southern men in his willingness publicly to support the cause of women's suffrage, and he used the pages of his magazine to question suffrage opponents. "A well-educated woman is surely as well able to understand a political question, and to form sound conclusions upon it, as the small shop-keeper or the tenant-farmer.... Seeing that she has to obey the laws, it seems only reasonable that she should have some hand in making them.... [Such women] may safely be trusted to exercise the privilege of voting with discretion."[11] Stark returned to the subject of women's rights often, remarking on advances in England and Portugal and publishing a seventeen-page poem on the issue.[12] Still, not all readers responded favorably to Stark's pro-suffrage views. Stark also opened the pages of his paper to opposing opinions. One correspondent agreed that female suffrage advocates were unusual in the region, but attributed that sentiment to the notion that it was "somewhat repugnant to the shrinking modesty of our Southern women to go to the polls to gain their rights."[13] Postwar southerners often harkened back to notions of the antebellum belle as the ideal woman, neglecting the fact that the early nineteenth-century South harbored its own female radicals and politicos. For these post-Civil War men and women, the Old South represented not just the Lost Cause of southern nationhood but a more traditional set of gender relations as well.

Interestingly, postwar women sometimes directly challenged the belief that the antebellum southern woman represented the ideal, and instead pointed to the Old South belle as a myth. Postwar women resented the implication that their antebellum mothers and grandmothers were consumed with leisure and devoid of substance, and that somehow the region was rescued by a new wave of more forward-looking women. In 1891, Maude Andrews, a columnist for the *Atlanta Constitution* wrote a column stating that "the indolent Southern woman of ante-bellum days will give place to the industrious, alert, thrifty daughter of the new South." Andrews's words generated controversy among her readers, who defended the antebellum woman. One reader responded angrily to the "false idea of our own Southern ante-bellum life"

[10] A. B. Stark, "Woman Suffrage," *The Home Monthly* 5 (July 1868), 59.

[11] *Ibid.*, 60.

[12] Stark, "Woman's Rights," 138–9, and H. S. Foote, "Essay on Woman's Rights," *The Home Monthly* 5 (August 1868), 85–102.

[13] S. E. Peck, "Woman," *The Home Monthly* 5 (September 1868), 195.

and claimed that before the war southern women were anything but "idlers of indolence."[14]

The prominence of postwar female journalists received a great deal of attention in both the North and South, a development generally praised as evidence of significant progress in the intellectual life of women. A South Carolina newspaper published a highly complimentary essay on New York women journalists, remarking "that there are no less than ten thousand earning some sort of return" as correspondents or editors.[15] Prompted by the growing number of female members of the press in the 1880s and early 1890s, New York's Margaret H. Welch suggested that although the field was promising, it was not without hazards. "I can recall," she reported, "with two minutes thinking, a dozen newspaper women of my acquaintance who are struggling with some form of nervous exhaustion directly consequent upon their newspaper duties."[16] Still, Welch believed, there was "no career opening more of honor and of promise for a woman than in the field of newspaper work."[17]

Women gained experience through special editions of newspapers, in which male editors would hand over the operations for a day to women, sometimes to raise money for charity. In these special editions, women assumed control over editing, selling advertising, selecting articles, and printing illustrations.[18] *The Journalist*, a New York weekly magazine that began in the early 1880s, was largely devoted to men in the field but frequently printed news about women editors and columnists. In fact, an 1889 issue was completely given over to women editors and authors and included news about female members of the press in New England and the South.[19] Similarly, the *Hillsboro* [Texas] *Mirror* gave women complete control over an issue of the paper, in which "everything in it will be written and edited by the ladies."[20] Women's editions in Columbia, Louisville, New Orleans, Atlanta, Knoxville, and Memphis in the 1890s dealt with a range of issues from the economy to women's suffrage.[21]

Although the 1870s and 1880s witnessed advances in female journalism, the cause of women's rights, the belief in the intellectual equality of the sexes, and the respect for women journalists advanced after the World's Columbian Exposition in Chicago in 1893. The effect of the 1893 fair on women nationwide, and especially on women in the New South, can hardly be overestimated. Alas, African American women were largely excluded from the fair,

[14] "A Misrepresentation. The Ante-bellum Southern Woman Not What She is Said to Have Been," *Macon Weekly Telegraph* (November 2, 1891), 6.

[15] "Notable Women," *Columbia State* (June 4, 1895), 2.

[16] Welch, "Is Newspaper Work Healthful for Women?" 110.

[17] *Ibid.*, 116.

[18] Ann Colbert, "Philanthropy in the Newsroom: Women's Editions of Newspapers, 1894–1896," *Journalism History* 22 (Autumn 1996), 91.

[19] *The Journalist* 8 (January 26, 1889).

[20] "Women Editors," *Dallas Morning News* (January 19, 1896), 20.

[21] Colbert, "Philanthropy in the Newsroom," 94–6.

and their participation was limited due to discrimination.[22] For white female intellectuals, authors, activists, and journalists, however, the fair was an unusual opportunity. Soon after they became aware that there would be a Woman's Building at the fair that would display literary and artistic contributions by women, activists sprang into action. Excited by the prospect of this national exposure, women from throughout the South either attended the fair as delegates or sent items for exhibition. Southern women organized into state and local clubs to help coordinate efforts, and to be elected to chair or serve in some other official capacity was deemed a great honor. As historian Anne Firor Scott has demonstrated, the fair was held in the midst of the movement for women's clubs, in which southern women participated with a vigor that matched their northern sisters.[23] Indeed, soon "Columbian fever" broke out with great excitement among women in southern towns and cities and in many rural areas.[24] The Woman's World Fair Association of Texas, for example, led by Bernadette Tobin, gathered books, poems, and other items for the Woman's Building Library.[25] "Columbian Clubs" were organized throughout Arkansas.[26] The Woman's Building consisted of 80,000 square feet of displays, and women often hosted displays alongside men's exhibits in other buildings, such as the agriculture building. The displays drew attention to women's work in the New South, particularly work by journalists and authors, and were harbingers of a new era of importance for women members of the press. Equally important, the fast-growing club movement was further spurred by the Columbian Exposition, giving rise to magazines and newsletters designed to highlight club activity. One such journal, Ida Marshall Lining's *The Keystone*, a Charleston periodical begun in 1899, was the voice of the South Carolina General Federation of Women's Clubs. Until its demise in 1913, *The Keystone* "chronicled the activities of civic-minded women in South Carolina, North Carolina, Mississippi, Virginia, and Florida."[27]

Even after "Columbian fever" broke out, there was some ambivalence about employing the title "journalist" for women who worked in the newspaper business. Although appealing to many because of the standards of professionalism the term connoted, "journalist" seemed even to some women to be more than a bit pretentious. "It is the young girl fresh from school," remarked Helen M. Winslow in an 1896 essay, "who insists upon her title of journalist; the woman who has labored side by side with men for years and whose work

[22] Robert Rydell, *The Reason Why the Colored American is not in the World's Columbian Exposition* (Urbana-Champagne, 1999).

[23] Anne Firor Scott, *Natural Allies: Women's Associations in American History* (Urbana, 1991).

[24] Jennie June Croly, *The History of the Woman's Club Movement in America* (New York, 1998), 233.

[25] Jeanne Madeline Weimann, *The Fair Women* (Chicago, 1981), 133–4.

[26] Croly, *The History of the Woman's Club Movement*, 210.

[27] Kathleen L. Endres, "The Keystone," in Endres and Therese L. Lueck, eds., *Women's Periodicals in the United States: Social and Political Issues* (Westport, CT, 1996), 142.

will stand the strain of comparison is content to be a 'newspaper woman.'"[28] Yet at the same time, Winslow asserted that the late nineteenth century was in fact a time of tangible progress, not only for female members of the press, but for women in general. "The evolution of the woman journalist, pure and simple, was left for this age – women regularly on a daily newspaper; women to take editorial and reportorial positions and stand side by side with the men with whom they compete." Most importantly for Winslow and her peers was the key point that these journalists were not merely covering topics such as household duties, new recipes, and child-rearing advice. She pointed out "that they do write on all topics of interest – politics, finance, and even baseball (O crucial test!), as well as literature, art, and so-called woman's interests – and that they draw equal pay for the same quality work with men, are established facts."[29] Despite the questionable assumption that male and female members of the press earned equal pay, Winslow's point is an important one. Although the antebellum journalistic pioneer occasionally ventured into discussions of politics, the number of women covering political issues and current events was small. By the turn of the twentieth century, however, as Winslow suggests, the number of women writing on a range of topics, and the willingness of the reading public to support their efforts, had grown dramatically, especially by the 1880s and 1890s.

By the late nineteenth century, white southern women had been contributing to and editing periodicals for many decades. For African American women, however, the act of writing prose or poetry for magazine publication was a new phenomenon, especially for those native to the South. Black women editors and journalists were rare until the last two decades of the 1800s. Yet, within a remarkably short period of time after the end of slavery, black women forged careers as writers and journalists. Although Ida B. Wells is perhaps the best known of these new journalists, she was by no means the only one. By the turn of the twentieth century, African American women could be found at the helm of several periodicals, and many more contributed essays, poems, and short stories to magazines aimed primarily at a black audience.

Black women faced considerably more obstacles than white southern women journalists and were at best ignored and at worst scorned by white members of the press. White editors, male or female, saw little to interest them in the growing number of black newspapers founded during and after Reconstruction. Yet, if they had bothered, white female journalists would have found much of interest in African American newspapers and magazines, and in fact would have seen a great deal that was familiar to those writing against discrimination in the antebellum era. Postwar African American editors, for example, confronted a problem all too familiar among their white journalist counterparts: the stubborn refusal of subscribers to pay bills. As

[28] Helen M. Winslow, "Some Newspaper Women," *The Arena* 17 (December 1896), 127.
[29] *Ibid.*, 127–8.

Virginia's *The People's Advocate* complained in 1882, "If the colored people of this city who regularly *read* the two newspapers published here will subscribe and *pay* for them," the papers would be financially successful.[30] Such laments were ubiquitous in the white southern press as well, suggesting that many of the challenges of southern journalism were the same for blacks and whites. Although they sometimes seemed to have existed in parallel universes, when take together, black and white women authors and journalists provided a persistent and often vigorous voice in favor of expanded rights and responsibilities for women. Indeed, black women's involvement in the club movement, in reform efforts like temperance, the church, and literary activities all combined to raise dramatically the visibility of African American women in the postwar South. As Elizabeth McHenry has argued, "As the clubs recreated the atmosphere of culture from which black women were isolated, they also prepared black women to interact with other women of culture in mixed-race social groups."[31] Charlotte Hawkins Brown, for example, helped organize the North Carolina State Federation of Negro Women's Clubs, and other southern women founded the Women's Improvement League in Charleston, West Virginia, and the Chautauqua Circle in Atlanta.[32] Like their white counterparts, black women would also use this experience in literature and the club movement to forge careers in journalism.

After emancipation, black women entered the press with remarkable speed and boldness, becoming a recognizable force in the field in a matter of years. As scholar Noliwe M. Rooks has pointed out, "The explosion of African American newspapers after the Civil War resulted from increases in African American literacy and mobility combined with a need for advocacy in the battle against segregation, disfranchisement, and lynching."[33] Once southern black women began to write for and edit their own newspapers and magazines, they quickly became influential in the black community, contributing to debates over race and gender through editorials and articles. Building on work by African American women pioneers who contributed poetry, short stories, and serialized novels to periodicals, journalists published editorials and articles in black newspapers beginning in the 1880s. Among the dozen or so prominent post-Civil War female editors and journalists, Ida B. Wells is best known to modern scholars, and she was unique in her boldness and visibility as an anti-lynching activist. Other African American women, although not as widely known as Wells, were nonetheless leaders in the field, providing models for the rapid growth of black female journalists in the early twentieth century. Whereas scholars have focused much of their attention on black women journalists in the postwar North, southern black

30 "Our Papers," *The People's Advocate* 6 (March 4, 1882).

31 McHenry, *Forgotten Readers*, 226.

32 *Ibid.*, 226, 240.

33 Nowlie M. Rooks, *Ladies' Pages: African American Women's Magazines and the Culture That Made Them* (New Brunswick, 2004), 6.

journalists aside from Ida B. Wells have been largely neglected. Yet, according to one scholar's analysis, of the twenty-three African American journalists of prominence by 1890, sixteen were native southerners, a trend that continued into the early twentieth century. As the number of black women journalists rose in the late 1800s and early 1900s, southerners continued to dominate their ranks.[34]

Like white southern women, African Americans were actively involved in the women's club movement of the late nineteenth century.[35] The National Association of Colored Women (NACW), which represented hundreds of clubs, was truly national in scope; southern black women took leadership roles in the organization from the beginning. For example, Cornelia Bowen of Alabama, Mary E. Stewart of Louisville, Josephine H. Smith of Atlanta, and Sylvanie Williams and Alice Ruth Moors of New Orleans occupied leadership posts in the association in the late 1800s and early 1900s.[36]

Still, racism in the South kept black women from meeting with their white counterpart, the National Association of Women. In 1903, New Orleans threatened successfully to withdraw its invitation to the white group if, as was rumored, black delegates from the NACW were permitted to meet with whites. Josephine Yates, president of the NACW, sought to avoid controversy by declining to attend herself, and instead sending New Orleans native Sylvanie Williams as her proxy. When word leaked out that black representatives might attend the mostly white meeting, city leaders reacted angrily. Williams, of course, was hardly surprised by white leaders' reaction. "I am a southern woman," Williams remarked, "born and reared, and I understand local conditions thoroughly. I am fully cognizant that it will be impossible for me to attend a meeting."[37] She knew all too well the strict racial separation southern cities demanded.

In part because such racism persisted and intensified, the NACW annual meetings became forums for often bold rhetoric. Black women were aware that newspapers across the nation reported on their meetings and reprinted speeches delivered at the conventions. In 1907, for example, NACW President Mary Church Terrell of Washington, D.C., angrily denounced the sexual abuse and violence inflicted on domestic servants. She harshly criticized southern courts for their unwillingness to punish abusers and protect young black workers, and she denounced white southern women for claiming that black

[34] Gloria Wade-Gayles, "Black Women Journalists in the South, 1880–1905," *Callaloo* 13 (October 1981), 138–52.

[35] Michelle Rief, "Thinking Locally, Acting Globally: The International Agenda of African American Clubwomen, 1880–1940," *The Journal of African American History* 89 (Summer 2004), 203–22.

[36] "National Association of Colored Women," *Knoxville Journal* 12 (July 24, 1896), 6; "Election of Negro Women," (Omaha, Nebraska) *Sunday World-Herald* 42 (July 17, 1904), 16. See also "Colored Women's Clubs," *The Grand Rapids Herald* (August 13, 1899), 14.

[37] "Women and the Race Question," (Omaha, Nebraska) *Morning World Herald* 39 (March 23, 1903), 8.

women were devoid of honor. South Carolina's newspaper *The State*, reported the speech, claiming that Terrell was "furious" and "bitter."[38]

Through her determination to be heard and her courage in the face of virulent racism, Ida B. Wells proved perhaps more than any other individual in the late nineteenth century the power of women in journalism. Although she gained respect as a speaker and also worked for racial justice in other ways, her career as a journalist helped to propel her into the status of one of the most important Americans of the nineteenth century.

As one of her biographers, Patricia A. Schechter, has noted, Ida B. Wells-Barnett used skills as an editor and journalist to promote justice. As early as 1885, while living in Memphis, observers had taken notice of her talents and suspected an illustrious life in journalism lay in her future.[39] However, although there were numerous white women who had earned a living and a reputation as editors throughout the South, there were few African American women in journalism. Nearly all of the black members of the press during and after the Civil War were men, and in the New South only black men had joined the press during Reconstruction, mostly to work on Republican Party newspapers. As the editor of the *Washington Bee* argued in 1887, "There is no question but intelligent colored women of our race should become adept in journalism as much so as white women."[40] But Wells-Barnett had precious few models of black women to follow and instead became a pioneer.

Like many women editors in the nineteenth century, Wells-Barnett began her career in 1887 as a writer for periodicals, particularly columns for a church weekly that drew readers for their clarity and boldness. These led to other contributions to religious and literary periodicals. Signing her contributions "Iola," Wells-Barnett became known in her adopted town of Memphis and increasingly throughout the South. As she recalled in her autobiography, Wells-Barnett received an offer from William J. Simmons of the Negro Press Association to become a correspondent for "the lavish sum of one dollar a letter weekly!" "It was the first time," she recalled, "anyone had offered to pay me for the work I had enjoyed doing.... I had been too happy over the thought that the papers were giving me space." Wells-Barnett did not set out to become a professional journalist, but once it was clear she could supplement her income as a teacher by writing and editing, she became freer in expressing her opinions, to the detriment of her career as a teacher.

Wells-Barnett parlayed her reputation as a writer into a position as editor with the same level of boldness and straightforwardness that characterized her writings for racial justice. In 1889, she was invited to join a small Memphis

[38] "Furious Address Against the South," (Columbia, South Carolina) *The State* (November 2, 1907), 6.

[39] Patricia A. Schechter, *Ida B. Wells-Barnett & American Reform, 1880–1930* (Chapel Hill, 2001), 20.

[40] Calvin Chase, *Washington Bee* (April 23, 1887), quoted in Schechter, *Ida B. Wells-Barnett*, 60.

periodical, the *Free Speech and Headlight*, as an author. Wells-Barnett, however, had grander designs and regarding her position with the journal's male editors said in her autobiography, "I refused to come in except as equal with themselves, and I bought a one-third interest."[41] She became coeditor of the paper, with J. L. Fleming as business manager and F. Nightingale as sales manager. When she became editor, the *Free Speech and Headlight* sold about 500 copies, mostly to Baptist church-goers in Nightingale's Memphis church on Beal Street.[42] She was wise to demand a piece of the paper's ownership, for one of her editorials criticizing the state of the city's black schools led the school board to decline appointing her to another term as a teacher.[43]

In one sense her firing proved a benefit, for Wells-Barnett was now free to pursue journalism unfettered by her teaching duties. She faced numerous acts of racial prejudice and was dismissed by whites as well as many male black journalists. But as Wells-Barnett stated in her autobiography, she had a largely positive experience when she traveled throughout the South in search of subscribers and contributors to the newly named *Free Speech*. "Newspaper folks then," she wrote, "rode on passes everywhere, so it was easy to get around the country." She ventured into Tennessee, Arkansas, Mississippi, and other states: "Wherever there was a gathering of the people, there I was in the midst of them, to solicit subscribers for the *Free Speech* and to appoint a correspondent to send us weekly news." In her home state of Mississippi, Wells-Barnett received the warmest reception. "At Greenville, Mississippi," she proudly wrote in her autobiography, "I attended the state bar association, made a short appeal to them, and came out with the subscription of every man present.... I was very proud of my success because up to that time very few of our newspapers had made any money."[44] By 1891, Wells-Barnett believed that "my travels were so successful that I felt I had at last found my real vocation."[45]

Wells-Barnett was well aware of her uniqueness as a black woman editor. As she later acknowledged about her travels in support of the magazine, "It was quite a novelty to see a woman agent who was also an editor of the journal for which she canvassed."[46] Schechter has remarked in her study that "journalism neatly captured the new freedoms and constraints facing educated African American women in the 1880s."[47] Yet Wells-Barnett employed the gender-specific terms of the period; she referred to fellow female editors as "editress" or the even more cumbersome "journalistess."[48] Whatever term

[41] Alfreda M. Duster, ed., *Crusader for Justice: The Autobiography of Ida B. Wells* (Chicago, 1970), 35.

[42] *Ibid.*

[43] *Ibid.*, 37. See also Jinx Coleman Broussard, *Giving a Voice to the Voiceless: Four Pioneering Black Women Journalists* (New York, 2004), 25–54.

[44] Duster, *Crusader for Justice*, 39.

[45] *Ibid.*, 41.

[46] *Ibid.*

[47] Schechter, *Ida B. Wells-Barnett*, 62.

[48] *Ibid.*

she selected, however, Wells-Barnett took pride in her accomplishments. The *Free Speech* reached a circulation of four thousand, and with satisfaction she pointed out that as editor her "salary came to within ten dollars of what I had received as teacher."[49]

As editor, Wells-Barnett continued to attack racism in Memphis, especially the lynchings that occurred there and throughout the South. She spoke out against black disfranchisement and even advised African Americans to settle in the western territories.[50] Realizing the danger her outspokenness posed, she refused to give in, purchasing a gun for protection, and she left the South, lending her talents to the *New York Age* in 1892. She continued to rail against racism and racist violence until her death.

Though Wells is certainly the most noticed by modern observers, other black female journalists dotted the landscape of the former slave states. Mary V. Cook, born a slave in Bowling Green, Kentucky, became a professor of Latin and mathematics at Kentucky Baptist College in 1883. In addition to speaking before the American Baptist National Convention in Mobile in 1887 and the Baptist Home Mission Society in Nashville in 1888, Cook became an active participant in professionalizing journalism for women. She presented speeches at the National Press Convention in Louisville in the late 1880s, and in 1887 she began editing a column for the *South Carolina Tribune* and the *American Baptist*.

Under the name "Grace Ermine," Cook earned considerable national recognition as a journalist. As one contemporary biographer summed up her reputation, "She has crossed swords with our man editors, [and] in fact, she may be styled the equal of many of our *boasted* editors."[51] Like Wells-Barnett, Cook stood boldly in favor of racial and gender equality and was not afraid to fight injustice. As a journalist in the late 1880s, she reacted angrily to racial violence. "White faces," she declared, "seem to think it their heaven-born right to practice civil war on negroes, to the extent of bloodshed and death. They look upon the life of their brother in black as a bubble to be blown away at their pleasure.... This outrage cannot endure. God still lives, and that which has been sown shall be reaped."[52] Through articles in Louisville's *Our Women and Children* and other periodicals, Cook earned a journalistic reputation second perhaps only to that of Ida B. Wells. Perhaps most important for our purposes, Cook saw the power of journalism in promoting racial and gender justice. Like Tennessee's Virginia Broughton, Cook promoted women's rights vocally in her newspaper and magazine contributions and in her role as a leader in the Baptist church.[53] Her journalistic work in the black Baptist press convinced Cook that Christianity and the Bible were important

[49] *Ibid.*
[50] *Ibid.*, 69, 77.
[51] Majors, *Noted Negro Women*, 196.
[52] Cook quoted in Garland, *The Afro-American Press*, 373–4.
[53] Higginbotham, *Righteous Discontent*, 124.

to expanding rights for women. As Evelyn Brooks Higginbotham has argued, Cook "termed the Bible an 'iconoclastic weapon' that would destroy negative images of her sex and overcome the popular misconceptions of woman's place in the church and society."[54] Cook could be heavy-handed in her advocacy of the Baptist Church, proclaiming in an 1887 speech that "every woman in the world ought to be a Baptist, for in this blessed denomination men are even freer than elsewhere."[55] But she was also keen to reveal to the world racial and gender injustices. In the same 1887 speech, she pointed to examples of women in history who served with distinction "as writers, linguists, poets, physicians, lectures, editors, teachers and missionaries."[56] It is telling that Cook placed editors among the other vaunted professions in which both black and white women made lasting contributions.

At the same time that Cook was building her career, Kentucky was also home to prominent journalists Mary E. Britton and Lucy Wilmot Smith. Born just before the Civil War, Britton was raised in Lexington and, like many black women who became journalists, began her professional life as a public school teacher. After getting her start in newspaper writing in the late 1870s, Britton became well known in Kentucky, Ohio, and Indiana for her trenchant criticism of the status quo. She published essays on a wide range of political topics, including suffrage. Her 1887 essay "Woman's Suffrage as an important factor in Public Reforms," published in a Cincinnati paper, garnered Britton considerable attention. Indeed, one Lexington paper remarked that Britton was an example of the fact that "the colored race possesses many women of brain, nerve, and energy, who, when left to wage a hand-to-hand combat with adversity, fight along bravely and well and in the end come off victorious."[57] Britton contributed to over a dozen African American periodicals, often to protest the unjust treatment of her race in postwar Kentucky.[58]

Britton, along with Lucy Wilmot Smith of Lexington and Lavinia B. Snead of Louisville, helped to make Kentucky notable for harboring black women journalists and solidified the public's notion of female journalists as prominent advocates of equal rights.[59] Smith, like Britton a Lexington native, was a persistent advocate of female suffrage. In 1890, for example, she challenged those who opposed gender equality. "It is said by many," Smith argued, "that women do not want the ballot. We are not sure that the 150,000 women of voting age would say this; and if they did, majorities do not always establish

[54] *Ibid.*, 125.

[55] Philip S. Foner and Robert James Branham, eds., *Lift Every Voice: African American Oratory, 1787–1900* (Tuscaloosa, 1998), 668.

[56] *Ibid.*, 669.

[57] Lexington's *Christian Soldier* quoted in Alice Allison Dunnigan, ed., *The Fascinating Story of Black Kentuckians: Their Heritage and Traditions* (Washington, 1982), 286.

[58] Majors, *Noted Negro Women*, 218.

[59] Dunnigan, *The Fascinating Story*, 187–8.

the right of a thing. Our position is, that women should have the ballot, not as a matter of expediency, but as a matter of pure justice."[60]

As in the case of white women journalists, black female members of the press appeared more prominently in some southern states than others. Kentucky and Alabama seem to have built networks of support that helped to make those states significant in terms of the numbers of African American women journalists. C. C. Stumm, for example, a Kentucky native, moved from teaching to journalism and contributed to numerous black periodicals, including the Bowling Green *Watchman*, Boston's *Advocate*, Brooklyn's *National Monitor*, and *Our Women and Children*.[61]

Among the Deep South states, Alabama harbored a significant number of black women journalists and writers. Amelia L. Tilghman, a musician and vocalist, was the only African American woman to edit a musical journal, the *Musical Messenger*, a monthly that she published in Montgomery beginning in 1886. Tilghman was born to a free black family in Washington, D.C., who ensured she received an education in music, in schools as well as at Howard University. After graduating from college in 1870, Tilghman became a teacher in local black public schools while also earning acclaim as a pianist and singer. She was soon touring the South as a soloist, settling in Montgomery in early 1886. In this former Confederate capitol, Tilghman began the *Musical Messenger*. Clearly she recognized the importance of the endeavor. Her magazine, Tilghman hoped, was a "new step that has for its object the further advancement and progress of our race in all the intellectual avenues of life."[62] As scholar Juanita Karpf has pointed out, this journal marked an important maturation of the southern black press, from general periodicals to more specialized ones.[63] Yet, in keeping with the eclectic nature of southern periodicals, Tilghman's journal, according to Karpf, contained information on "artists with whom she shared the stage, black composers, and teaching – spiced with occasional editorial excursions into social commentary."[64] Tilghman moved back to the nation's capitol in 1888 but continued to edit and publish the *Musical Messenger* until 1891.

Whereas Tilghman migrated to Alabama from the nation's capital, Mattie Allison Henderson was an Alabama native, born in Frankfort in 1868. Despite a troubled upbringing, including being orphaned as a child, her determination to become a teacher led her to the Le Moyne Normal Institute in Memphis. She

[60] Penn, *The Afro-American Press*, 380.

[61] Majors, *Noted Negro Women*, 203.

[62] Juanita Karpf, "'As with Words of Fire:' Art, Music, and Nineteenth-Century African-American Feminist Discourse," *Signs* 24 (Spring 1999), 620. See also Allen Woodrow Jones, "Alabama," in Henry Lewis Suggs, ed., *The Black Press in the South, 1865–1979* (Westport, 1983), 34–5.

[63] Karpf, "The Early Years of African American Music Periodicals, 1886–1922: History, Ideology, Context," *International Review of the Aesthetics and Sociology of Music* 28 (December 1997), 143.

[64] *Ibid.*, 144.

graduated in 1885 and taught at Le Moyne and in other schools in Tennessee and Arkansas.[65] In the southwest, Henderson became known as a competent writer, publishing articles in the *Headlight*, printed in Marion, Arkansas. Much of her production may be lost, for as a contemporary observer put it, "From time to time [she was] acting as correspondent and occasionally contributing an article to different papers, under assumed names."[66] Such haphazard participation in the world of journalism hardly amounted to a career, but after leaving the South and eventually settling in Kansas City, she edited a weekly newspaper titled *The Future State*. According to one author, "She manages every department of that paper with the ability of a man."[67]

Henderson was like many black women journalists, who, though born in the southern states, earned fame while working in the North. Such transplants, although nonetheless southerners, carved out prominent journalistic careers in northern towns. As Glenda Gilmore has reminded us, if one leaves out southerners who left the region to make careers elsewhere, one misses a great deal of the South's history and legacy.[68] Gilmore's comments pertained to the radicals and activists who were born and raised in the South, but who left the region for cities in the North and West. Yet her point is a good one, for the lives and careers of many southern women have been forgotten because they elected to leave the region. Sarah Gibson Jones, for example, was born a free black in Alexandria, Virginia, in 1845 and schooled in Cincinnati. Like many black women journalists, she began her career as a teacher and then started writing for magazines and newspapers. During the war, she helped to edit *The Colored Citizen* newspaper in Ohio and continued to write articles for the prominent African American paper *The Christian Recorder* and the *Indianapolis World*.[69] In addition to impressive careers in teaching and editing, Jones was also a respected speaker who delivered lectures across Ohio.

Lecturing in public was a new endeavor for black women like Wells and Jones, but as these women broke new ground they opened a field for others. Frances Ellen Watkins Harper, a Baltimore native, earned prominence as a lecturer throughout the North beginning in 1854 and continuing in the postwar period. One modern observer has praised her poetry as "stylistically diverse" and peppered with "socio-political content concerned with slavery, temperance, and suffrage."[70] Like other women, both white and black, Harper used her skills as a poet and speaker in support of expanding women's rights. She delivered lectures at the International Council of Women in 1888 as well as the Columbian Exposition in 1893; at the latter gathering she spoke

[65] Majors, *Noted Negro Women*, 122.
[66] *Ibid.*, 123.
[67] *Ibid.*
[68] Glenda Gilmore, *Defying Dixie: The Radical Roots of Civil Rights: 1919–1950* (New York, 2008).
[69] Majors, *Noted Negro Women*, 139.
[70] Erlene Stetson, *Black Sister: Poetry by Black American Women, 1746–1980* (Bloomington, 1981), xiv.

on "Woman's Political Future."[71] Unlike her white sisters, however, Harper protested racial inequality while devoting equal vigor to promoting women's rights. In a speech before the National Council of Women in 1891, Harper chastised whites for calling African Americans ignorant after enslaving and suppressing the race. "It comes with ill grace from a man," she argued, "who has put out my eyes to make a parade of my blindness – to reproach me for my poverty when he has wronged me of my money."[72]

Josephine Turpin Washington, like Jones a southerner who ventured North, was born in Virginia in 1861 and trained as a teacher at the Richmond Institute and later at Howard University. Unlike Jones, however, Washington returned to the South as a correspondent for newspapers, writing on racial controversies. When Annie Porter published an essay highly critical of the achievements and abilities of black women in the pages of the *Independent*, Washington followed with a defense in the New York *Freeman*. "All of the prominent Negro newspapers," a biographer wrote at the time, "have stood by her in her bold assertions, and applauded her achievements."[73] Like many white and black women writers and journalists, Washington engaged in many different pursuits. After graduating from Howard in 1886, she became a teacher at Selma University in Alabama. Yet, she continued to write for periodicals, including the *Christian Recorder* and the *A. M. E. Church Review*.[74]

Washington and other black women journalists could often boast of a college education, and Alice McEwen attended Fisk University in her native Tennessee. Like Washington, McEwen moved to Alabama where she was to earn local renown as "a brilliant lady journalist."[75] As her father was editor of the *Montgomery Herald*, McEwen had an open path to publishing, and in 1886 she authored "The Progress of the Negro" for the paper. In the late 1890s, her career really rose to prominence, and she became associate editor of the *Montgomery Baptist Leader*, read papers before the National Colored Press Association, and aided Amelia Tilghman in editing the *Musical Messenger*.

One of the most respected African American writers and journalists was Amelia E. Johnson. Though her place of birth has not been documented, she lived during her productive career as an author and editor in Baltimore. Like many southern women editors, Johnson began her journalistic career by writing poems. In 1887 Johnson, having married a minister in Baltimore, edited a new magazine for children titled *The Joy*, an eight-page monthly that published original works as well as reprinted articles.[76] Observers called attention to the quality of the stories published in *The Joy*, with a fellow editor

[71] Bert James Loewenberg and Ruth Bogin, eds., *Black Women in Nineteenth-Century American Life* (University Park, 1976), 244.

[72] *Ibid.*, 249.

[73] Majors, *Noted Negro Women*, 201.

[74] Jones, "Alabama," in Suggs, ed., *The Black Press*, 34.

[75] *Ibid.*

[76] Penn, *Afro-American Press*, 422–4.

remarking that the themes explored were "original, and the general tone very creditable to the author."[77] After the demise of her magazine, she continued her work as an editor, heading the "Children's Corner" section of a Baltimore paper. Her work was praised by white and black journalists.[78]

As we have seen, it was common for both white and black women to conduct careers in journalism, literature, and teaching at the same time. While Amelia Johnson developed a reputation as a leading black woman member of the press, she published two novels, *Clarence and Corrine; or, God's Way* (1890) and *The Hazeley Family* (1894). Printed with the aid of the American Baptist Publication Society, *Clarence and Corrine* was a moral tale that would have found much in common with the views of Victoria Earle Matthews and other black women active in the Women's Christian Temperance Union. According to one scholar, *Clarence and Corrine* asserted "the dangers that alcoholism poses to women as wives and mothers, and to their children in particular."[79] *The Hazeley Family*, another moralistic story brought out under the auspices of the American Baptist Publication Society, emphasized the importance of a virtuous mother in keeping a family together and in promoting domestic happiness.[80] Many of these black women journalists were also prominent public speakers and delivered lectures on racism, gender inequality, temperance reform, and a host of other topics. We have seen how female authors and teachers like Anna Julia Cooper earned fame as lecturers.

Matthews was one of the postbellum period's most prolific female contributors to periodicals. The youngest of nine children born in slavery to her mother and white master in Macon County, Georgia, Matthews is perhaps best known today for her work in New York City missions. Yet, she had grown up in Georgia and went to New York only in 1873. After receiving limited schooling, she worked as a domestic servant but relished the chance to work in journalism. Married in 1879, she lived in Brooklyn and began writing for local newspapers and magazines. In 1897, after considering a return to the South, Matthews decided to stay in New York and help found a charitable organization to protect young women workers. The purpose of the mission was "to establish and maintain [a] Christian, industrial, and nonsectarian home for Afro-American and Negro working women and girls."[81] (Alice Dunbar-Nelson, another prominent black author, cofounded and taught in the White Rose Mission as well.)[82] In addition to establishing the White Rose Industrial League for young working girls, Matthews became a leader in the

[77] *Ibid.*, 424, reprinted in Hortense Spillers, ed., "Introduction," *Clarence and Corrine; or, God's Way* (reprint, New York, 1988), xxx.

[78] *Ibid.*, 425.

[79] Spillers, ed., "Introduction," xxxi.

[80] Barbara Christian, "Introduction," *The Hazeley Family* (reprint, New York, 1988), xxvii.

[81] "Certificate of Incorporation of the White Rose Mission and Industrial Association," White Rose Mission Records, Schomburg Center for Research in Black Culture, New York.

[82] Gloria Hull, ed., *The Works of Alice Dunbar-Nelson* (New York, 1988), lvii.

women's club movement, cofounding the Woman's Loyal Union in 1892 and the National Federation of Afro-American Women in 1895.[83]

Like her white counterparts, Matthews wrote on a range of political and cultural topics, refusing to be bound by traditional feminine fare like fashion and housekeeping. Indeed, literary scholar Shirley Wilson Logan envisions Matthews "as a prototype of the emerging black woman public intellectual."[84] In 1888 and 1889, Matthews published essays in newspapers such as Washington's *National Leader*. In one such essay, she enlightened readers on the activities of Republican women.[85] In the 1890s, she also supported Ida B. Wells' anti-lynching movement, becoming known as an excellent orator at iconic events such as the Columbian Exposition in Chicago in 1893. She denounced her native region for its "systematic outrages which have been perpetrated upon the negro during the last twenty-five years."[86] Thus, African American journalists like Matthews fought racial injustice as they simultaneously symbolized black advancement.

Matthews published many of her most important writings in the widely read periodical *The Woman's Era*. In 1896, for example, she authored several pieces on the Atlanta Colored Woman's Congress, particularly its debate on a lynch law resolution.[87] In these essays, Matthews worked diligently to denounce racism and lynching and call for racial equality. Yet she also worked hard to elevate the cause of gender equality, pointing to women like Harriet Tubman as models for female activists.[88] In early 1897, Matthews issued "An Open Appeal to Our Women for Organization," which would become the National Association of Colored Women.[89] As a journalist, Matthews knew that her profession as a journalist provided a vehicle for a call to action: "Sisters! In all earnestness let me ask, will you actively take hold with heart and brain and place our association on a foundation second to none in America?"[90] In a similar speech titled "The Awakening of the Afro-American Woman," Matthews called for an end to segregation in public accommodations, especially in railroad cars, whose "entire operation tends to degrade Afro-American womanhood."[91]

[83] Gerda Lerner, "Early Community Work of Black Club Women," *Journal of Negro History* 59 (April 1974), 161.

[84] Shirley Wilson Logan, "*We Are Coming:" The Persuasive Discourse of Nineteenth-Century Black Women* (Carbondale, 1999), 150.

[85] Victoria Earle Matthews, "Our New York Letter," *The National Leader* 1 (December 22, 1888). See also (January 5, 1889).

[86] Matthews quoted in Steve Kramer, "Uplifting our 'Downtrodden Sisterhood:' Victoria Earle Matthews and New York City's White Rose Mission," *Journal of African American History* 91 (Summer 2006), 245.

[87] Matthews, "Note on the Atlanta 'Lynch Law Resolution,'" *Woman's Era* (February 1896), 9.

[88] Matthews, "Harriet Tubman," *Woman's Era* (June 1896), 8, and (July 1896), 3.

[89] Matthews, "An Open Appeal to Our Women for Organization," *Woman's Era* (January 1897), 2–3.

[90] *Ibid.*, 3.

[91] Foner and Branham, *Lift Every Voice*, 839.

After working with T. Thomas Fortune, one of the nation's best-known black editors, Matthews moved back to the South. In Atlanta she helped Fortune by working on his paper the *Southern Age*.[92] Like other women journalists, Matthews was itinerant, almost restless, and always in search of new adventures and opportunities. Along with many of her fellow female members of the press, Matthews made her literary and journalistic career in more than one state.

The 1890s proved to be crucial years for black female journalists in promoting gender equality, not just for individuals like Matthews, but for black women members of the press more broadly. As Rosalyn Terborg-Penn has argued, "By the 1890s, the growth in the number of Black women journalists with feminist perspectives writing for Black newspapers became more evident."[93] As she argues in *African American Women in the Struggle for the Vote*, Terborg-Penn notes the importance of activists in the 1890s like Mary McCurdy, who edited the temperance newspaper the *National Presbyterian*. In her paper, McCurdy explicitly blamed white men for preventing black men and women of both races from enjoying suffrage.[94]

Although black female members of the press could be bold and vigorous advocates of racial and gender equality, few questioned outright the legitimacy of capitalism and advocated anarchy or an alternate economic system. One of the most unusual southern black women of the late nineteenth and early twentieth centuries was Lucy Parsons, born (perhaps in slavery) in Waco, Texas, in 1853. She married Albert Parsons, a former Confederate soldier turned advocate for black civil rights, and together they proved powerful supporters of anarchism throughout the nation. Attracting scorn and caustic press coverage wherever she went, Parsons became one of the best known black radicals of her era. In addition to backing the eight-hour workday and denouncing the injustices of capitalism, she wrote for and edited key revolutionary periodicals, such as *The Alarm*, *The Socialist*, and the *Liberator*.[95]

Parson's work as a journalist mainly served her desire for racial, gender, and economic justice, and her speeches and writings reflect her unwavering commitment to fighting all on all three fronts. In one speech, delivered in 1886, she defended the Haymarket "Riot" as "a peaceable meeting" and the subsequent witch hunt for perpetrators of violence as a "judicial farce."[96] Before the crowd, she declared, "I am an anarchist," and explained why she rejected capitalism. "When the red flag floats over the world the idle shall be called to work," she declared. "There will be an end of prostitution for women, of slavery for man, of hunger for children."[97] Not surprisingly, such passion

[92] Roland E. Wolseley, *The Black Press, U.S.A.* (second ed., Ames, IA, 1990), 41.

[93] Rosalyn Terborg-Penn, *African American Women in the Struggle for the Vote, 1850–1920* (Bloomington, 1998), 58.

[94] *Ibid.*, 59.

[95] Foner and Branham, *Lift Every Voice*, 655.

[96] *Ibid.*, 658, 659.

[97] *Ibid.*, 657, 660.

earned only contempt from most of her fellow journalists, who criticized her as a dangerous radical. But even as she called for economic justice, Parsons also repeatedly demanded the expansion of woman's sphere. As she wrote in a Chicago newspaper in 1905, "The sooner men learn to make companions and equals of their wives and not subordinates, the sooner the marriage relation will be one of harmony."[98] Like other advocates of gender equality, Parsons understood well the importance of the press in promoting justice.

Whereas African American journalists proliferated in southern states like Kentucky and Alabama, white female members of the press counted Georgia as a stronghold. By the end of the nineteenth century, the state could boast of a long history of editors and reporters. After the Civil War, and particularly in the latter two decades of the 1800s, the prominence and number of Georgia's white female members of the press increased noticeably. Spurred in part by positive responses they received from southern readers and from a growing female readership, women journalists entered a new and important phase of visibility and influence in Georgia. At the same time, white female members of the press fashioned careers, earned income, and managed businesses.

That the new women editors of the postwar South could be astute businesswomen as well as literary figures is demonstrated by the life and career of Ellen J. Dortch. Born in Georgia in 1868, she hailed from a middle-class family and received a thorough education. In 1888, she took over the Carnesville, Georgia, *Tribune* as owner and editor when the newspaper experienced financial trouble. When she assumed control, the *Tribune* "consisted of one-hundred-fifty pounds of long primer type ... a few cases of worn advertising type and a subscription book whose credit column had been conscientiously neglected."[99] However, just a few years after taking over the paper, the subscription list numbered in the thousands and boasted new presses and type. Other Georgians, including men, thought Dortch's successes boded well for the New South. Another Georgia newspaper remarked in 1891 that Dortch "can write an editorial, put it in type, take a proof, and, if need be place it properly in the 'form.' She hustles up subscribers [and] talks advertising in a business-like way." As "an enterprising, wide-awake young lady," according to the paper, Dortch was a prime "example right here at home of woman's progressiveness."[100]

[98] Parsons, "The Woman Question Again?" *The Liberator* (October 3, 1905), reprinted in Gale Ahrens, ed., *Lucy Parsons: Freedom, Equality, & Solidarity* (Chicago, 2003), 103.

[99] Willard and Livermore, *American Women*, 255.

[100] "A Georgia Lady Journalist," *Macon Weekly Telegraph* (February 20, 1891), 3. Interestingly, as editor, Dortch did not shrink from fierce literary battles that often erupted between neighboring papers in the South. In April 1891, Dortch was locked in a "bitter newspaper war" with a local newspaper called the *Register*. In the war of words, other Georgia periodicals sided with Dortch, claiming that "the spirited, bright little woman has the full sympathy of the Georgia Press in her fight." "Carnesville," *Columbus Daily Enquirer* 32 (April 22, 1891).

In the midst of her editorial career, personal tragedy and considerable embarrassment struck Dortch when her father, James Dortch, the Franklin County School Commissioner, was thrown from his buggy and killed in 1891. The tragedy was made all the more painful when the community learned that Dortch was drunk when he fell from his cart. His "besetting weakness was intemperance," remarked a local paper, but Ellen remained deeply loyal to her father and sought to keep favorable memories of him alive.[101] Despite her pain and humiliation, she still moved on to edit the Milledgeville *Recorder* shortly after her father's death. Dortch's new position in Milledgeville, once the state capital, was a step up from the village of Carnesville and provided her with a more conspicuous platform. Like many women editors, Dortch sought to open new opportunities for southern women. She helped to form the Georgia Normal and Industrial College and in 1893 offered free scholarships through her paper.[102] In 1894, she competed with men and women for the position of private secretary for the Georgia governor, and many of her fellow members of the press endorsed her as "brainy, industrious, and capable."[103]

Such statewide fame earned her a position writing a weekly column for the *Columbus Daily Enquirer* beginning in 1895. In her column, "Ellen Dortch's Weekly Chat," she expressed opinions on politics, current events, gender roles, and journalism. She also sought to enlarge women's sphere and praised those who ventured beyond traditional gender boundaries. Dortch commented on economic matters, such as the silver issue, grain crops, and guano.[104] In one column, Dortch defended "the modern woman" against charges that such women were uninterested in marriage. "Cultivated, advanced, modern (whatever you choose to call them) women," she wrote in one of her weekly columns in 1895, "fall in love and get married" just like traditional women.[105] She took every opportunity to praise women's advancement. "What women have done," she proclaimed in an 1895 column, "in the latter half of this century has been an eye-opener as to her capabilities in science, art, statecraft – in every field where brains and energy count for success – and just what she will finally accomplish none but a seer can pretend to predict."[106] Such public statements made Dortch a leading spokesperson for gender equality in the Deep South.

For all of her progressiveness on gender issues, however, Dortch defended segregation and believed in the inferiority of African Americans. She rejected any analogies between the movements for gender and racial equality. She

[101] "To a Higher Tribunal," *Macon Weekly Telegraph* (September 1, 1891), 2.

[102] "Miss Ellen Dortch," *Columbus Daily Enquirer* 34 (April 11, 1893); "An Applicant was Selected," *Macon Weekly Telegraph* (September 12, 1893), 5.

[103] "Editor Ellen Dortch," *Columbus Daily Enquirer* 35 (September 9, 1894); see also "Last Days of the Campaign," 35 (September 30, 1894).

[104] "Ellen Dortch's Bright Chat," *Columbus Daily Enquirer* 36 (May, 5, 1895) and (July 7, 1895).

[105] "Ellen Dortch's Weekly Chat," *Columbus Daily Enquirer* 36 (June 9, 1895).

[106] "Fair Woman's Achievements," *Columbus Daily Enquirer* 36 (August 11, 1895).

railed against an acquaintance who insisted on the connection between gender and "social equality between the races," claiming that "if that is what woman agitation means at the North ... [then] no honorable white woman ... would touch the hand of an advocate of such rotten principles in friendliness and good will."[107] Although out in front of southern readers on gender equality, Dortch was no radical when it came to civil rights for African Americans.

Neither did Dortch break with standard Democratic Party ideology. In the 1880s and 1890s, Georgia was fertile ground for the anti-monopoly, anti-bank attitudes of the growing agrarian movement, but Dortch remained a staunch Democrat, believing the Farmers' Alliances and Populists to be mere demagogues who preyed on the plight of farmers for political gain.[108] She was not opposed to the benevolent, cooperative efforts of these groups, only to their intrusion into the political process.[109] Dortch was most critical of leading Alliance politicians like Leonidas Livingston and Charles W. Macune for their political ambitions and charged them with corruption. The mutual hostility lasted from 1890 to 1892 and was especially heated in the spring of 1890 when smaller, local Alliance groups boycotted her newspaper. Despite the boycott from Franklin County sub-Alliance members, the *Carnesville Tribune* survived, and the following year Dortch announced triumphantly that the newspaper had come through the boycott unscathed.[110] As she wrote in her paper in the fall of 1891, "The boycotters who seek to kill the *Tribune* have a hopeless task before them. The *Tribune* is strong and brave and fearless. The men who are boycotting us are weak and cowardly and would go around and burn up men's houses while they are asleep."[111] She viewed the People's Party as a continuation of the Alliance's demagoguery.

Dortch's devotion to the Democratic Party and her fame as a journalist provided the foundation for other opportunities. She was appointed assistant state librarian, one of the first women to serve in an official position in the state government, and in the fall of 1896 she ran for state librarian against the male incumbent, Capt. John Milledge.[112] Dortch was instrumental in persuading the state legislature to change the law to allow women to serve as state librarians.[113] She was defeated in 1896 and was deciding whether to run again in 1897 when she met and married Confederate General James Longstreet. Rumors of a courtship between the former general and

[107] "Ellen Dortch's Weekly Chat," *Columbus Daily Enquirer* 36 (June 16, 1895).

[108] Matthew Hild, *Greenbackers, Knights of Labor, and Populists: Farmer-Labor Insurgency in the Late-Nineteenth-Century South* (Athens, 2007).

[109] William F. Holmes, "Ellen Dortch and the Farmers' Alliance," *Georgia Historical Quarterly* 69 (Summer 1985), 156.

[110] *Ibid.*, 158.

[111] Ellen Dortch, "Editorial," *Carnesville Tribune* (September 30, 1891), reprinted in Holmes, "Ellen Dortch and the Farmers' Alliance," 162.

[112] *Columbus Daily Enquirer* 37 (October 14, 1896).

[113] "Southern Gleanings," *Biloxi Herald* 13 (November 14, 1896), 2; "Gen. Evans or Miss Dortch," *Columbus Daily Enquirer* 38 (August 27, 1897).

the assistant state librarian attracted considerable attention.[114] The marriage between the seventy-six-year-old Longstreet and Dortch, who was then thirty-four, was a sensation, and many papers reported that the general had been "conquered" by Dortch.[115] Through her husband and through her own writings Dortch remained faithful to the Lost Cause, becoming one of the chief examples of the new powerful southern woman of the late nineteenth century. Utilizing her position as editor, Dortch denied the social and intellectual equality of the races while simultaneously advocating (and indeed demonstrating herself) greater roles and responsibilities for white women.

Like Dortch, Georgia journalist Elia Goode Byington provided a model for other aspiring white female members of the press. Born in Thomaston in 1858, Byington and her husband served as editors and owners of the Columbus *Evening Ledger* in the 1880s and 1890s. Educated at the female colleges in Americus and Madison, including the respected Georgia Female College, Byington and her husband purchased the *Evening Ledger* in 1888.[116] The newspaper carried her husband's name as publisher, E. T. Byington & Co. However, as a neighboring paper pointed out, readers recognized that "Mrs. Byington is the 'Co.,' and is said to have been largely instrumental in making the Ledger what it is."[117] Most importantly, the paper consciously employed only women. As one observer reported, "A woman is employed as foreman, a woman artist makes the illustrations for the paper, a woman reads the proofs, a woman manipulates the type-writer, a woman is mailing clerk, and all the type is set by women, all of whom receive equal pay with men who are employed in similar capacities."[118] Byington earned a national reputation for her work, and her picture and biography appeared in New York's *Illustrated American* in 1891.[119] She also helped to found the Women's Press Club of Georgia and served as its president.[120]The public roles played by editors and

[114] "General Longstreet Denies," *Columbus Daily Enquirer* 38 (August 18, 1897) and "And a Marriage it will be," 38 (September 7, 1897).

[115] "The Conquest of Gen. Longstreet," *Columbus Daily Enquirer* 38 (September 9, 1897). Despite their age difference, Dortch tirelessly defended her husband's military reputation, especially against charges that he was largely responsible for the Confederate defeat at Gettysburg, and in 1905 she published such a defense in *Lee and Longstreet at High Tide.* Even while married, Dortch remained active in politics and in 1898 was one of the first women appointed postmaster in Georgia. Throughout her long life (she died in 1962 at the age of ninety-nine), Dortch supported Theodore Roosevelt and the Progressive Party, advocated conservation of natural resources in northern Georgia, and even eventually supported expanded civil rights for African Americans. Dortch was inducted in 2004 into the Georgia Women of Achievement memorial association for her life's work.

[116] "Mrs. E. T. Byington," *Macon Weekly Telegraph* (January 21, 1888), 2.

[117] "Her Talent Recognized," *Macon Weekly Telegraph* (March 22, 1891), 6.

[118] Willard and Livermore, *American Women*, 143.

[119] "Mrs. E. C. Byington," *Macon Weekly Telegraph* (April 17, 1891), 3.

[120] "The Editors' Frolic," Columbia, South Carolina *State* (May 2, 1894), 5. Byington and Dortch, although unusually popular literary celebrities, were hardly alone in nineteenth-century Georgia. Emily Verdery Battey, an editor and journalist, acquired considerable notice in her native state and in New York. Like Mary Edwards Bryan, Battey wrote for

authors like Dortch and Byington are a testament to the power of the women's press in late nineteenth-century Georgia.

Although not as numerous as the women editors of Georgia, Louisiana female members of the press were as significant. Home to writers like Kate Chopin, Louisiana, and particularly New Orleans, earned a reputation as an important center of female journalistic activities.[121] As was true in the antebellum period, many postwar women who had assisted their editor husbands in conducting a newspaper or magazine took control of the enterprise when their spouses died. New Orleans' *Picayune* was headed by George Nicholson, whose wife, Eliza J. Poitevent, took over when he passed away. Born in Mississippi, Nicholson took a local geographical feature of her childhood as her pen name, "Pearl Rivers."[122] However, she did not simply fall into the editorship of the *Picayune* because she married the owner of the paper, A. M. Holbrook, and then the paper's business manager, George Nicholson; she was first employed at the paper as literary editor for a substantial salary of twenty-five dollars per week.[123]

When Holbrook died in 1876, Nicholson had to decide whether to continue the paper or sell it to businessmen. She did not receive much encouragement

newspapers, such as Atlanta's *Ladies Home Gazette*, that attracted the attention of New York publishers. She moved to New York in 1870 and lived there for the next several years, editing the *Tablet*, the *Home Journal*, and the *Telegram*. Willard and Livermore, *American Women*, 64; Margherita Arlina Hamm, "Southern Literary Women," *Peterson's Magazine* 5 (November 1895), 1176. Like many female journalists of the late nineteenth century, Battey earned money by delivering lectures that attracted large audiences. Her lectures "The Woman of the Century" and "Twenty Years on the Press" were delivered in both the North and South. "Georgia," *Macon Weekly Telegraph* (July 3, 1891), 4. Battey also wrote for the New York *Sun* and received a generous salary. See Frank Michael O'Brien, *The Story of the Sun, New York, 1833–1918* (New York, 1928), 286. Corinne Stocker and Lollie Belle Wylie helped to edit the *Atlanta Journal*; Wylie also edited a journal between 1890 and 1892 titled *Society* and helped to found the Women's Press Club, serving as its vice president. Florence B. Williams became editor of the Statesboro *Eagle*, which became the county's official paper. After leaving the *Eagle*, she edited the Valdosta *Telescope*. Finally, Marie Louise Myrick became editor of the Americus *Times Recorder* after the death of her husband in 1895. After her husband's passing, she pledge to readers to continue the paper "on the same high plane that has characterized it." "Mrs. Marie Louise Myrick," *Columbus Daily Enquirer* 36 (August 17, 1895), 2. As one contemporary observer wrote, Myrick was "editor as well as manager of the paper. Her ability as a political writer is such that the paper is one of the most influential in Georgia, and Mrs. Myrick's opinion is sought upon all questions of importance effecting the politics or official conduct of affairs in the state." George Byron Merrick, *Genealogy of the Merrick-Mirick-Myrick Family* (Madison, WI, 1902), 392. Hamm, "Southern Literary Women," 1179.

121 Carmen Lindig, *The Path from the Parlor: Louisiana Women, 1879–1920* (Lafayette, 1986), especially pp. 95–109.

122 B. H. Gilley, "A Woman for Women: Eliza Nicholson, Publisher of the New Orleans *Daily Picayune*," *Louisiana History* 30 (1989), 235. Nicholson's use of the pen name "Pearl Rivers" was a reference to a local waterway and town in her native Mississippi.

123 *Ibid.* See also "Hymeneal," *New Orleans Times* 14 (June 28, 1878) and *Biographical and Historical Memories of Louisiana* (vol. 2, Chicago, 1892), 277–8; Ishbel Ross, *Ladies of the Press: The Story of Women in Journalism by an Insider* (New York, 1936), 591.

from her family; her brother urged her to "come home and behave herself."[124] By her own admission she suffered from considerable self-doubt, remarking that when she took over the debt-ridden and legally troubled paper, "I never felt so lonely and little and weak in my life ... and for months afterward my lack of confidence was so great that I used to wonder why the staid old Picayune ... didn't just role over and split its sides laughing at me."[125] Women editors often privately revealed a lack of self-confidence, afraid to appear weak and unsure of themselves, particularly in front of male employees and colleagues. Thus they internalized much of the stress, so much that some suffered physically. As one female editor confidentially admitted to a colleague, she "never turned the knob of the office door without a fluttering of the heart that cost her an effort to subdue." "I suppose," the woman observed, "it is because I lack the confidence born of training and long experience. I feel always that something may lie beyond the threshold that I have not yet encountered, something that my small stock of business knowledge may be unequal to."[126] Nicholson felt similar pangs of inadequacy. However, with the encouragement of her future husband, George Nicholson, and others, she later reported, "I swam and floated the best I could and have succeeded beyond all expectations."[127]

Far from generating resentment, Eliza Nicholson drew praise and respect throughout the region. The *Dallas Morning News* reported in 1894 that "she is, perhaps, the only woman in the world who is at the head of a great daily political newspaper, shaping its course, suggesting its enterprises, and actually holding in her slender hands the reins of its government."[128] Nicholson's reputation spread north, and a New York paper admired the fact that "she loves to give personal supervision to her business ... and there is no part of the *Picayune* that she does not keep her eye on."[129] Nicholson maintained a tight control over the paper and managed the business closely. In fact, Nicholson's meticulous approach to editing her periodical parallels that of other southern women journalists. But Nicholson, in common with Byington and other female editors, earned devotion from her employees even as she carefully governed the paper.

Male and female workers at the papers do not seem to have resented either the gender of their editors nor the micromanaging approach taken by Byington and Nicholson. After deciding to remain in control of the paper, Nicholson gathered her employees for the announcement. "Some of you," she

[124] Quoted in Dallas Criss, "Eliza Nicholson, Elizabeth Gilmer, and the New Orleans *Daily Picayune*, 1876–1901," (M.A. Thesis, University of Southern Mississippi, 1994), 17, and Elsie Farr, *Pearl Rivers* (New Orleans, 1951), 6–7.

[125] Nicholson quoted in John Kendall, "Journalism in New Orleans Between 1880 and 1900," *Louisiana Historical Quarterly* 8 (October 1925), 558–9.

[126] Welch, "Is Newspaper Work Healthful for Women?" 112.

[127] Nicholson quoted in Criss, "Eliza Nicholson," 18.

[128] *Dallas Morning News* (September 30, 1894), 16; Willard and Livermore, *American Women*, 537.

[129] New York newspaper quoted in "New York," *Columbus Daily Enquirer* 32 (July 3, 1891), 2.

acknowledged, "may not wish to work for a woman. If so, you are free to go, and no hard feelings. But you who stay – will you give me your undivided loyalty, and will you advise me truly and honestly?"[130] She oversaw many male reporters and department editors, including men who served as city editor.[131] In fact, a biography of Nicholson reprinted in the *Dallas Morning News* in 1893 remarked that "it speaks volumes for her as an admirable character that those who assisted her in her demanding task [of running the paper] are her staunch and faithful co-workers still and unstinted in their praise of her as an employer and a friend."[132] One of her staff members claimed that "there is not a man of us who would not lay down his life for her" and another challenged anyone who reacted against her to a duel.[133]

Under Nicholson's leadership, the *Picayune* offered readers unvarnished political opinions. Like Dortch, Nicholson remained a staunch Democrat and frequently endorsed Democratic candidates for state and local government positions. Although hardly radical in promoting reforms, the paper supported temperance, protection for animals, and laws against convict leasing and child labor.[134] In appealing to female readers, the *Picayune* offered a column, "As Viewed by a Woman," and reported on women's association and club activities in a special Sunday edition. Like other late nineteenth-century southern women editors, Nicholson was a vigorous and persistent advocate of educational opportunities for women.[135] Nicholson used her highly visible role as a journalist to promote greater rights for her sex.

As editor of a major daily newspaper, one might have expected Nicholson to be reticent to call openly for expanded prospects for women for fear of offending male and traditional female readers. Such was not the case, however: She seized both editorial space as well as news articles to expose her readers to broader views of women's abilities. For example, in 1895 she remarked that a female bank president had arrived at the *Picayune's* offices to meet Nicholson and her staff. She commented that the visitor was "altogether a type of what a true Southern woman can do when confronted with a position she must master."[136] Nicholson commented favorably on female physicians, teachers, and state officials. She believed that improved opportunities for women would make them "more independent and self-reliant," qualities she advocated (and modeled herself) tenaciously. Furthermore, though her early tenure as editor of the *Picayune* took a skeptical approach to suffrage, by the 1880s and 1890s Nicholson was persistent in her support of women's rights.

[130] Nicholson quoted in Gilley, "A Woman for Women," 236.

[131] Kendall, "Journalism in New Orleans," 562–3.

[132] "Mrs. E. J. Nicholson," *Dallas Morning News* (August 13, 1893), 6.

[133] Criss, "Eliza Nicholson," 18.

[134] Madelon Golden Schilpp and Sharon M. Murphy, *Great Women of the Press* (Carbondale, IL, 1983), 100–1.

[135] Criss, "Eliza Nicholson," 27–9.

[136] *Ibid.*, 30.

In 1883, the *Picayune's* articles began to evince a change in opinion toward active promotion of the women's movement. A column that year argued that women and men should be viewed as equal under the law when married. Husband and wife "are both individual souls, each with its own sacred responsibility" and "neither ... can be subordinated to the other."[137] The following year, Nicholson expressed support for women's suffrage but complained that men stood in the way. "Man will never surrender the domain of American politics to women while there is a dollar to be made.... There will be money in it just so long as there are one hundred thousand Federal offices and several hundred thousand more of State and municipal places to be filled."[138] By the 1890s, Nicholson was pointing out the absurdity of not granting suffrage to women. "There is an undercurrent of strong feeling," she observed in 1896, "among our intelligent women against the injustices of a law that shuts them aside ... [but] gives every ignorant and drunken hoodlum the right to vote."[139] Nicholson had warm words for Susan B. Anthony, and the famous suffragist lauded Nicholson in return.

New Orleans female members of the press considered Nicholson a mentor and a pioneer in the field. One of Nicholson's colleagues was Martha R. Field, who often wrote under the pen name "Catherine Cole." Shortly after leaving school, Field went to work for Nicholson and the *Picayune*; she also worked at the *San Francisco Post* and later at the *New Orleans Times*, where she became one of the first female reporters to earn a regular salary.[140] In part because of her work as a journalist, Field became, in the words of one Georgia newspaper, "one of the best known literary women of the South."[141] In addition to her daily reporting for the *Picayune*, Field wrote the Sunday column "Catherine Cole's Letter," which was read widely outside of New Orleans.[142] Her depictions of rural Louisiana and extensive travel narratives of Europe earned Field even greater numbers of readers.[143] Newspapers across the South, from the *Charlotte Observer* to the *Mobile Register*, marked her passing in 1898 with great sadness for the loss of a female journalist who "never wrote a dull line."[144]

Like Nicholson, Field promoted a wider range of paid work for women outside the home. In response to a local preacher who had scorned women for being employed, she demanded for women "broader fields in which to work." Job opportunities not only brought in income to help support a family, but

[137] *Picayune* (December 2, 1883), quoted in *ibid.*, 34 and Wheeler, *New Women*, 4.

[138] Nicholson, "A Word for the Woman Candidate," *Picayune* (September 30, 1884), quoted in Gilley, "A Woman for Women," 245.

[139] *Picayune* (January 15, 1896), quoted in Criss, "Eliza Nicholson," 34.

[140] Willard and Livermore, *American Women*, 289; Schilpp and Murphy, *Great Women*, 98.

[141] "Catherine Cole and Jumbo," *Columbus Daily Enquirer* 28 (April 30, 1886).

[142] Martha R. Field, *Louisiana Voyages: The Travel Writings of Catherine Cole* (Jackson, MS, 2006), ix.

[143] Winslow, "Some Newspaper Women," 130.

[144] *Mobile Register* article was reprinted in the *Charlotte Observer* (December 27, 1898), 2.

also provided women with a chance to use their minds. Women, Field argued, have "not only been starving to death, but rusting to death" as well.[145] She shared with Nicholson an admiration for Susan B. Anthony and the suffragists and used her literary talents to support women's rights. She repeatedly clashed with conservative male readers in the newspaper, telling them at one point that "you will be obliged to recognize our souls, to respect our existence and admit that ... our natures must burst the bonds and limitations with which you would confine us in doll's houses."[146]

Nicholson mentored Field while also appointing other women to write for the paper, some of whom became nationally known. She hired Elizabeth Gilmer, known as Dorothy Dix, who became a leading advice columnist in the early twentieth century.[147] Nicholson also relied heavily on her staff of apprenticing female journalists. As she remarked in 1887, "I believe almost any woman who has brain enough to recognize good newspaper work, and heart enough to appreciate it, could manage the up stairs department of a newspaper, especially if she had such a staff of honorable and competent editors and reporters as I am proud to lean on."[148] Nicholson's legacy lies with resurrecting an important and venerable major newspaper and using her authority as editor to call for expanded rights and responsibilities for women.

At the same time that pioneering female members of the press began advocating expanded rights for women during and after Reconstruction in the Deep South, similar women journalists made headway in the southwest. Before the Civil War, Eleanor Spann edited the *Texian Monthly Magazine*, but beginning in the 1870s, the number of female journalists in Texas rose to more than a dozen. Not surprisingly, given Texas' frontier status even after the Civil War, many female editors had emigrated from other states. Bella French, for example, began a monthly literary magazine titled *The American Sketch Book* in 1874 in Wisconsin. When she moved to Austin in 1878, French began editing the journal from her new home while retaining the name. Like most postwar southern women editors, she married; in Austin she wed John M. Swisher shortly after moving there. As an enterprising editor and reporter, French was determined to use the local color of Texas frontier life and capture the people and places of her adopted state. The mission of her magazine, French stated in her first number, was "not only to collect histories of different localities, and reminiscences of old times in Texas, but to give sketches and incidents of later days, together with truthful descriptions of various portions

[145] Field quoted in Criss, "Eliza Nicholson," 31.

[146] Field quoted in *Louisiana Voyages*, xii.

[147] On Gilmer, see Barbara Belford, *Brilliant Bylines: A Biographical Anthology of Notable Newspaperwomen in America* (New York, 1986), 70–8, and Schilpp and Murphy, *Great Women*, 112–20.

[148] Nicholson, "The *Picayune*: Its Semi-Centennial," *Picayune* (January 25, 1887), quoted in Gilley, "A Woman for Women," 237.

of the State, regarding their business facilities, healthfulness, location, etc."[149] French was born in Georgia in 1837 but moved to the upper Midwest with her family at a young age. In her early thirties, she edited and owned the *Western Progress* in Minnesota and edited a second periodical titled the *Busy West* in Wisconsin.[150] Thus, French had considerable experience as a businesswoman and editor before she emigrated to Texas.

French was to experience a mixed record of success and failure as an editor and a businesswoman in Austin. Publishing a monthly magazine proved difficult in the frontier town; lining up reliable printers was a constant concern. In an 1880 issue of *The American Sketch Book*, she lamented, "we have had a great deal of trouble and delay in getting out this issue of the *Sketch Book*, and are much later with it than we expected."[151] At the same time, French experienced frustration with the reliability of the postal service; she suspected copies of the magazine were being stolen before they reached subscribers. In discussing "What Ails the Mails," she asked "if postmasters and mail agents want the *Sketch Book* why do they not subscribe for it, and not steal it from people who do pay for it?"[152] Her questionable business decisions exacerbated her financial difficulties. She attempted to solve her printing problems by starting her own company, the Sketch Book Publishing House, which met with little success. In 1880, while she was still editing her magazine, French opened the Thermo Water Cure or Hot Air Bath and Hygienic Institute. The spa was supposed to help cure physical maladies such as rheumatism.[153] In addition, French published two novels. *Struggling Up to the Light* tells the story of an abused woman who divorces her husband and embarks on a successful career as a female poet, a career in which she writes about the abilities of women.[154] French's versatility was a common trait among literary women of the nineteenth century. Like most editors she was a wife and mother and carried on those duties as she worked as an author and journalist. As one contemporary observer wrote, she was "a sort of universal genius, – she cooks a dinner, makes a dress, nails up a broken fence, harnesses her horses for a drive, edits a paper, writes a story, and then entertains with her verses in the afternoon."[155]

[149] Bella French, "Mission," *American Sketch Book* 4 (1878), 65, quoted in Imogene Bentley Dickey, *Early Literary Magazines of Texas* (Austin, 1970), 11.

[150] Julia L. Vivian, "Bella French Swisher," *The Handbook of Texas Online* http://64.233.169.104/search?q=cache:b9ZGOJF03noJ:www.tsha.utexas.edu/handbook/online/articles/SS/fsw18.html+%22bella+french+swisher%22&hl=en&ct=clnk&cd=1&gl=us accessed December 9, 2007.

[151] French, "Editorial," *American Sketch Book* 6 (1880), 82, quoted in Dickey, *Early Literary Magazines of Texas*, 12.

[152] French, "What Ails the Mails," *American Sketch Book* 6 (1880), 242, quoted in Dickey, *Early Literary Magazines of Texas*, 12.

[153] Vivian, "Bella French Swisher."

[154] Bella French Swisher, *Struggling Up to the Light: The Story of a Woman's Life* (Chicago, 1876).

[155] R. J. P, "Bella French Swisher," *Magazine of Poetry: A Quarterly Review* 1 (October 1889), 475. Texas periodicals edited by women presented the same content found in journals

The nineteenth-century woman author and editor had to be multifaceted to succeed as a journalist.

Postwar women journalists and authors often engaged in other professions as well. Bessie Agnes Dwyer, a Texas native, was "heir to naught but her father's mental gifts."[156] For six years she worked as a postmaster in Texas, and then beginning in 1868 she spent time traveling widely along the southwestern frontier regions of Arizona and New Mexico. Based on those experiences, Dwyer contributed to southern periodicals with news of life on the frontier and became a congressional correspondent for the Washington-based periodical, the *National Economist*.[157] After attending business college in San Antonio, she continued to write for southern newspapers such as the *Galveston News* and the *Texas Baptist and Herald*.[158] In 1893 she was honored as the first female assistant librarian of the Library of Congress. Dwyer still found time to write for the National Farmer's Alliance periodicals, engaging in political discourse on a wide range of economic questions. Although she traveled to the Philippines in the early twentieth century to establish libraries there, she remained active in politics, serving as a delegate to the 1920 Democratic National Convention representing the Philippines.[159]

It was rare for two or more women to embark on a new periodical together; editing seems to have been a largely solitary endeavor. One exception to this

throughout the late nineteenth-century South. *The Round Table*, for example, edited by Mrs. Sidney Smith in Dallas, devoted a section of each issue to updates on women's club activities and literary associations. Dickey, *Early Literary Magazines of Texas*, 21. *The Prairie Flower*, run by Mrs. C. M. Winkler in Corsicana, Texas, in the 1880s, promised readers monthly issues of forty-eight pages containing "short stories, poems, essays, current events, historical sketches, Masonic notes, recipes, and advertisements." *Ibid.*, 15. See also, Sylvia Grider and Lou Rodenberger, eds., *Let's Hear It: Stories by Texas Women Writers* (College Station, TX, 2003), 15, and Willard and Livermore, *American Women*, 790. Mrs. E. C. Kent, who edited Austin's monthly literary magazine *The Repository* in 1889, taught for more than two decades in the Texas public schools. See Dickey, *Early Literary Magazines of Texas*, 19.

156 Francis E. Willard and Mary E. Livermore, eds., *A Woman of the Century* (Buffalo, 1893), 267.

157 *Ibid.*

158 Melissa G. Wiedenfeld, "Elizabeth Agnes Dwyer," *Handbook of Texas Online* http://www.tshaonline.org/handbook/online/articles/DD/fdw3.html (accessed 1/1/08)

159 The diversity of women's interests can also be seen in the career of Anna J. Hamilton. Born in Kentucky right before the Civil War, Hamilton was educated in Louisville public schools and at a young age began writing for local periodicals. In addition to her work in editing the children's section of an educational magazine, Hamilton helped to edit the *National Encyclopedia of America* and worked with the Filson Club. A prominent advocate for women's education, she managed between 1900 and 1915 the Semple Collegiate School in Louisville. John E. Kleber, ed., *The Encyclopedia of Louisville* (Lexington, 2000), 802. Similarly versatile, Emma Churchman Hewitt, born in New Orleans in 1850, moved north at a young age to make her career as a member of the press and author. Joining the *Daily Evening Reporter* of New Jersey in 1884, Hewitt soon after became the associate editor of the *Ladies' Home Journal* and contributed hundreds of stories and essays to numerous periodicals, including *Golden Days*, *Wide Awake*, *Home Guard*, and *Lippincott's Magazine*. Willard and Livermore, *Woman of the Century*, 375.

general rule was the business partnership of Laura E. Foute and Sara Hartman, who met in 1891 and cofounded *The Gulf Messenger* in San Antonio. The partnership between these two friends endured only two years, for Foute died in 1893. The magazine merged with New Orleans' *Current Topics* in 1897, and Fannie Reese Pugh, Margaret H. Foster, and May W. Mount became coeditors. Friendships as well as business partnerships no doubt formed among these women engaged together in the common struggle to keep a literary journal afloat.[160]

As we have seen it was quite common for southern women to be both novelists and editors or journalists at the same time, or to switch easily between the two careers. Annie Marie Barnes, born in Columbia, South Carolina, in 1857, was one southern intellectual who became a successful novelist and a member of the press. Between 1877 and 1884, she edited a periodical for children titled *The Acanthus*, which proved popular with southern families. Even while she conducted her magazine, Barnes also worked as a correspondent for the *Atlanta Constitution* and contributed to other periodicals in the region and in northern publications such as *Godey's Lady's Book*.[161] Barnes also embarked on a successful profession as a novelist, publishing novels such as *Izilda: A Story of Brazil* (1896) and *Chonita: A Story of the Mexican Mines* (1896). All of this literary and journalistic activity Barnes undertook while remaining active in her community and in the club movement, including the Women's Board of Missions for the Methodist Episcopal Church.[162]

These middle- and upper-class white women were afforded the support and freedom to engage their literary and journalistic interests. For Barnes and other southern women, editing a children's periodical seemed a safe way to adhere to traditional notions of motherhood while also pushing the boundaries of women's sphere. Then there were women who burst through the sphere altogether with little regard for tradition. Elizabeth Bisland was born in Louisiana in 1863, and her family "lost its entire property while she was a child," persuading Bisland as she grew up, "the necessity of doing something toward the support of herself and her relatives."[163] Using her considerable literary talent, she worked her way up to the position of literary editor of the New Orleans *Times-Democrat* and ventured to New York where she served in the

[160] Grider and Rodenberger, eds., *Let's Hear It*, 15–16. That such women editors could be bold advocates for women's equality is exhibited in the life and career of Maria I. Johnston. After her birth in Fredericksburg, Virginia, in 1835 her family moved to Vicksburg, Mississippi, where they remained for the next several decades. Johnston earned regional fame by publishing her Civil War experiences in fictional form in *The Siege of Vicksburg* in 1869. Johnston became editor of a family weekly titled the *St. Louis Spectator*, a paper that lasted from 1880 to 1893. See Willard and Livermore, *Woman of the Century*, 424.

[161] See, for example, her short story "The Spectre Castle," *Godey's Lady's Book* 120 (June 1890), 468–71.

[162] Willard and Livermore, *Woman of the Century*, 54.

[163] *Ibid.*, 86.

same position with *The Cosmopolitan Magazine*.[164] She wrote more than a hundred short stories, reviews, and other pieces for periodicals, from her story "The Confessions of a Reformed Cannibal" in New York's *Outing* magazine to an essay on "Women at Oxford" in *Harper's Bazaar*.[165] Far from shrinking from public consideration, women like Bisland reveled in the attention. In fact, Bisland was one of the guests at Mark Twain's seventieth birthday celebration at Delmonico's restaurant in New York.[166]

Black and white women writers and journalists pose challenges to our understanding of gender dynamics in the late nineteenth century. Seeking to understand the roots of the southern women's rights movement of the early twentieth century, historians have rightly turned to the club movement and its importance for women entering the fray of public life. Yet the region's fertile periodical and literary culture should be considered at least as significant to the emergence of calls for racial and gender equality. We are only beginning to value these women's contributions to the South and the nation, but their roles in shaping the region's literary and political culture are no doubt worthy of further study.

For all their boldness, however, southern women journalists lacked a sense of professional community. Rigid and unrelenting racism divided the black and white female press. Although newspapers and periodicals continued to be relatively affordable, readers still tended to be middle and upper class. Despite such social and racial chasms, white and black journalists tried to create a sense of professional community through the establishment of regional and state press associations. The formation of such associations marked a new and important step on the path to professionalization.

164 *Ibid.*

165 Bisland, "The Confessions of a Reformed Cannibal," *Outing; an Illustrated Monthly Magazine of Recreation* 12 (September 1888), 546–51; "Women at Oxford," *Harper's Bazaar* 24 (March 21, 1891), 210–11.

166 "Celebrate Mark Twain's Seventieth Birthday," *New York Times* (December 6, 1905).

Epilogue

Women's Press Associations and Professional Journalism

Toward the end of her life in 1896, Eliza Nicholson lamented that she did not enjoy the fellowship experienced by her male peers. "As the proprietor of a newspaper," she admitted to a Boston audience, "my position is, in a way, lonesome and peculiar.... I miss the pleasure and encouragement men of our profession have in friendly association."[1] Male editors in North Carolina formed their own press association in 1873.[2] However, until the late 1870s and 1880s no such organizations for women in the South existed. Given the personal and professional relationships formed among female members of the press, it is not surprising that in an age in which women across the country formed all kinds of organizations they should band together to form women's press clubs and associations. Perhaps even more importantly for the women's rights cause, female journalists and editors wished to be considered professionals, and forming press associations was a useful way to increase their professional status. The numbers of female journalists nationwide had risen from 288 in 1880 to 1,888 in 1890 and more than 2,000 in 1900 according to the federal census data, and the formation of press clubs was one avenue for prominent female members of the press to maintain standards and promote the status of their profession.[3]

The formation of press associations for southern women was part of a national movement to establish such clubs. Among the first was the New England Press Association, formed in 1885 by Marion McBride and several other Boston newspaperwomen.[4] In the 1880s and 1890s, women's press associations were formed in Utah, Ohio, Illinois, New York, California, Michigan, and Colorado; and the Women's Press Association counted 700 members by 1900.[5] Thus, the associations formed in the South in the last

[1] Nicholson quoted in Gilley, "A Woman for Women," 238.

[2] Thad Stem, Jr., *The Tar Heel Press* (Charlotte, 1973), 70.

[3] Census numbers are reported in Bradley, *Women and the Press*, 115.

[4] Elizabeth V. Burt, *Women's Press Organizations, 1881–1999* (Westport, CT, 2000), 154.

[5] Bradley, *Women and the Press*, 118.

two decades of the nineteenth century, particularly in Georgia, Texas, and Mississippi, were very much in line with their northern and western cousins.

The Woman's Press Association of the South, formed in 1886 in Greensboro, North Carolina, was apparently the first such organization in the region. Greensboro was a logical place for such a meeting, for in the 1850s Frances Bumpass had edited the *Weekly Message* newspaper in that city when her husband died. But the impetus for the association actually came from Mamie Hatchett, the editor of the *Southern Woman*, a journal published in Henderson, North Carolina.[6] Born in Virginia, Hatchett had attended the Mecklenburg Female College and by 1886 was already known in the South as a pioneer journalist.[7] Hatchett expressed optimism for the association because "the number of women pursuing journalism in the South as a profession is very large."[8] The first meeting attracted women from throughout the South as well as delegates from the New England Women's Press Association. The town welcomed these female members of the press, and in a precedent that would be repeated for later meetings of southern women's press clubs, the railroads offered lower rates for convention delegates. Sallie F. Chapin of South Carolina was elected the organization's first president from the thirty women present at the meeting.[9] Chapin, a Charleston native, had been active in the Women Christian Temperance Union as state president and wrote one novel after the Civil War destroyed her family's home. Like Hatchett and most female journalists, Chapin was active in the women's club movement.[10] The Women's Press Association seems to have disbanded soon after it was formed, for little archival evidence of its continuation exists. It left a vacuum soon filled by other women's press clubs throughout the region.

Just a few years later, newspaper women met in Dallas to organize the Texas Woman's Press Association in May 1893. Led by Houston journalist Aurelia Hadley Mohl, more than thirty writers and members of the press from eighteen different cities and towns across Texas formed the organization.[11] As was true with the Woman's Press Association of the South in Greensboro, southerners proved supportive of these women and their efforts to move beyond the traditional sphere. Little or no opposition was expressed toward these women; indeed, citizens opened their homes to visiting delegates. Hotel owners provided discounts for conference participants. The openness

[6] Karla K. Gower, "Women's Press Associations of the South, 1886–18(90)," in Burt, ed., *Women's Press Organizations*, 224.

[7] *Ibid.*, 227. Hatchett would later edit the *Orphan's Friend* in Oxford, North Carolina, and numerous other periodicals with her husband Al Fairbrother.

[8] *Greensboro North State* (September 16, 1886), 4, quoted in *ibid.*

[9] Gower, "Women's Press Associations," 224–8.

[10] Willard and Livermore, *Woman of the Century*, 168.

[11] Kate Pierce, "Texas Professional Communicators, 1893–Present," in Burt, ed., *Women's Press Organizations*, 207.

of southern communities to these bold, public women should cause historians to rethink the common perception of the New South as a bastion of gender conservatism.[12]

Mohl had considerable experience as a journalist even before she helped organize the Texas Woman's Press Association. She volunteered at the *Houston Tri-Weekly Telegraph* 1856 when she was in her early thirties and then joined the paper's paid staff in 1863. After serving as a Washington correspondent for a number of Texas periodicals, Mohl resumed her journalistic career in Texas until her death in 1896. She was remembered by her peers as a prominent advocate for women's rights; she called for the formation of the Texas Equal Rights Association in 1893 and was active in many literary clubs in Houston.[13] When Mohl called for a state-wide press club for women, there was little basis on which to hope for a sustained or meaningful gathering. Texas women participated in the club movement of the late nineteenth century with a fervor equal to their southern sisters. However, no professional group for women had succeeded to any great extent. And yet, the Texas Woman's Press Association did indeed make its mark, helping to lay the groundwork in organizing and public advocacy that would later be helpful to the cause of women's suffrage. At just the third meeting of the association, Austin papers called the convention "the most notable gathering of women ever assembled in the state."[14]

In addition to holding professional meetings, the Texas club also had its own library for women journalists and writers. In this way the association functioned much like antebellum lyceums and debating societies, many of which kept libraries for members' use. The reading room of the Texas Women's Press Association offered the latest issues of northern and European magazines such as the *North American Review*, *Lippincott's*, *Public Opinion*, and the *Ladies' Home Journal*.[15] As was true of all such women's organizations, both single and married women joined, providing both with an unusual opportunity to read casually and discuss various topics from suffrage to temperance. The state association also spawned local organizations. Like the Texas club, the Waco Woman's Press Club organized a reading room and library that held "dailies, weeklies, magazines and all the news works of fiction, as fast as they appear."[16]

[12] Southerners opened churches, homes, and public buildings to female journalists at their annual meetings. F. M. B. Hughes, *The History of the Texas Woman's Press Association* (Huntsville, TX, 1935), 1. See also "At Galveston. The Women Pencil Pushers had their Innings Yesterday," *Fort Worth Morning Register* 1 (February 19, 1897).

[13] Grider and Rodenberger, eds., *Let's Hear It*, 17; Judith N. McArthur, "Aurelia Hadley Mohl," *Handbook of Texas Online* http://www.tsha.utexas.edu/handbook accessed December 9, 2007.

[14] *Dallas Morning News* (May 31, 1896), 15, quoted in Pierce, "Texas Professional Communicators," in Burt, ed., *Women's Press Organizations*, 208.

[15] "Texas Woman's Press Club," *Dallas Morning News* (January 3, 1897), 15.

[16] "Women's Press Club," *Dallas Morning News* (March 24, 1897), 5.

Similarly, the Mississippi Women's Press Club was organized in Greenwood in 1894 and held its first meeting in the summer of 1895. Membership grew from an original group of just eleven women to more than forty a few years later. Importantly, the Mississippi club, in common with other southern women's press associations, welcomed a wide range of women involved in the newspaper and magazine business, including illustrators, typesetters, and writers.[17] Typical of its membership was Kate Power, a Jackson native who served as city editor and in many other positions with the *Jackson Clarion-Ledger* in the 1880s and 1890s. Between 1894 and 1895, she published *Kate Power's Review*, a Sunday paper that offered book reviews, poems, recipes, and short stories.[18] Most unusual was the editor's name in the title of the periodical; as we have seen, southern women frequently signed their names to contributions and often put their names on the title page of magazines they edited, but it was rare for women in the nineteenth-century North or South to incorporate their names into the title of a newspaper or journal. In her magazine, she promoted women's rights, including suffrage: "After asking men why they object to allowing women to vote," Power wrote, "I have yet to hear one single, sound logical reason."[19] Power helped to promote the Mississippi Women's Press Club in her publications, as did newspapers throughout the state. The *Biloxi Herald*, for example, published an account of the club's initial meeting.[20]

Like Texas and Mississippi, Georgia harbored one of the region's leading press associations for women. Led by club president Elia Goode Byington, the Woman's Press Club of Georgia featured many of the leading authors and journalists of the state, including Rebecca Latimer Felton, Corinne B. Stocker, Lollie Belle Wylie, Mary Louise Wylie, Ellen Dortch, Florence Williams, and Rosa Woodbury.[21] Women were also active as auxiliary members of the male Georgia Press Association but recognized the value of a club of their own.[22] Founded in 1889, the club boasted forty-five members just five years later.[23] At their first annual meeting in Atlanta, and then at later meetings in Columbus and Indian Springs, women held discussions, delivered papers, and debated the ways in which they could help women in Georgia. Dortch, for example, at the 1893 meeting of the association made a motion to appropriate more than

[17] Susan Weill, "Women's Press Organizations in Mississippi, 1894–Present," in Burt, ed., *Women's Press Organizations*, 302.

[18] *Ibid.*, 301.

[19] Power quoted in *ibid.*

[20] "The Woman's Press Club," *Biloxi Herald* 11 (May 18, 1895), 8.

[21] "The Editorial Bouquet," *Macon Weekly Telegraph* (May 27, 1892), 4, and "Women of the Newspapers," *Macon Weekly Telegraph* (June 25, 1893), 5. See also "The Woman's Press Club," *Columbus Daily Enquirer* 35 (June 17, 1894), 7.

[22] "The Georgia Editors," *Columbus Daily Enquirer* 34 (May 16, 1893), 1; "Editors Took Possession," *Macon Weekly Telegraph* (May 16, 1893), 1.

[23] "The Woman's Press Club," *Columbus Daily Enquirer* 35 (June 17, 1894), 7.

$50,000 to the Industrial College for girls in Milledgeville.[24] In addition, the Georgia club sent delegates to the National League of Press Clubs.[25]

White women formed press associations in the 1870s and 1880s, but although proposals were made for similar organizations for black women, no such societies emerged. Rather, African American journalists like Wells attended the meetings of male press associations, which were formed in beginning in 1880. Like newspapers themselves, the black press associations formed in the late nineteenth century came to symbolize political power and the advancement of the race. As one black newspaper argued in 1889, "With a Press united and fearless, any cause has a powerful instrument with which to make itself felt in the land."[26] Thus, African Americans formed their own press associations, in addition to the white organizations they sometimes attended. Though comprised mostly of men, African American press associations were significant, not only because they provided a forum for increasing numbers of professional black editors and journalists, but also because magazines became essential vehicles for expression. The association meetings often proved contentious as African Americans debated their responses to racism, the KKK, party politics, and myriad other issues. Through these specialized organizations, we get a sense of how journalism was viewed as a professional career for both men and women, and we understand better the extent to which African Americans fought for recognition and respect in Jim Crow America.

Although the church was the locus of power and prominence in the black community after the Civil War, the press would come to rival that power. With the increasing literacy of African Americans rose the importance of newspapers and magazines, and editors competed with the clergy for the attention of black citizens. "It is not to be denied," remarked the editor of the *Christian Recorder*, one of the nation's most prominent African American periodicals, "that henceforth the press is destined to be a most influential factor that will altogether stand abreast with the pulpit itself." The paper directed readers' attention to the upcoming meeting of the new Colored Press Association. "The press, then, among us, is fast becoming a power, and any assembly of those engaged in it cannot but command the respect of the great public."[27]

Annual conventions for black journalists, which began in 1880, were deemed vitally important by the African American community. "Let the members of the coming convention remember," one paper reminded attendees, "that they are to wield an instrument for creating public opinion in favor of a despised

[24] Lollie Belle Wylie, "Women Workers of the Press," *Macon Weekly Telegraph* (June 18, 1893), 5. See also Rebecca Latimer Felton, *Country Life in Georgia in the Days of My Youth* (Atlanta, 1919), 213–8.

[25] "National League Press Clubs," *Macon Weekly Telegraph* (April 29, 1894), 1.

[26] "The Press Convention," *The National Leader* 2 (February 2, 1889). See also 2 (March 9, 1889).

[27] "The Press Annual Association," *The Christian Recorder* (June 1, 1882).

people."[28] Thus, African Americans expected a great deal of the annual conventions of the black press. The first national meeting of the Colored Press Association took place in 1880, and the group immediately became a seminal organization for African Americans. From the beginning, the organization included newspapers from all sections of the country, and southern editors participated actively in the committees and meeting deliberations. The *Christian Advocate* reported that the first meeting, in Louisville, Kentucky, included male editors from Virginia, Georgia, Louisiana, Tennessee, and the Carolinas.[29] Whether from the North or South, the black members of the press expressed their anger and frustration with racism in the South. Though their rhetoric probably had little effect on the white South, their debates and resolutions were printed in southern white newspapers. At one meeting in the 1880s, the Colored Press Association complained bitterly of segregation, lamenting "that the act recently passed by the Georgia Legislature making it a felony ... to teach a colored child in a white school, or vice versa, is the work of unreasonable and unprincipled men, who are a disgrace to the position they hold."[30] The strident attacks on white supremacy were reprinted in papers nationally, including in the *Dallas Morning News*. Criticisms of racism and segregation continued to be an important part of the association's national meetings in the 1890s.[31]

Though the association was comprised almost entirely of men in its early stages, women joined the group and gradually became more prominent participants by the end of the nineteenth century. At the second national meeting in 1882, the *Recorder* noted that the sixty delegates in attendance, "mostly if not entirely young men ... may be said to represent a constituency of a full hundred thousand; for are we not six millions strong?"[32] Among the speakers was Frederick Douglass, who delivered a speech "declared by all present to have been eloquent, thoughtful and timely." The attendees devised committees, established rules for a permanent organization, and debated resolutions. No women appeared prominently either as committee members or speakers in these early meetings. Rather, women were welcomed to the evening receptions, and the newspapers remarked in detail on the ladies' fashions.[33] It was assumed in black newspapers like the *Arkansas Weekly Mansion* that the president and leadership of these press associations would be men.[34]

[28] "The Press Convention," *The National Leader* 2 (February 2, 1889).

[29] "Colored Press Association," *Christian Advocate* 55 (June 24, 1880), 412.

[30] "The State Press," *Dallas Morning News* (August 20, 1887), 4; "Colored Press Association," *Daily Inter Ocean* 16 (August 11, 1887), 140.

[31] John Mitchell of Richmond, president of the Colored Press Association in 1891, complained angrily of "the increase of outrages in the South – to the plain violation of the rights of citizens as guaranteed by the Constitution of the United States." See "Colored Press Association," *Daily Inter Ocean* 19 (March 18, 1891), 3.

[32] "The Press Convention," *The Christian Recorder* (July 6, 1882).

[33] "Colored Press Reception," *Daily Inter Ocean* 10 (August 26, 1881), 5.

[34] "Colored Press Convention," *Arkansas Weekly Mansion* 4 (June 30, 1883).

If the Colored Press Association largely excluded women in its first two years, it nonetheless was a bold advocate for African American causes. At an early meeting, in St. Louis in 1883, the association debated resolutions "in favor of the co-education of the races and of mixed schools and teachers, urging the pursuits of the industrial arts by negroes, [and] advising negroes to pre-empt or purchase public lands." The association also believed that the Republican Party took African Americans for granted and encouraged "the colored voters of the country to exercise their right of suffrage untrammeled by party claims."[35] Resolutions also passed urging editors to begin printing the word "negro" with a capital "N." Equally important, the convention in St. Louis was the first to feature women participants, as Alice Peterson and Annie C. Sneed of Kentucky addressed the association on temperance.[36] Until the 1890s and early 1900s, however, active participation by black women at the national meetings was unusual. Until that time, black women appeared sporadically in leadership positions within the National Colored Press Association. At the 1883 meeting in St. Louis, which was reported on in black papers throughout the nation, Sarah G. Patton of the Galveston *Spectator* was named secretary pro tem.[37] However, until the later years of the nineteenth century, such appointments were rare. Men comprised the vast majority of editors, a fact reflected in the press association's membership.

In the white female press associations, black women experienced a similar outsider status. Still, although considerable racism no doubt pervaded southern press associations for women, it is clear that in the late 1880s and early 1890s African American women belonged to such organizations. By the late nineteenth century, numerous press associations for men had formed, and sometimes these even welcomed African Americans. Wells-Barnett attended a meeting of the National Press Association in 1889.[38] Victoria Earle Matthews, the Georgia-born journalist who was a correspondent for papers such as the *Southern Christian Recorder*, was a leading member of the Women's National Press Association.[39] Alice E. McEwen, an associate editor of the *Baptist Leader* and a Nashville native, read a paper before the National Press Association in Washington in the late 1880s titled "Women in Journalism."[40] Other black women joined fellow female press members to found associations for African American journalists. Kentucky's Lucy Wilmot Smith, for example, editor of the "Woman's Department" of *Our Women and Children Magazine*, belonged to the Afro-American Press Convention. This organization, for which Wells-Barnett served as secretary in 1887, was a leading voice for black journalists across the country. As August Meier has pointed out, the Afro-American Press

[35] "Co-Education of the Races," *Macon Weekly Telegraph* (July 14, 1883), 1.

[36] *Ibid.*

[37] "National Colored Press Association," *Arkansas Weekly Mansion* 4 (July 14, 1883).

[38] Duster, *Crusader for Justice: The Autobiography of Ida B. Wells*, 32.

[39] Garland, *The Afro-American Press*, 375–6.

[40] *Ibid.*, 397–8.

Convention "denounced railroad segregation, and all discrimination practices in places of public amusement and accommodation."[41]

The National Colored Press Association began allowing more active participation of women in the 1890s. At the 1891 gathering in Cincinnati a woman, Mrs. W. H. Heard of Philadelphia, was elected secretary.[42] And in 1893, at the national meeting in Chicago, Miss J. E. Anderson read a paper titled "The Colored Journalist and His Success."[43]

Not all black editors were pleased with the notion of a colored press association, for they knew that such organizations were necessary only because they were excluded from white clubs. As a result some, like the editor of *The Christian Recorder*, believed that the black press should set a precedent that white editors could join their press associations. "No white man," the editor remarked in 1882, "would have been allowed to enter the [colored association's] Washington convention, save as a favor. Out, we say again, upon such color lines."[44] Indeed, the association itself lamented the fact that such a separate grouping by race was necessary. At its 1887 meeting in Louisville, the organization stated,

> We deplore the conditions that make this convention a necessity, and while it shall be our effort to secure equal and common privileges for all nationalities in places of public instruction ... we have no other reason to offer for the meeting of the colored press association than the realization of privileges, pleasures, and benefits that should be common to the country, regardless of nationalities.[45]

Black editors resented the fact that they were unwelcome in white organizations and viewed the colored press clubs as a last resort to advancing their profession.

Despite the ambivalence some black editors felt over maintaining an African American national press association, the group was a remarkable step forward in promoting gender and racial equality, and southern blacks also established state clubs that were also significant in professionalization. Through these associations, African American journalists could meet and discuss issues of importance. The Colored Press Association of South Carolina devoted much of its meeting in November 1899 to a debate about how to prevent the stealing of black papers by white postmasters who refused to deliver them. "A great number of postmasters in the rural districts," association members complained, failed to deliver papers, and the group resolved to take the matter up with railroad companies and post office officials.[46] The Negro Press

[41] August Meier, *Negro Thought in America, 1880–1915: Racial Ideologies in the Age of Booker T. Washington* (new edition, Ann Arbor, 1988), 72.

[42] "Colored Press Association," *Dallas Morning News* (March 20, 1891), 6.

[43] "Colored Editors in Session," *Daily Inter Ocean* (September 14, 1893).

[44] No title, *The Christian Recorder* (July 13, 1882).

[45] "Colored Press Association," *Daily Inter Ocean* 16 (August 11, 1887), 1.

[46] "Colored Press Association," [South Carolina] *State* (November 11, 1899), 6.

Association of Virginia debated at a "heated" meeting in 1893 whether to capitalize "negro" or not.[47]

In 1887, black editors from Birmingham, Montgomery, and other cities met in Selma to form the Alabama Colored Press Association.[48] The group, under the leadership of Jesse Duke of the *Montgomery Herald*, drafted a constitution, but despite the auspicious beginning the association soon came under fire from whites. Duke was well-known in Alabama journalism for loudly criticizing racism in the 1880s. Born a slave in 1853, Duke owned a grocery store and became a teacher in the 1870s until he founded the *Herald* in 1886.[49] In its first year, Duke pulled no punches in condemning in editorials the brutal treatment of southern blacks, especially lynching. He admonished his fellow black southerners to exhibit "race pride ... and manhood" and to stop "crawling on your belly to lick the white men's boots."[50] He and his colleagues carried this anger into the press clubs, and the groups became targets for white fears of black insurrection and insubordination. In common with other national black press associations, the Alabama journalists were outspoken and condemned racial violence and intimidation in papers read before the meetings, which were reported in the white press. Duke and his colleagues were forced to disband the first incarnation of the organization.

In the spring 1891, the press association visited with President Benjamin Harrison at the White House, an event that attracted nationwide attention. The *Macon* [Georgia] *Weekly Telegraph*, for example, published a lengthy account of the historic meeting, in which the male editors respectfully asked Harrison to appoint African Americans to "representative and prominent positions in the Columbian World's Fair commission."[51] As we have seen, the 1893 fair would be significant in helping to spur greater calls for women's rights, and white women came to play a highly visible role in the event. The black press association understood the fair's importance and sought firmly but politely to persuade the president to make the commission more racially inclusive. Harrison responded half-heartedly and without making commitments, but the persistence of the group was impressive. They felt their loyalty to the Republican Party warranted more visible roles in national events like the fair.

With persistence, however, the group was reconstituted in 1894 as the Afro-American Press Association and included sixteen black editors. At its first meeting the following summer, the journalists recorded their anger at segregation, lynching, and especially the unwillingness of the state government to

47 No title, *Charlotte News* 9 (July 15, 1893), 2. See also "Negro Press Association," [Baltimore] *Sun*, 62 (April 5, 1893), 2.

48 Allen Woodrow Jones, "Alabama," in Henry Lewis Suggs, ed., *The Black Press in the South, 1865–1979* (Westport, 1983), 35.

49 Allen W. Jones, "The Black Press in the 'New South:' Jesse C. Duke's Struggle for Justice and Equality," *Journal of Negro History* 64 (Summer 1979), 216.

50 Duke quoted in *ibid.*, 221.

51 "Ask for a Circuit Court Judge," *Macon Daily Telegraph* (March 24, 1891), 1; see also "Called on the President," *The Knoxville Journal* 7 (March 24, 1891), 1.

protect black citizens from racial violence. Such boldness contrasts with white press gatherings in the South, which sought to promote the profession but seldom registered any radical or iconoclastic protests. Clubs for black journalists, however, were frequently unyielding in their demands for justice, even at the risk of inflaming whites. The Alabama meeting in 1895 discussed suggestions to institute a black newspaper union in addition to denouncing white politicians for complicity in the KKK's reign of terror.[52] Although women apparently did not play leadership roles within the organization, they read papers and served on organizing committees, such as the one charged with hosting and feeding the guests.[53]

Other state black press clubs appear to have welcomed women journalists. The Texas Colored Press Association held its first meeting in 1888, and women delivered papers at its meetings in the 1890s.[54] The Negro Press Association of Kentucky, for example, met in 1907 and heard a paper by Julia Young of Louisville, who also served as secretary of the group.[55] The Negro Press Association of Virginia included women as members and endorsed Theodore Roosevelt for president in 1904.[56] Press associations specifically for African American women were established later than those for white women. *The Christian Recorder* reported in 1886, "Over fifty women, it is stated, are connected with newspapers in the South and it is proposed that they organize a Southern Women's Press Association."[57]

"There is no longer any question," wrote Helen M. Winslow near the end of the nineteenth century, "whether women shall enter journalism. They *have* entered and occupied the field, and they are 'there to stay.' There is but one standard by which their work must be judged: that is the standard which decides whether man's work is good or bad."[58] Of course Winslow's pronouncement was more than a little premature, as female journalists, writers, and editors would continue to fight sexism and discrimination to the present day. Although female television broadcasters and political commentators are no longer unusual, they still must fight audience complaints about hairstyles and dress. Still, the remarkable body of work by nineteenth-century southern women journalists, and the equally remarkable number of newspapers and magazines they left behind, would prove valuable, perhaps even essential, to the suffrage and equal rights battles of the twentieth century. The U.S. Census

[52] Jones, "Alabama," 35.

[53] See reports of the three-day meeting in the Birmingham *Age-Herald* 21 (August 30, 31, and September 1, 1895).

[54] "Colored Press Association," *Dallas Morning News* (October 4, 1888), 8; "Negro Press Association," *Dallas Morning News* (Sept 15, 1899), 10.

[55] "Kentucky Negro Press Association to Meet," *The Lexington Herald* (September 19, 1907), 8. See also "Negro Press Association in Politics," (September 28, 1907), 1.

[56] "Negroes for Roosevelt," *Philadelphia Inquirer* 150 (February 6, 1904), 9.

[57] No title, *The Christian Recorder* (November 11, 1886).

[58] Winslow, "Some Newspaper Women," 142.

listed just 288 women editors across the country in 1880, a number that rose dramatically to nearly 12,000 by 1920.[59] Many of these authors and members of the press would go on to be key activists themselves, with Georgia's Felton being just one example. Other individuals who did not join the forefront of the movement, either because they passed away or passed on the opportunity for ideological reasons, nonetheless laid the groundwork for women activists. From the editors and writers of the early nineteenth century like Mary Chase Barney to the later authors and journalists of the late 1800s like Mary Edwards Bryan, these southern women bequeathed to their daughters precious models of powerful, smart, public women. For African American women like Ida B. Wells-Barnett, the legacy is doubly significant, for in leaving behind for their daughters a valuable example of strong black womanhood they also left behind indispensible lessons for their sons as well.

Despite advances made by southern women editors by the 1880s, one should avoid the urge to impart a "Whiggish" depiction of literary and journalistic success on the nineteenth century. To be sure, southern women had made great strides over the course of the 1800s, and by the turn of the twentieth century women could be found in places and positions that would have seemed highly unlikely in the early nineteenth century. Women like Eliza Nicholson no doubt built on the successes of earlier women editors like Mary Edwards Bryan, Mary Chase Barney, and Frances Bumpass. However, even in the late 1800s and early 1900s, women battled the same worn stereotypes of woman's proper sphere. The mere editing of a periodical did not necessarily guarantee a progressive or forward-looking approach to women's rights or the suffrage question.[60]

Although the development of southern women's journalism was not a tale of unbroken advancement over the nineteenth century, and although the progress was uneven and intermittent, there were important pieces in place by the 1890s that could not have been dreamed of in the early part of the century. The achievements of female editors of the Early Republic like Royall, Barney, Gilman, Holton, and others are noteworthy, but for the most part they toiled in isolation, with little sense of camaraderie with fellow journalistic pioneers and little professional sisterhood. By the turn of the twentieth century, southern women members of the press could begin to see progress toward establishing professional organizations that would provide fellowship, mentoring,

[59] Mary Ellen Zuckerman, *A History of Popular Women's Magazines in the United States, 1792–1995* (Westport, CT, 1998), 54.

[60] Riley, *Magazines of the American South*, 271. Anna M. Marcotte, for example, edited *The Tatler of Society in Florida* in St. Augustine beginning in 1892 until finally closing down the paper in 1908. *The Tatler* consisted mostly of society news, word of the comings-and-goings of Florida visitors, reports of golf scores, and other light fare. Despite the hardly groundbreaking content of this seasonally published paper, however, Marcotte should be recognized for her business acumen; her paper was offered for sale at hotels throughout the state, from Jacksonville to Tampa to Miami.

and lay the groundwork for greater advancement for women in literature and journalism in the next century.

As Mr. Compson suggested in *Absalom, Absalom!*, the South has often viewed its women as ghosts, with little rootedness to the red clay and moss-covered trees of the real southern landscape. Historians also have often seen the southern woman as the product of the peculiarities of the southern plantation, assuming that the relatively few women who experienced life in gothic mansions somehow represented the lives and careers of the southern woman more broadly. Fortunately, a wide range of scholars in different disciplines continue the work of transforming the gauzy biographical remnants of professional southern women into more substantial and tangible knowledge. Much more work awaits.

Southern women authors and journalists played a central role in creating a foundation for the broader equal rights agenda of late nineteenth-century and early twentieth-century reformers. Literary careers were one of the very few avenues open to educated and ambitious women. Southern society regarded writing as a pursuit in which women could achieve personal fulfillment, develop a regional or national reputation, and earn money to supplement the family income. For women writers, literature was a safe endeavor that allowed a chance for self-expression within accepted bounds of femininity.

It would be a mistake, however, to view these women as merely adhering to traditional gender boundaries. Many female writers used their literary careers to earn respect and public acclaim. In doing so, in carving out an individual identity separate from their husbands and fathers, separate from their duties as wives and mothers, they were implicitly challenging the conservative notion of a woman's place in society. By putting themselves before the public as authors, by laying out for public consumption and critical review their own work in poetry, essays, and fiction, these southern women helped lay the foundation for the consideration of women as political actors.

Bibliography

I. Primary Documents

A. Manuscripts

Southern Historical Collection, Chapel Hill, North Carolina
John Lancaster Bailey Papers
Beale-Davis Papers
Carr, Barnes, and Branch Family Papers
Gordon-Hackett Family Papers
Lenoir Family Papers
Ella Nolland MacKenzie Papers
Lucy McIver Papers
Caroline O'Reilly Nicholson Reminiscences
Sigourney Club Records
John Francis Speight Papers
Marcus Cicero Stephens Letters
Margaret A. Ulmer Diary
Sarah Lois Wadley Diary
Webb Family Papers

Historic New Orleans Collection
Walton-Glenny Family Papers

North Carolina State Archives, Raleigh
Alexander Brevard Papers
John W. Hill Collection
Mrs. Scott R. Newton Papers
James Norcum Family Papers
Sawyer Papers
Robert H. Smith Papers
Zollicoffer Papers

Perkins Library, Duke University, Durham, North Carolina
James L. Boardman Papers
Amy Morris Bradley Papers

Sarah Magill Papers
William Reavis Papers
Lucy Spooner Ruggles Diary

South Carolina Historical Society, Charleston
Diary of Anna C. Lesesne
William A. Morrison Account Book

Alabama Department of Archives and History, Montgomery
B. T. Williams Letters

Clements Library, University of Michigan, Ann Arbor
Burwell-Guy Papers
Crittenden Papers
Maury Family Papers

Virginia Historical Society, Richmond
Cooper Family Papers
Nannie Armistead Storrs Grant Papers

B. *Newspapers and Magazines*

American Sketch Book
Aurora
Bouquet
Carrier Dove
Christian Index
Columbus (Georgia) Daily Enquirer
Daily Republican Banner
Dallas Morning News
De Bow's Review
Family Christian Album
Family Companion and Ladies' Mirror
Floral Wreath, and Ladies' Monthly Magazine
Fort Worth Morning Register
Graham's Magazine
Guardian
Hurricane
Ladies' Garland
Ladies' Pearl
Land We Love
Macon Weekly Herald
Macon Weekly Telegraph
Magazine of Poetry: A Quarterly Review
Magnolia
Mistletoe
Nashville Banner and Nashville Whig
National Magazine, or Ladies' Emporium
New Orleans Miscellany
North-Carolina Journal of Education
Orion

Our Living and Our Dead
Russell's Magazine
Scott's Monthly Magazine
Southern Cultivator
Southern Field and Fireside
Southern Illustrated News
Southern Ladies' Book
Southern Lady's Companion
Southern Lady's Magazine (Baltimore)
Southern Light
Southern Literary Journal
Southern Literary Messenger
Southern Monthly
Southern Patriot (Charleston)
Southern Planter
Southern Quarterly Review
Southern Review (Columbia)
Southern Review (Baltimore)
Southern Rose
Southern Teacher
Southern Weekly Post
Southron (Tennessee)
Sumter Mirror
Texian Monthly Magazine
Weekly Message
Young Ladies' Journal of Literature and Science

C. *Nineteenth- and Early Twentieth-Century Published Sources*

Felton, Rebecca Latimer. *Country Life in Georgia in the Days of My Youth* (Atlanta, 1919).

Forrest, Mary. *Women of the South Distinguished in Literature* (New York, 1861).

Garnett, James M. *Seven Lectures on Female Education* (Richmond, 1824).

Majors, M. A. *Noted Negro Women: Their Triumphs and Activities* (Chicago, 1893).

Nixon, John Travis. *History of the National Amateur Press Association* (Crowley, LA, 1900).

Picquet, Louisa. *Inside Views of Southern Domestic Life* (New York, 1861).

Richings, G. F. *Evidences of Progress among Colored People* (Philadelphia, 1902).

Rutherford, Mildred Lewis. *The South in History and Literature* (Athens, 1906).

Tucker, Nathaniel Beverley. "A Discourse on the Dangers that Threaten the Free Institutions of the United States, being an address to the Literary Societies of Hampden Sidney College, Virginia," (Richmond, 1841).

Welch, Margaret H. "Is Newspaper Work Healthful for Women?" Journal of Social Science 32 (November 1894), 110–16.

Willard, Frances E. and Mary A. Livermore, eds. *A Woman of the Century: Fourteen Hundred-Seventy Biographical Sketches Accompanied by Portraits of Leading American Women in All Walks of Life* (Buffalo, 1893).

II. Secondary Sources

A. Books

Ahrens, Gale, ed. *Lucy Parsons: Freedom, Equality, & Solidarity* (Chicago, 2003).

Alexander, Adele Logan. *Ambiguous Lives: Free Women of Color in Rural Georgia, 1789–1879* (Fayetteville, AR, 1991).

Ammons, Elizabeth, ed. *Short Fiction by Black Women, 1900–1920* (New York, 1991).

Aronson, Amy Beth. *Taking Liberties: Early American Women's Magazines and their Readers* (Westport, 2002).

Baggett, James Alex. *The Scalawags: Southern Dissenters in the Civil War and Reconstruction* (Baton Rouge, 2002).

Baker, Jean H. *Sisters: The Lives of America's Suffragists* (New York, 2005).

Bay, Mia. *To Tell the Truth Freely: The Life of Ida B. Wells* (New York, 2009).

Baym, Nina. *Woman's Fiction: Popular Novels by and about Women, 1820–1870* (Ithaca, 1978).

Belford, Barbara. *Brilliant Bylines: A Biographical Anthology of Notable Newspaperwomen in America* (New York, 1986).

Bennett, Paula Bernat. *Poets in the Public Sphere: The Emancipatory Project of American Women's Poetry, 1800–1900* (Princeton, 2003).

Bennion, Sherilyn Cox. *Equal to the Occasion: Women Editors of the Nineteenth-Century West* (Reno, 1990).

Bernath, Michael T. *Confederate Minds: The Struggle for Intellectual Independence in the Civil War South* (Chapel Hill, 2010).

Bernhard, Virginia. *Hidden Histories of Women in the New South* (Chapel Hill, 1994).

Boyd, Anne E. *Writing for Immortality: Women and the Emergence of High Literary Culture in America* (Baltimore, 2004).

Boyd, Melba Joyce. *Discarded Legacy: Politics and Poetics in the Life of Frances E. W. Harper, 1825–1911* (Detroit, 1994).

Bradley, Patricia. *Women and the Press: The Struggle for Equality* (Evanston, 2005).

Braxton, Joanne M. *Black Women Writing Autobiography: A Tradition within a Tradition* (Philadelphia, 1989).

Broussard, Jinx Coleman. *Giving a Voice to the Voiceless: Four Pioneering Black Women Journalists* (New York, 2004).

Bullock, Penelope L. *The Afro-American Periodical Press, 1838–1909* (Baton Rouge, 1981).

Burr, Virginia Ingraham, ed. *The Secret Eye: The Journal of Ella Gertrude Clanton Thomas, 1848–1889* (Chapel Hill, 1990).

Burt, Elizabeth V., ed. *Women's Press Organizations, 1881–1999* (Westport, 2000).

Bynum, Victoria. *Unruly Women: The Politics of Social and Sexual Control in the Old South* (Chapel Hill, 1992).

Carby, Hazel V. *Reconstructing Womanhood: The Emergence of the Afro-American Woman Novelist* (New York, 1987).

Carter, Christine Jacobson. *Southern Single Blessedness: Unmarried Women in the Urban South, 1800–1865* (Urbana, 2006).

Cashin, Joan E. *Our Common Affairs: Texts from Women in the Old South* (Baltimore, 1996).

Chambers, Deborah Linda Steiner, and Carole Fleming. *Women and Journalism* (London, 2004).

Christian, Barbara. *Black Women Novelists: The Development of a Tradition, 1892–1976* (Westport, 1980).

Clark, Thomas D. *The Southern Country Editor* (reprinted edition, Columbia, 1991).

Clinton, Catherine. *The Other Civil War: American Women in the Nineteenth Century* (New York, 1999).

The Plantation Mistress: Woman's World in the Old South (New York, 1982).

Cohen, Sidney. *Three Notable Ante-Bellum Magazines of South Carolina* (Charleston, 1925).

Collier-Thomas, Bettye. *Jesus, Jobs, and Justice: African American Women and Religion* (New York, 2010).

Coultrap, Susan. *Doing Literary Business: American Women Writers in the Nineteenth Century* (Chapel Hill, 1990).

Crane, Gregg D. *Race, Citizenship, and Law in American Literature* (Cambridge, UK, 2002).

Crowe, Terrell Armistead, and Mary Moulton Barden, eds. *Live Your Own Life: The Family Papers of Mary Bayard Clarke, 1854–1886* (Columbia, SC, 2003).

Daniel, Walter C., ed. *Black Journals of the United States* (Westport, 1982).

Davidson, Cathy N. *Revolution and the Word* (New York, 1986).

Delfino, Susanna, and Michele, Gillespie. *Neither Lady Nor Slave: Working Women of the Old South* (Chapel Hill, 2002).

Dickey, Imogene Bentley. *Early Literary Magazines of Texas* (Austin, 1970).

Dooley, Patricia L. *Taking their Political Place: Journalists and the Making of an Occupation* (Westport, CT, 1997).

Dunnigan, Alice Allison, ed. *The Fascinating Story of Black Kentuckians: Their Heritage and Traditions* (Washington, DC, 1982).

Duster, Alfreda M., ed. *Crusader for Justice: The Autobiography of Ida B. Wells* (Chicago, 1970).

East, Charles, ed. *Sarah Morgan: The Civil War Dairy of Southern Woman* (New York, 1992).

Elbert, Monika M., ed. *Separate Spheres No More: Gender Convergence in American Literature, 1830–1930* (Tuscaloosa, 2000).

Endres, Kathleen L., and Therese L. Lueck, eds. *Women's Periodicals in the United States: Social and Political Issues* (Westport, CT, 1996).

Women's Periodicals in the United States: Consumer Magazines (Westport, CT, 1995).

Fairclough, Adam. *Better Day Coming: Blacks and Equality, 1890–2000* (New York, 2001).

Farnham, Christine Anne. *The Education of the Southern Belle: Higher Education and Student Socialization in the Antebellum South* (New York, 1994).

Farrar, Hayward. *The Baltimore Afro-American, 1892–1950* (Westport, 1998).

Faust, Drew Gilpin. *A Sacred Circle: The Dilemma of the Intellectual in the Old South, 1840–1860* (Baltimore, 1977).

Fidler, William Perry. *Augusta Evans Wilson, 1835–1909* (University, AL, 1951).

Flanders, Bertram Holland. *Early Georgia Magazines: Literary Periodicals to 1865* (Athens, 1944).

Foner, Philip S., and Robert James Branham, eds. *Lift Every Voice: African American Oratory, 1787–1900* (Tuscaloosa, 1998).

Fought, Leigh. *Southern Womanhood and Slavery: A Biography of Louisa S. McCord, 1810–1879* (Columbia, MO, 2003).

Foster, Francis Smith. *Witnessing Slavery: The Development of Ante-Bellum Slave Narratives* (second ed., Madison, 1979).

Written by Herself: Literary Production by African American Women, 1746–1892 (Bloomington, 1993).

Fox-Genovese, Elizabeth. *Within the Plantation Household: Black and White Women of the Old South* (Chapel Hill, 1988).

Fox-Genovese, Elizabeth, and Eugene Genovese. *The Mind of the Master Class: History and Faith in the Southern Slaveholders' Worldview* (Cambridge, 2005).

Fraser, Hilary, et al. *Gender and the Victorian Periodical* (Cambridge, 2003).

Freehling, William. *The South vs. the South: How Anti-Confederate Southerners Shaped the Course of the Civil War* (New York, 2002).

Friedman, Jean E. *The Enclosed Garden: Women and Community in the Evangelical South, 1830–1900* (Chapel Hill, 1985).

Giddings, Paula J. *Ida A Sword among Lions: Ida B. Wells and the Campaign Against Lynching* (New York, 2008).

Gilmer, Gertrude. *Checklist of Southern Periodicals to 1861* (Boston, 1934).

Gray, Janet. *She Wields a Pen: American Women Poets of the Nineteenth Century* (Iowa City, 1997).

Griffith, Louis Turner, and John Erwin Talmadge. *Georgia Journalism 1763–1950* (Athens, 1951).

Gwin, Minrose. *Black and White Women of the Old South: The Peculiar Sisterhood in American Literature* (Knoxville, 1985).

Habermas, Jurgen. *The Structural Transformation of the Public Sphere: An Inquiry into a Category of Bourgeois Society* (translated by Thomas Burger, Boston, 1989).

Hahn, Steven. *A Nation Under Our Feet: Black Political Struggles in the Rural South from Slavery to the Great Migration* (Cambridge, MA, 2003).

Harris, Sharon M., ed., *Blue Pencils & Hidden Hands: Women Editing Periodicals, 1830–1910* (Boston, 2004).

Higginbotham, Evelyn Brooks. *Righteous Discontent: The Women's Movement in the Black Baptist Church, 1880–1920* (Cambridge, 1993).

Hine, Darlene Clark, and Kathleen Thompson. *A Shining Thread of Hope: The History of Black Women in America* (New York, 1998).

Hobson, Fred. *Tell about the South: The Southern Rage to Explain* (Baton Rouge, 1983).

Hoffert, Sylvia D. *Jane Grey Swisshelm: An Unconventional Life 1815–1884* (Chapel Hill, 2004).

Holman, Hugh. *The Roots of Southern Writing: Essays on the Literature of the American South* (Athens, GA, 1972).

Homestead, Melissa J. *American Women Authors and Literary Property, 1822–1869* (Cambridge, 2005).

Horsman, Reginald. *Josiah Nott of Mobile* (Baton Rouge, 1987).

Hubbell, Jay B. *The South in American Literature, 1607–1900* (Durham, 1954).

Hughes, F. M. B. *The History of the Texas Woman's Press Association* (Huntsville, TX, 1935).

Humphries, Nancy K. *American Women's Magazines: An Annotated Historical Guide* (New York, 1989).
Hunter, Tera W. *To 'Joy My Freedom: Southern Black Women's Lives and Labors after the Civil War* (Cambridge, 1997).
Huntzicker, William E. *The Popular Press, 1833–1865* (Westport, CT, 1999).
Hutton, Frankie. *The Early Black Press in America, 1827–1860* (Westport, 1993).
Hutton, Frankie, and Barbara Straus Reed, eds. *Outsiders in 19th-Century Press History: Multicultural Perspectives* (Bowling Green, OH, 1995).
Inscoe, John C., and Robert C. Kenzer, eds. *Enemies of the Country: New Perspectives on Unionists in the Civil War South* (Athens, 2004).
Jackson, Blyden. *A History of Afro-American Literature* (Baton Rouge, 1989).
Jackson, Leon. *The Business of Letters: Authorial Economies in Antebellum America* (Stanford: Stanford University Press, 2008).
Johanningsmeier, Charles. *Fiction and the American Literary Marketplace: The Role of Newspaper Syndicates, 1860–1900* (Cambridge, 1997).
John, Richard R. *Network Nation: Inventing American Telecommunications* (Cambridge, MA, 2010).
Spreading the News: The American Postal System from Franklin to Morse (Cambridge, MA, 1995).
Johnson, Karen. *Uplifting the Women and the Race: The Lives, Educational Philosophies and Social Activism of Anna Julia Cooper and Nannie Helen Burroughs* (New York, 2000).
Jones, Anne Goodwyn. *Tomorrow is Another Day: The Woman Writer in the South, 1859–1936* (Baton Rouge, 1995).
Joyce, Donald Franklin. *Black Book Publishers in the United States: A Historical Dictionary of the Presses, 1817–1990* (Westport, 1991).
Kelley, Mary. *Learning to Stand and Speak: Women, Education, and Public Life in America's Republic* (Chapel Hill, 2006).
Kerber, Linda. *Women of the Republic: Intellect and Ideology in Revolutionary America* (Chapel Hill, 1980).
Kielbowicz, Richard B. *News in the Mail: The Press, Post Office, and Public Information, 1700–1860s* (New York, 1989).
Kleber, John E., ed. *The Encyclopedia of Louisville* (Lexington, 2000).
Klein, Stacey Jean. *Margaret Junkin Preston: Poet of the Confederacy* (Columbia, SC, 2007).
Lang, Marjory. *Women Who Made the News: Female Journalists in Canada, 1880–1945* (Montreal, 1999).
Lebsock, Suzanne. *The Free Women of Petersburg: Status and Culture in a Southern Town, 1784–1860* (New York, 1984).
Lee, Maurice S. *Slavery, Philosophy, & American Literature, 1830–1860* (Cambridge, UK, 2005).
Leeman, Richard W. *African-American Orators: A Bio-Critical Sourcebook* (Westport, 1996).
Lehuu, Isabelle. *Carnival on the Page: Print Media in Antebellum America* (Chapel Hill, 2000).
Lemert, Charles, and Esme Bhan, eds. *The Voice of Anna Julia Cooper* (Lanham, MD, 1998).
Lindig, Carmen. *The Path from the Parlor: Louisiana Women, 1879–1920* (Lafayette, LA, 1986).

Loewenberg, Bert James, and Ruth Bogin. *Black Women in Nineteenth-Century American Life* (University Park, PA, 1976).
Logan, Shirley Wilson. "*We Are Coming:*" *The Persuasive Discourse of Nineteenth-Century Black Women* (Carbondale, 1999).
Long, Elizabeth. *Book Clubs: Women and the Uses of Reading in Everyday Life* (Chicago: 2003).
Lounsbury, Richard C., ed. *Louisa S. McCord: Political and Social Essays* (Charlottesville, VA, 1995).
Loveland, Anne C. *Southern Evangelicals and the Social Order, 1800–1860* (Baton Rouge, 1980).
Lutes, Jean Marie. *Front Page Girls: Women Journalists in American Culture and Fiction, 1880–1930* (Ithaca, 2006).
Manning, Carol, ed. *The Female Tradition in Southern Literature* (Urbana, 1993).
Marks, Jason. *Around the World in 72 Days: The Race Between Pulitzer's Nellie Bly and Cosmopolitan's Elizabeth Bisland* (New York, 1993).
Marzolf, Marion. *Up From the Footnote: A History of Women Journalists* (New York, 1977).
McAlexander, Hubert Horton. *The Prodigal Daughter: A Biography of Sherwood Bonner* (Baton Rouge, 1981).
McGill, Meredith L. *American Literature and the Culture of Reprinting, 1834–1853* (Philadelphia, 2003).
McHenry, Elizabeth. *Forgotten Readers: Recovering the Lost History of African American Literary Societies* (Durham, 2002).
Meier, August. *Negro Thought in America, 1880–1915: Racial Ideologies in the Age of Booker T. Washington* (new edition, Ann Arbor, 1988.)
Mitchell, Catherine C. *Margaret Fuller's New York Journalism: A Biographical Essay and Key Writings* (Knoxville, 1995).
Montgomery, Rebecca S. *The Politics of Education in the New South: Women and Reform in Georgia, 1890–1930* (Baton Rouge, 1996).
Morris, Christopher, and Steven G. Reinhardt, eds. *Southern Writers and their Worlds* (Arlington, TX, 1996).
Moss, Elizabeth. *Domestic Novelists in the Old South: Defenders of Southern Culture* (Baton Rouge, 1992).
Moss, Hilary. *Schooling Citizens: The Struggle for African American Education in Antebellum America* (Chicago, 2005).
Mott, Frank Luther. *A History of American Magazines* (5 vols., Cambridge, MA, 1938–1968).
Nash, Margaret A. *Women's Education in the United States, 1780–1840* (New York, 2005).
O'Brien, Michael. *Conjectures of Order: Intellectual Life and the American South, 1810–1860* (Chapel Hill, 2004).
ed., *An Evening When Alone: Four Journals of Single Women in the South, 1827–67* (Charlottesville, VA, 1993).
Rethinking the South: Essays in Intellectual History (Baltimore, 1988).
O'Brien, Michael, and David Moltke-Hansen, eds. *Intellectual Life in Antebellum Charleston* (Knoxville, TN, 1986).
Okker, Patricia. *Our Sister Editors: Sarah J. Hale and the Tradition of Nineteenth-Century American Women Editors* (Athens, GA, 1995).

Onslow, Barbara. *Women of the Press in Nineteenth-Century Britain* (New York, 2000).

Phegley, Jennifer. *Educating the Proper Woman Reader: Victorian Family Literary Magazine and the Cultural Health of the Nation* (Columbus, 2004).

Price, Kenneth M., and Susan Belasco Smith, eds. *Periodical Literature in Nineteenth-Century America* (Charlottesville, 1995).

Pryse, Marjorie, and Hortense J. Spillers, eds. *Conjuring: Black Women, Fiction, and Literary Tradition* (Bloomington, 1985).

Raymond, Ida, ed. *Southland Writers* (Philadelphia, 1870).

Reed, David. *The Popular Magazine in Britain and the United States, 1880–1960* (Toronto, 1997).

Riley, Sam G. *Magazines of the American South* (Westport, CT, 1986).

Roberts, Giselle. *The Confederate Belle* (Columbia, MO, 2003).

The Correspondence of Sarah Morgan and Francis Warrington Dawson (Athens, GA, 2004).

Rooks, Noliwe M. *Ladies' Pages: African American Women's Magazines and the Culture That Made Them* (New Brunswick, 2004).

Ross, Ishbel. *Ladies of the Press: The Story of Women in Journalism by an Insider* (New York, 1936).

Rubin, Louis D., Jr., et al., eds. *The History of Southern Literature* (Baton Rouge, 1985).

Rydell, Robert. *The Reason Why the Colored American is not in the World's Columbian Exposition* (Urbana-Champagne, 1999).

Sachsman, David B., ed. *The Civil War and the Press* (New Brunswick, 2000).

Schechter, Patricia A. *Ida B. Wells-Barnett & American Reform, 1880–1930* (Chapel Hill, 2001).

Schilpp, Madelon Golden, and Sharon M. Murphy. *Great Women of the Press* (Carbondale, IL, 1983).

Schwalm, Leslie A. *A Hard Fight for We: Women's Transition from Slavery to Freedom in South Carolina* (Urbana, 1997).

Scott, Anne Firor. *Natural Allies: Women's Associations in American History* (Urbana, 1991).

Sherman, Joan R. *The Black Bard of North Carolina George Moses Horton and His Poetry* (Chapel Hill, 1997).

Shevelow, Kathryn. *Women and Print Culture: The Construction of Femininity in the Early Periodical* (London, 1989).

Simmons, Charles A. *The African American Press: With Special Reference to Four Newspapers, 1827–1965* (Jefferson, NC, 1998).

Smith, Valerie. *Self-Discovery and Authority in Afro-American Narrative* (Cambridge, MA, 1987).

Smith-Rosenberg, Carroll. *Disorderly Conduct: Visions of Gender in Victorian America* (New York, 1985).

Smythe, Ted Curtis. *The Gilded Age Press, 1865–1900* (Westport, CT, 2003).

Solomon, Martha M., ed. *A Voice of Their Own: The Woman Suffrage Press, 1840–1910* (Tuscaloosa, 1991).

Spencer, Truman J. *Amateur Journalism* (New York, 1957).

Stem, Thad, Jr. *The Tar Heel Press* (Charlotte, 1973).

Stetson, Erlene, ed. *Black Sister: Poetry by Black American Women, 1746–1980* (Bloomington, 1981).

Storey, Margaret M. *Loyalty and Loss: Alabama's Unionists in the Civil War and Reconstruction* (Baton Rouge, 2004).
Stover, Johnnie M. *Rhetoric and Resistance in Black Women's Autobiography* (Gainesville, 2003).
Stowe, Steven M. *Intimacy and Power in the Old South: Ritual Lives of the Planters* (Baltimore, 1987).
Streitmatter, Rodger. *Raising Her Voice: African-American Women Journalists Who Changed History* (Lexington, KY, 1994).
Suggs, Henry Lewis, ed. *The Black Press in the South, 1865–1979* (Westport, 1983).
Sweeney, Patricia. *Women in Southern Literature: An Index* (New York, 1986).
Tebbel, John, and Mary Ellen Zuckerman. *The Magazine in America, 1741–1990* (New York, 1991).
Terborg-Penn, Rosalyn. *African American Women in the Struggle for the Vote, 1850–1920* (Bloomington, 1998).
Tomlinson, Stephen. *Head Masters: Phrenology, Secular Education, and Nineteenth-Century Social Thought* (Tuscaloosa, 2005).
Tracy, Susan J. *In the Master's Eye: Representations of Women, Blacks, and Poor Whites in Antebellum Southern Literature* (Amherst, 1995).
Varon, Elizabeth R. *We Mean to be Counted: White Women and Politics in Antebellum Virginia* (Chapel Hill, 1998).
Warner, Michael. *The Letters of the Republic: Publication and the Public Sphere in Eighteenth-Century America* (Cambridge, MA, 1990).
Weaks, Mary Louise, and Carolyn Perry, eds. *Southern Women's Writing: Colonial to Contemporary* (Gainesville, FL, 1995).
Weimann, Jeanne Madeline. *The Fair Women: The Story of the Woman's Building, World's Columbian Exposition, Chicago 1893* (Chicago, 1981).
Wellman, Judith. *The Road to Seneca Falls: Elizabeth Cady Stanton and the First Woman's Rights Convention* (Urbana, 2004).
Wells, Daniel A. *The Literary Index to American Magazines, 1850–1900* (Westport, CT, 1996).
Wells, Daniel A., and Jonathan Daniel Wells, eds. *The Literary and Historical Index to American Magazines, 1800–1850* (Westport, CT, 2004).
Wells, Jonathan Daniel. *The Origins of the Southern Middle Class, 1800–1861* (Chapel Hill, 2004).
Wheeler, Marjorie Spruill, ed. *Votes for Women! The Woman Suffrage Movement in Tennessee, the South, and the Nation* (Knoxville, TN, 1995).
Whitt, Jan. *Women in American Journalism: A New History* (Urbana, 2008).
Willard, Frances E., and Mary E. Livermore, eds. *American Women: Fifteen Hundred Biographies* (two volumes, New York, 1897).
Williams, Heather Andrea. *Self-Taught: African American Education in Slavery and Freedom* (Chapel Hill, 2005).
Wilson, Clint C. *Black Journalists in Paradox: Historical Perspectives and Current Dilemmas* (New York, 1991).
Winegarten, Ruthe. *Black Texas Women: 150 Years of Trial and Triumph* (Austin, 1995).
Winship, Michael. *American Literary Publishing in the Mid-Nineteenth Century: The Business of Ticknor and Fields* (Cambridge, MA, 1995).
Wolseley, Roland E. *The Black Press, U.S.A.* (second ed., Ames, IA, 1990).

Zuckerman, Mary Ellen. *A History of Popular Women's Magazines in the United States, 1792–1995* (Westport, CT, 1998).

B. Articles

Bainbridge, Judith T. "A 'Nursery of Knowledge': The Greenville Female Academy," South Carolina Historical Magazine 99 (January 1998), 56–63.

Bakker, Jan. "Caroline Gilman and the Issue of Slavery in the Rose Magazines, 1832–1839," Southern Studies 24 (Fall 1985), 275–83.

Brady, Patricia. "Literary Ladies of New Orleans in the Gilded Age," Louisiana History 33 (Spring 1992), 147–56.

Clark, E. Culpepper. "Sarah Morgan and Francis Dawson: Raising the Woman Question in Reconstruction South Carolina," South Carolina Historical Magazine 81 (January 1980), 8–23.

Colbert, Ann. "Philanthropy in the Newsroom: Women's Editions of the Newspapers, 1894–1896," Journalism History 22 (Autumn 1996), 90–9.

Davis, Curtis Carroll, "Dr. Caruthers Aids a Lady," Georgia Historical Quarterly 56 (Winter 1972), 583–7.

Garnsey, Caroline. "Ladies' Magazines to 1850," Bulletin of the New York Public Library 58 (January 1954), 74–88.

Gilley, B. H. "A Woman for Women: Eliza Nicholson, Publisher of the New Orleans *Daily Picayune*," Louisiana History 30 (1989), 233–48.

Ginzberg, Lori D. "'Moral Suasion is Moral Balderdash': Women, Politics, and Social Activism in the 1850s," Journal of American History 73 (December 1986), 601–22.

Griffin, Max L. "A Bibliography of New Orleans Magazines," Louisiana Historical Quarterly 17 (July 1935), 491–556.

Howe, Daniel Walker. "A Massachusetts Yankee in Senator Calhoun's Court: Samuel Gilman in South Carolina," New England Quarterly 44 (June 1971), 197–220.

Hubbell, Jay B. "Ralph Waldo Emerson and the South," in *South and Southwest: Literary Essays and Reminiscences* (Durham, 1965), 123–52.

Hunt, Robert E. "Home, Domesticity, and School Reform in Antebellum Alabama," Alabama Review 39 (October 1996), 253–75.

Jabour, Anya. "'Grown Girls, Highly Cultivated': Female Education in an Antebellum Southern Family," Journal of Southern History 64 (February 1998), 23–64.

Jones, Allen W. "The Black Press in the 'New South:' Jesse C. Duke's Struggle for Justice and Equality," Journal of Negro History 64 (Summer 1979), 215–28.

Jones, Beverly W. "Mary Church Terrell and the National Association of Colored Women, 1896 to 1901," Journal of Negro History 67 (Spring 1982), 20–33.

Junker, Clara. "Behind Confederate Lines: Sarah Morgan Dawson," Southern Quarterly 30 (Fall 1991), 7–18.

Karpf, Juanita. "The Early Years of African American Music Periodicals, 1886–1922: History, Ideology, Context," International Review of the Aesthetics and Sociology of Music 28 (December 1997), 143–68.

"'As with Words of Fire:' Art, Music, and Nineteenth-Century African-American Feminist Discourse," Signs 24 (Spring 1999), 603–32.

Kelley, Mary. "Reading Women/Women Reading: The Making of Learned Women in Antebellum America," Journal of American History 83 (September 1996), 401–24.

Kendall, John. "Journalism in New Orleans Between 1880 and 1900," Louisiana Historical Quarterly 8 (October 1925), 550–62.

Kerber, Linda. "Separate Spheres, Female Worlds, Woman's Place: The Rhetoric of Women's History," Journal of American History 65 (June 1988), 9–39.

Kerrison, Catherine. "The Novel as Teacher: Learning to be Female in the Early American South." Journal of Southern History 69 (August 2003), 513–48.

Kramer, Steve. "Uplifting our 'Downtrodden Sisterhood:' Victoria Earle Matthews and New York City's White Rose Mission," Journal of African American History 91 (Summer 2006), 243–66.

Lerner, Gerda. "Early Community Work of Black Club Women," Journal of Negro History 59 (April 1974), 158–67.

List, Karen. "Magazine Portrayals of Woman's Role," Journalism History 13 (Summer 1986), 64–70.

Luker, Ralph E. "God, Man and the World of James Warley Miles, Charleston's Transcendentalist," Historical Magazine of the Protestant Episcopal Church 39 (June 1970), 101–36.

Orth, Geoffrey C. "Mary E. Lee, Martha Fenton Hunter and the German Connection to Domestic Fiction in the Southern Literary Messenger," Southern Quarterly 34 (Summer 1996), 5–13.

Patty, James S. "A Georgia Authoress Writes Her Editor: Mrs. Mary E. Bryan to W. W. Mann (1860)," Georgia Historical Quarterly 41 (December 1957), 416–31.

Prior, Linda T. "Ralph Waldo Emerson and South Carolina," South Carolina Historical Magazine 79 (October 1978), 253–63.

Porter, Dorothy B. "The Organized Educational Activities of Negro Literary Societies, 1828–1846," The Journal of Negro Education 5 (October 1936), 555–76.

Rees, Robert A., and Marjorie Griffin, "Index and Author Guide to the *Family Companion*, 1841–1843," Studies in Bibliography 25 (1972), 205–12.

Rief, Michelle. "Thinking Locally, Acting Globally: The International Agenda of African American Clubwomen, 1880–1940," The Journal of African American History 89 (Summer 2004), 203–22.

Rogers, William Warren. "Seraphena Speaks with a Southern Accent," Alabama Historical Quarterly 37 (Spring 1975), 64–7.

Smith, Marion B. "South Carolina and *The Gentleman's Magazine*," South Carolina Historical Magazine 95 (April 1994), 102–29.

Stearns, Bertha-Monica. "Southern Magazines for the Ladies, 1819–1860," South Atlantic Quarterly 31 (January 1932), 70–87.

Thornbrough, Emma Lou. "American Negro Newspapers, 1880–1914," The Business History Review 40 (Winter 1966), 467–90.

Wade-Gayles, Gloria. "Black Women Journalists in the South, 1880–1905: An Approach to the Study of Black Women's History," Callaloo (February–October 1981), 138–52.

Walker, Elinor An. "Tradition and Innovation: Southern Women Writers," Southern Literary Journal 28 (Fall 1985), 149–54.

Warner, Michael. "Publics and Counterpublics," 88 Quarterly Journal of Speech (November 2002), 413–25.

Watson, Helen R. "A Journalistic Medley: Newspapers and Periodicals in a Small North Carolina Community, 1859–1860," North Carolina Historical Review 60 (October 1983), 457–85.

Wesley, Dorothy Porter. "The Organized Educational Activities of Negro Literary Societies, 1828–1846," Journal of Negro Education 5 (October 1936), 555–76.
Weyant, Jane G. "The Debate over Higher Education in the South, 1850–1860," Mississippi Quarterly 29 (Fall 1976), 539–57.

C. *Theses and Dissertations*

Atchison, Ray Morris. "Southern Literary Magazines, 1865–1887," (Ph.D. diss., Duke University, 1956).
Cutler, Ronald E. "A History and Analysis of Negro Newspapers in Virginia," (MA Thesis, University of Richmond, 1965).
Criss, Dallas. "Eliza Nicholson, Elizabeth Gilmer, and The New Orleans *Daily Picayune*, 1876–1901," (M.A. thesis, University of Southern Mississippi, 1994).
Grose, Charles William. "Black Newspapers in Texas, 1868–1970," (Ph.D. diss., University of Texas, 1972).
McLean, Frank. "Periodicals Published in the South before 1880," (Ph.D. diss., University of Virginia, 1928).

Index